Arbitration Clauses and Their Design in
Standard Form Contracts

格式合同中的
仲裁条款研究

钟皓珺◎著

厦门大学出版社 国家一级出版社
XIAMEN UNIVERSITY PRESS 全国百佳图书出版单位

图书在版编目（CIP）数据

格式合同中的仲裁条款研究 / 钟皓珺著. -- 厦门：
厦门大学出版社，2022.11
ISBN 978-7-5615-8679-2

Ⅰ．①格… Ⅱ．①钟… Ⅲ．①合同－经济纠纷－仲裁
－研究 Ⅳ．①D915.704

中国版本图书馆CIP数据核字(2022)第130464号

出 版 人	郑文礼
责任编辑	甘世恒

出版发行 厦门大学出版社

社　　址	厦门市软件园二期望海路 39 号
邮政编码	361008
总 编 办	0592-2182177　0592-2181253(传真)
营销中心	0592-2184458　0592-2181365
网　　址	http://www.xmupress.com
邮　　箱	xmupress@126.com
印　　刷	厦门集大印刷有限公司

开本	787 mm×1 092 mm　1/16
印张	9.75
字数	268 千字
版次	2022 年 11 月第 1 版
印次	2022 年 11 月第 1 次印刷
定价	55.00 元

本书如有印装质量问题请直接寄承印厂调换

厦门大学出版社
微信二维码

厦门大学出版社
微博二维码

缩略语
Abbreviations

AAA	American Arbitration Association
ACICA	Australia Center for International Commercial Arbitration
BIMCO	The Baltic and International Maritime Council
EU	European Union
GATT	General Agreement on Tariffs and Trade
HKIAC	Hong Kong International Arbitration Center
IBA Guidelines	International Bar Association Guidelines on Conflicts of Interest in International Arbitration 2004
ICC	International Chamber of Commerce
ICC Court	ICC International Court of Arbitration
ICC Rules	The Rules of Arbitration of the ICC
ICDR	International Center for Dispute Resolution
ICSID	International Center for Scttlement of Investment Disputes
LCIA	London Court of International Arbitration
NAFTA	North American Free Trade Agreement
SIAC	Singapore International Arbitration Center
UCC	Uniform Commercial Code
UNCITRAL	United Nations Commission on International Trade Law
UNCITRAL Model Law	UNCITRAL Model Law on International Commercial Arbitration 1985
UNCITRAL Rules	UNCITRAL Arbitration Rules (1976 (revised in 2010))
UPICC	UNIDROIT Principles of International Commercial Contracts
WIPO	World Intellectual Property Organization
WTO	World Trade Organization

目　录

TABLE OF CONTENTS

前　言

第二次世界大战后，国际贸易的业务量急剧增长。[①]这一趋势在1994年世界贸易组织扩充关税及贸易总协定（General Agreement on Tariffs and Trade, GATT）的内容后变得更加明显，特别是在服务贸易领域。[②]与此同时，更多的欧盟和北美自由贸易协定签订，区域之间的贸易正在不断深化。随着世界各国贸易交流日益频繁，人们需要找到一种更有效的方式来进行商业交易，因此在国际商业中经常采用标准形式的格式合同。

格式合同在各个商业领域有着悠久的历史，在商品贸易、服务贸易中都普遍存在。[③]格式合同对交易双方都很方便。此外，格式合同的起草者可以充分利用合同中的条款和条件，以此避免一些不必要的法律或商业风险。

Preface

After the Second World War, international trade has had a dramatic increase.[①] This tendency is shown in the expansion of the GATT with the adoption of the 1994 WTO Agreements into other areas, such as trade in service.[②] Meanwhile, regional trading is deepening with the establishment of many organizations, such as the EU and the NAFTA. With more frequent economic and trade exchanges in the world, people need to find a more efficient way to do their commercial transactions, and therefore standard form contract is often adopted in international business.

Standard contracts are pervasive in most consumer and business transactions involving commodities and services. Standard contracts have a long history in various fields of commerce.[③] Standard form contract is convenient for both parties involved in the transaction. Furthermore, standard form contract drafters can take full advantage of the terms and conditions in the contract to avoid some unnecessary legal or business risks.

[①]　DiMatteo, L., Dhooge, L., & DiMatteo, L. (2006). *International Business Law: A Transactional Approach.* Mason, OH: Thomson/Southwestern, at 28.

[②]　Available at: https://www.wto.org/ (Last visited on May 12, 2016).

[③]　Sales, H.B. (1953). Standard Form Contracts. *The Modern Law Review*, 16(3), 318-342, at 319.

Therefore, more and more standard form contracts are applied to international trade. Some scholars even think 99% of contracts are standard form contracts in modern business.[①] The convenience of the standard form contract has made it irreplaceable. It is necessary to do further research about standard form contracts in order to better develop them.

Arbitration is faster, more informal and less expensive than other dispute resolution mechanisms.[②] The parties may achieve autonomy through arbitration agreements and facilitate the resolution of disputes in international trade. Many standard form contract drafters prefer to use arbitration for their future dispute resolution.

In international business practice, an arbitration clause is often included in the standard form contract.[③] The arbitration clause is the arbitration agreement in the contracts, and the arbitration agreement is the foundation of arbitration,[④] so a perfect arbitration clause design and full knowledge of the details regarding the clause are very important in business dispute resolution.

The key issue of design is to ensure the validity of the arbitration agreement. If the arbitration agreement is invalid, the arbitration cannot start and the final award may be challenged.[⑤]

因此，越来越多的格式合同被应用于国际贸易中。一些学者甚至认为99%的合同是现代商业中的格式合同。[①]格式合同的便利性使其不可替代。为了更好地开发格式合同，有必要对其进行进一步的研究。

仲裁这一争端解决机制比其他争端解决机制结案的效率更高、具有自治性，解决纠纷的成本更低。[②]案件争议的双方可以通过自愿地达成仲裁协议进行纠纷的解决，促进国际贸易争端的解决。许多格式合同起草者更喜欢使用仲裁来解决他们未来的纠纷。

在国际商业实践中，仲裁条款通常包含在格式合同中。[③]仲裁条款是合同中的仲裁协议，仲裁协议是仲裁的基础，[④]因此，完善的仲裁条款设计和对该条款细节的充分了解是解决商业纠纷中非常重要的内容。

仲裁条款设计的关键问题是确保仲裁协议的有效性。无效的仲裁协议，不能开启仲裁程序。基于无效的仲裁协议而作出的仲裁裁决，当事人可以对最终裁决结果提出质疑。[⑤]

---

① Korobkin, R. (2003). Bounded Rationality, Standard Form Contracts, and Unconscionability. *The University of Chicago Law Review*, 70(4), 1203-1225, at 1207.

② Dore, I. I. (1986). Arbitration and Conciliation under the UNCITRAL Rules. A Textual Analysis. Dordrecht: Martinus-Nijhoff Publishers, at 7.

③ Redfern, A. (2004). *Law and Practice of International Commercial Arbitration*. London: Sweet & Maxwell, at 135.

④ Lew, J.D., Mistelis, L.A., & Kröll, S. (2003). *Comparative International Commercial Arbitration*. The Hague: Kluwer Law International, at 167.

⑤ Id.

本书讨论了在格式合同中的仲裁条款的设计和仲裁协议的有效性方面存在的主要问题。它可以帮助当事人在格式合同中设计合适的仲裁条款，为商业纠纷的解决提供参考，为格式合同中设立仲裁条款提供范本。

This book discusses the main problems regarding the design of standard contract terms and the validity of the arbitration agreement. It can help the parties to design suitable arbitration clauses in standard contracts, provide a reference for the commercial dispute resolution and build a model for future arbitration clauses in standard form contracts.

更具体地说，本书主要关注三个研究问题：什么是格式合同？仲裁协议是什么？如何保证格式合同中的仲裁条款的有效性？

More specifically, this book focuses on three research questions: What is a standard contract? What is the arbitration agreement? How do we ensure the validity of arbitration clauses in standard form contracts?

本书对现有资料进行了一些研究，如相关著作、论文，仲裁裁决和国家法院的判决等。本书还讨论了当事人在格式合同中起草仲裁条款时可能出现的主要问题及解决问题的方法，并采用了比较法的研究方法，探讨了世界各地不同的法律法规，对不同的法律制度进行了比较。本书最后以 GENCON 1994（金康 1994 合同）为例，说明如何在格式合同中设计一个合理的仲裁条款。

In this book, some research has been done with reference to bibliographical sources, such as books, articles and the decisions of arbitral tribunals and national courts. The main problems which can arise when parties draft an arbitration clause in a standard contract and the methods to solve the problems are discussed. In addition, a comparative methodology is used in this research, and different worldwide laws and regulations are explored to make comparisons between different legal systems. At the end of the book, GENCON 1994 is taken as an example to show how to design a good arbitration clause in standard form contracts.

本书的第一章介绍了格式合同和仲裁的相关问题。首先分析了格式合同的概念和法律特征，并阐述了格式合同存在的必要原因。

As for the content of the book, in the first chapter relevant issues about standard form contracts and arbitration are introduced. Concepts and legal characteristics of standard form contracts are analyzed firstly, and then necessary reasons for standard form contracts to exist are stated.

第二章讨论了仲裁协议的概念和组成部分，以及仲裁协议在格式合同中的重要性。本章还介绍了在仲裁过程

In the second chapter the concept and components of arbitration agreements, and the importance of arbitration agreements in standard contracts are discussed. In this chapter the legal risks which may occur in arbitration are also presented. To avoid legal risks, a well-designed arbitration clause is very critical.

In the third chapter, relevant issues regarding the validity of the arbitration agreements are elaborated. Firstly, challenges to validity of the arbitration agreement are introduced briefly, and then key issues which may determine the validity of the arbitration agreement are discussed. These key issues include validity of arbitration agreements, and the recognition and enforcement of the arbitration agreement.

In the fourth chapter, the law applicable to standard contract terms is introduced. Some regulations about arbitration in different countries including China, the United States, and Germany are discussed. The regulation of this issue is interpreted at international level, for example, according to the CISG (United Nations Covention on Contracts for the International Sale of Goods) and the New York convention.

In the fifth chapter GENCON 1994 is taken as a case in the study in order to explain how to design arbitration clauses in standard form contracts. Arbitration clauses in the GENCON 1994 contract are discussed and its pros and cons are evaluated.

Finally, suggestions about how to design arbitration clauses in standard form contracts are given. The conclusions are drawn in the last chapter. The main conclusions of this book are summarized and how to construct better arbitration clauses in standard form contracts is reiterated.

中可能发生的法律风险。为了避免法律风险，一个精心设计的仲裁条款是非常重要的。

第三章阐述了仲裁协议有效性的相关问题，首先简要介绍了影响仲裁协议有效性的法律风险，然后讨论了可能决定仲裁协议有效性的关键问题。这些关键问题包括仲裁协议的有效性，以及对仲裁裁决的承认和执行。

第四章介绍了仲裁和适用法条款，讨论了中国、美国、德国等不同国家有关仲裁的规定。在国际贸易的角度探讨了格式合同中的仲裁条款设计。

第五章中，以 GENCON 1994 为案例进行研究，以解释如何在格式合同中设计仲裁条款。讨论了 GENCON 1994 的仲裁条款，并评价了其优缺点。

最后，对格式合同中如何设计更好的仲裁条款提出了建议。

第一章
格式合同的介绍

Chapter I   Introduction of Standard Form Contracts

一、格式合同的概念

1. Concept of Standard Form Contracts

在几个世纪以前，当人们想做商品交易时，他们需要与另一方讨论价格和质量，以确保交易让人可接受和满意。在那个时候，"大宗交易"是相当罕见的。

For many centuries, when people wanted to do commodity trading, they needed to have a discussion about price and quality with the other party to assure the trade acceptable and satisfactory. At that time, "grand bargain" was quite rare.

19 世纪中叶以后，随着自由资本主义的扩张，部分商事交易的过程被模式化。但是对于大部分的生产和交易，没有统一的标准。[①]人们认识到当事人自主的重要性，他们按照当事人的真实意图形成合同。双方都有权就该业务的条款进行谈判，并根据其个人喜好订立合同。但是这样做交易成本高，效率低。

After the middle of the 19th century, with the expansion of laissez-faire capitalism, the transaction process was customized. There were no uniform standards for production and transaction.[①] People realized the importance of autonomy of parties, and they formed the contract in line with the true intentions of the parties. Both parties had rights to negotiate terms of the business. The parties concluded the contract according to their personal preferences. However, transaction costs were high, and efficiency was low this way.

在 19 世纪末和 20 世纪初，随着制造业和贸易产业的不断发展，资本开始集中，出现了一些大型公司。[②]制造业的发展提供了大量的商品，导致了程序化交易、产品标准化和系统营销的出现。渐渐地，制造商们开始控制这个市场，制造商决定了他们所生产的商品的

At the end of the 19th century and in the early 20th century, with the continuous development of manufacturing and trade industry, capital became centralized and a number of large-scale companies appeared.[②] The development of the manufacturing

---

① Kessler, F. (1943). Contracts of Adhesion—Some Thoughts about Freedom of Contract. *Columbia Law Review*, 43(5), 629-635, at 631.

② Šulija, G. (2011). Standard Contract Terms in Cross-Border Business Transactions: A Comparative Study from the Perspective of European Union Law. P. Lang, at 25.

industry supplied a lot of commodities, which led to a process of programmed trading, standardized products and systematic marketing. Gradually, manufacturers started to control the market. Manufacturers decided the model, size and classification of commodity they manufactured. Consumers could only choose goods which were closest to their own expectation.

The large-scale production model had a requirement for minimizing production cost, increasing productivity, and ensuring the products' quality in all production process, and manufacturers did not often have time and money to negotiate the terms of contracts and conclude them individually, so the solution appeared in the shape of standard form contract.[1]

As for the definition of the standard form contract, there are various opinions. Yates and Hawkins held that standard form contracts are like elephants, which may be easily recognized, but it is devilish to describe them.[2] Standard form contracts are also called "adhesion contracts" in some countries, like France and Japan.

For example, the French doctrine of the contract of adhesion defines standard form contracts as terms which are not intended to be amended by the other party.[3] In China, most scholars think that the standard form contract means a contract which is prepared by one party in advance, and when the other party receives the proposal, they can only accept or reject all contents of the contract.[4]

型号、尺寸和分类。消费者只能选择最接近他们自己期望的商品。

大规模生产模式要求最小化生产成本，提高生产率，并确保产品的质量。在生产过程中，需求方往往没有时间和实力与制造商单独谈判合同条款，因此格式合同应运而生。[1]

对于格式合同的定义，有不同的意见。耶茨和霍金斯认为，格式合同就像大象，它很容易被感知到，但很难具体描述。[2]在一些国家，如法国和日本，格式合同也被称为"粘附合同"（adhesion contract）。

例如，法国将格式合同定义为原则上不允许由另一方修改的合同。[3]在中国，大多数学者认为格式合同是指一方事先准备的合同，当另一方收到提案时，他们只能接受或拒绝合同的所有内容。[4]

[1] Marotta-Wurgler, F. (2007). What's in a Standard Form Contract? An Empirical Analysis of Software License Agreements. *Journal of Empirical Legal Studies*, 4(4), 677-713, at 677.

[2] Yates, D., & Hawkins, A. J. (1986). *Standard Business Contracts: Exclusions and Related Devices*. Sweet & Maxwell, at 5.

[3] Šulija, G. (2011). Standard Contract Terms in Cross-Border Business Transactions: A Comparative Study from the Perspective of European Union Law. P. Lang, at 26.

[4] Wang S. (2007), An Analysis of the Legal Effects of Arbitration Clauses in Standard from Contracts from the Mutual Consent of Parties. *Journal of Changchun University of Science and Technology* (Social Sciences Edition),s, 16-21, at 18.

例如中国的《合同法》第39条第2款规定：

"格式条款是当事人为了重复使用而预先拟定，并在订立合同时未与对方协商的条款。"[①]

总而言之，格式合同可以被认为是"接受或离开"的合同。[②]格式合同与普通合同具有一些共同点，但格式合同也有其特点。

第一，格式合同的标准格式、基本内容和条款由一方事先制定，格式合同双方不得对合同条款的细节进行检查和谈判。

第二，格式合同有大量的用户。例如，格式合同在电子商务或互联网上被广泛使用。[③]每次我们在网上购买商品，甚至安装软件程序时，我们可能会签订一份标准的合同。起草者应考虑不确定的各方的所有可能情况，以确保格式合同符合其交易的要求。

第三，格式合同可以节省交易的时间和成本。例如，有时在互联网交易的过程中，格式合同会以标准表单合同的方式在网上呈现，您只需要点击网络表单上的按钮"是"，就可以快速签订一份标准的格式合同并获得进一步的服务。这一特性可能是格式合同的一个

The supporting evidence can be found from Article 39 of China Contract Law, which states:

"Standard terms are clauses that are prepared in advance for general and repeated use by one party, and which are not negotiated with the other party when the contract is concluded."[①]

All in all, standard form contracts can be considered as "take it or leave it" contracts.[②] Standard form contracts have some same characteristics as those of common contracts, but they also have their own characteristics.

First, the standard format, the basic contents and the terms of standard contracts are drawn up by one party in advance, and the parties in standard form contracts may not have opportunities to check and negotiate the details of contract terms.

Second, there is a wide array of users of standard form contracts. For instance, standard form contracts are used widely in electronic commerce or on the Internet.[③] Every time we buy something online, or even install a software program, we may conclude a standard form contract. The drafters should consider all possible situations for uncertain parties in order to make sure that standard form contract meets the requirements of their transactions.

Third, standard form contract can save time and cost for transaction. For example, sometimes standard form contracts are presented online, you just need to click "yes",

① Article 39 of China Contract Law.
② Aghion, P., & Bolton, P. (1992). An Incomplete Contracts Approach to Financial Contracting. *The Review of Economic Studies*, 59(3), 473-494, at 474.
③ Hillman, R. A., & Rachlinski, J. J. (2002). Standard-Form Contracting in the Electronic Age. *NYUL Rev.*, 77, 429-495, at 430.

and then you are allowed to quickly conclude a standard form contract and receive further services. This feature could be an advantage of standard form contracts, because the normalized and simple process can save time and cost, which means that merchants can pass on part of the savings to customers.

Fourth, standard form contract drafters can use standard form contracts to allocate risks in transactions beforehand. Standard form contract drafters can take full advantage of the terms and conditions in the contract to avoid some unnecessary legal or business risks and make the rights and obligations between both parties clear in advance. In addition, standard form contracts can also help the parties to solve disputes under such contracts. Since the terms in standard form contract are the same in every contract, when disputes happen, they can be solved by application of the same regulations.

However, standard form contracts also have their own limitations. The drafters of standard form contracts may abuse their dominant position.[1] In practice, the drafters of standard form contracts usually have a dominant position in the transaction. If the other parties do not agree with standard form contracts, they will not get products or service from the stronger party.

For example, if we want to open an account and deposit some money in a bank, we have to sign a standard form contract which is provided by the bank. If we refuse to sign the standard form contract, we cannot have access to deposit service. In this case, we find that the parties in standard form contracts do not have an equal status. Standard form contracts may not express the autonomy of the parties. The stronger party may abuse their dominant position during the transaction.

优势，因为标准化和简单的流程可以节省时间和成本，这意味着顾客可以得到实惠。

第四，格式合同起草者可以事先使用格式合同在交易中进行风险分配。格式合同起草人可以充分利用合同的条款，避免不必要的法律或商业风险，提前明确双方之间的权利和义务。此外，格式合同还可以帮助当事人解决相同类型合同中的纠纷。由于每份合同的格式合同条款相同，当发生争议时，可以采用相同的规定来解决。

然而，格式合同也有它们自己的局限性。格式合同的起草者可能会滥用其主导地位。[1]在实践中，格式合同的起草者通常在交易中占有主导地位。如果其他各方不同意格式合同，格式合同起草者将不会提供产品或服务给对方当事人。例如，如果我们想开银行账户并存一些钱，我们必须签署由银行提供的格式合同。如果我们拒绝签署格式合同，我们就无法获得存款服务。在这种情况下，我们发现在格式合同中的当事人并不具有平等的地位。格式合同可能无法表达当事人的自主权。实力较强的一方可能会在交易过程中滥用其主导地位。

① Bilal, S., & Olarreaga, M. (1998). Regionalism, Competition Policy and Abuse of Dominant Position. *Journal of World Trade*, 32(3), 153-166, at 155.

大多数国家都有试图防止格式合同中强势的一方滥用其主导地位的法律法规。例如,《中华人民共和国合同法》①第40条规定,格式条款具有本法第52条和第53条规定情形的,或者提供格式条款一方免除其责任、加重对方责任、排除对方主要权利的,该条款无效。

英国的一个案例也阐明了这一观点:圣戈本建筑分销有限公司诉希尔米德木材有限公司案。②英格兰和威尔士高等法院在2015年作出了判决。该案中,圣戈本建筑分销有限公司起诉希尔米德,要求追回由圣戈本建筑分销有限公司提供的一些货物的款项。希尔米德以货物质量有缺陷为事实提出了反诉。他们争论的关键是圣戈本提供的格式合同中的条款是否有效。高等法院使用了适用该案的《1977年不公平合同条款法》③来检验该合同的合理性。该格式合同中的索赔条款包含了限制条款,合同中约定:④

"如果希尔米德在货物交付后3天内提出书面投诉,除提供替代品外,圣戈本建筑分销有限公司对任何"视觉缺陷"不承担任何责任;

圣戈本建筑分销有限公司将不承担任何间接或衍生的损失(包括业务损失)......"⑤

Most countries have regulations that seek to prevent abuses. For instance, the Article 40 of Contract Law of People's Republic of China① states that Chinese contract law will not protect standard form contracts which may increase the weaker parties' liabilities or deprive them of their material rights.

A case in England also elucidates this point: *St Gobain Building Distribution Ltd* (GBD) *v. Hillmead Joinery Ltd.*② It is a case that High Court of Justice of England and Wales ruled upon in 2015. In this case, GBD sued Hillmead for recovery of the payment for some goods which were supplied by GBD. Hillmead held a counter-claim based on the facts that the quality of goods was defective. The key point of their disputes was whether the standard terms provided by GBD were valid. The High Court used applicable Unfair Contract Terms Act 1977③ to test the reasonableness of the contract. The claimant's standard terms which contained limitation clauses specified that:④

"GBD would have no liability for any "visual defects", save for providing replacement goods if a written complaint was presented by Hillmead within 3 days after delivery;

GBD would not be liable for any indirect or consequential losses (including loss of business) ..."⑤

---

① Article 40 of the China Contract Law: "When standard terms are under the circumstances stipulated in Articles 52 and 53 of this Law, or the party which supplies the standard terms exempts itself from its liabilities, increases the liabilities of the other party, and deprives the material rights of the other party, the terms shall be invalid."

② St Gobain Building Distribution Ltd v Hillmead Joinery (Swindon) Ltd., [2015] EWHC B7, High Court of Justice of England and Wales, available at: http://www.myerson. co.uk/limitation-of-liability-when-is-a-standard-term-unreasonable-case-law-update/(Last visited on July 2, 2016).

③ The details about the claimant's standard terms are available at: (http://www.myerson.co.uk/limitation-of-liability-when-is-a-standard-term-unreasonable-case-law-update) (Last visited on July 2, 2016).

④ Id.

⑤ Id.

The court held the opinion that the claimant's standard terms had the effect of limiting or excluding liability, so these terms were invalid. The judge explained that the standard terms which excluded GBD from all liability for "visual defects" were fundamentally unreasonable, and there was no mechanism in claimant's standard terms for replacement goods. The limitation clauses were standard and allowed no negotiation from the other party.[①]

法院认为，该格式合同中的索赔条款具有限制或排除责任的效果，因此这些条款无效。法官解释说，圣戈本建筑分销有限公司免除自身对"视觉缺陷"的所有责任的标准条款在根本上是不合理的，限制条款是标准的，不允许与另一方协商。在格式合同中没有替换货品的条款也是不合理的。[①]

2. Arbitration Clauses in Standard Form Contracts

二、格式合同中的仲裁条款

When disputes occur between two parties of standard form contracts, they can follow the "dispute resolution" terms to resolve disputes. Litigation is a traditional way for dispute resolution.

当格式合同双方发生争议时，可以按照"争议解决"条款来解决争议。诉讼是解决纠纷的一种传统方式。

Due to different legal cultures and systems, litigation is usually not the best strategy for dispute resolution in international business. The parties are weary of international litigation because they need to handle foreign procedures under different substantive rules, and have to rely on different legal resources. Unfamiliar legal systems can also make extraneous mistakes. What is more, a foreign-related litigation usually requires a more complex suing procedure. For avoiding the delays and the expenses inherent in the complex procedures and practices of judicial systems, people tend to choose a more convenient way to settle their disputes.

由于不同的法律文化和制度，诉讼通常不是解决纠纷的最佳策略。当事人厌倦了国际诉讼，因为他们需要在不同的实质性规则下处理外国程序，并且必须依赖不同的法律资源。不熟悉的法律体系也可能导致当事人会犯无关的错误。此外，与外国有关的诉讼通常需要更复杂的诉讼程序。为了避免司法系统复杂的程序和做法中所固有的拖延和费用，人们往往选择一种更方便的方式来解决纠纷。

Compared with litigation, arbitration is considered as a better way for international dispute resolution[②],

与诉讼相比，仲裁被认为是解决国际争端的一种更好的方式，[②]仲裁裁决可以在国外得到认可和执行。已有150多个国家加入了《纽约公约》。此外，诉

---

① Id.
② Park, W. W. (1984). Arbitration of International Contract Disputes. *The Business Lawyer*, 1783-1799, at 1784.

讼程序还由经验丰富的仲裁员执行。在某些情况下，法官并不熟悉具有其自身特点和技术语言的某些类型的国际合同。①在国际商事仲裁中，当事人有权根据其在争议所涉及的特定贸易和法律领域的专业知识选择仲裁员。②因此，许多格式合同的起草者倾向于在格式合同中加入仲裁条款，③并倾向于选择仲裁来解决他们未来的纠纷。

仲裁条款可以包含在各种行业的格式合同中。④例如，国际工程师咨询联合会（法语缩写"FIDIC"）⑤是建筑行业的国际标准组织，以 FIDIC 系列合同模板而闻名，其中有《FIDIC 红皮书 1999》。⑥

《FIDIC 红皮书 1999》被广泛地用于主要的建筑和工程项目，被认为提供了公正平衡了各方之间法律风险的范本条款。红皮书也受到国际机构的青睐，为许多业内人士熟悉，颇具优势。⑦《FIDIC 红皮书 1999》第 20 条提供了两个主要的争端解决机制：第 20.4 款明确了当事人可以将争议提交争端裁决委员会 (DAB) 进行仲裁，第 20.6 款提供了国际仲裁示范条款。

and the arbitral awards can be recognized and enforced in foreign countries. More than one hundred fifty countries have joined in the New York Convention.① In addition, the proceedings are conducted by experienced arbitrators. In some cases, judges are not familiar with some types of international contracts which have their own characteristics and technical language. In international commercial arbitration, parties have rights to choose arbitrators in accordance with their expertise in particular areas of trade and law involved in the dispute.② Therefore, many drafters of standard form contracts are inclined to include an arbitration clause in the standard form contract③, and prefer to choose arbitration for their future dispute resolution.

Arbitration is included in standard form contracts in various industries.④ For instance, the International Federation of Consulting Engineers⑤ is an international standard organization for the construction industry, best known for the FIDIC family of contract templates; among them there is the *FIDIC Red Book 1999*.⑥

The FIDIC Red Book 1999 is the most widely used for major construction and engineering projects. It is perceived to offer a fair balance of risks between parties, is favored by international agencies and now has the advantage of being familiar to many in the industry.⑦ Clause 20 of the FIDIC Red Book 1999

① The New York Convention is short for the Convention on the Recognition and Enforcement of Foreign Arbitral Awards. It is one of the key instruments in international arbitration. The New York Convention applies to the recognition and enforcement of foreign arbitral awards and the referral by a court to arbitration. The details are available at: http://www.newyorkconvention.org.

② Simões, F. D. (2015). Harmonization of Arbitration Laws in the Asia-Pacific: Trendy or Necessary?217-231, at 218, available at: https://works.bepress.com/fernandodiassimoes/12/ (Last visited on May 12, 2016).

③ Piersol, C. V. (1984). Insurance Arbitration and the Standard Form Contract after Southland. *SDL Rev.*30,617-637, at 617.

④ Id.

⑤ It is commonly known as FIDIC, the acronym for its French name Fédération Internationale des Ingénieurs-Conseils.

⑥ FIDIC homepage, available at http://fidic.org/about-fidic (Last visited on May 12, 2016).

⑦ Available at:https://www.expertguides.com/articles/arbitration-arising-out-of-fidic-contracts/ar3ce26b (Last visited on May 12, 2016).

provides two primary tiers of dispute resolution: Sub Clause 20.4 provides a Dispute Adjudication Board (DAB) and Sub Clause 20.6 provides international arbitration.

For instance, the Sub Clause 20.6 on FIDIC Clause provides:

"Unless settled amicably, any dispute in respect of which the DAB's decision (if any) has not become final and binding shall be finally settled by international arbitration. Unless otherwise agreed by both Parties:

(a) the dispute shall be finally settled under the Rules of Arbitration of the International Chamber of Commerce,

(b) the dispute shall be settled by three arbitrators appointed in accordance with these Rules,

(c) the arbitration shall be conducted in the language for communications."

In maritime industry, arbitration clauses are also included in standard form contracts. The Baltic and International Maritime Conference (BIMCO) also provides the standard form contracts. For instance, the GENCON 1994 is the most popularly and widely used general purpose voyage charter party in the industry for all kinds of trades and for numerous types of cargoes.[①]

Article 19 of GENCON 1994 puts forward the arbitration clauses:

"(a) This Charter Party shall be governed by and construed in accordance with English law and any dispute arising out of this Charter Party shall be referred to arbitration in London in accordance with the Arbitration Acts 1950 and 1979 or any statutory modification or re-enactment thereof for the time being in force. Unless the parties agree upon a sole arbitrator,

例如，FIDIC条款的第20.6款规定：

"除非友好解决，否则有关争端裁决委员会的决定（如有）尚未成为最终决定并具有约束力的任何争议，应通过国际仲裁最终解决。除非双方另有约定：

(a) 该争议应最终根据国际商会的仲裁规则进行解决，

(b) 该争议应由根据本规则指定的三名仲裁员来解决，

(c) 仲裁应以通信的语言进行。"

在海事业，仲裁条款也包括在格式合同中。波罗的海和国际海事会议（BIMCO）也提供了格式合同。例如，GENCON 1994（金康1994合同）是该行业中最广泛使用的通用航次租船合同，用于各种贸易和各种类型的货物。[①]

金康1994合同第19条提出仲裁条款：

"(a) 本租约应受英国法律管辖并按其解释，因本租约引起的任何争议应提交伦敦仲裁，仲裁法律可选择使用1950年仲裁法案和1979年仲裁法案，或任何在当时生效的法定修改或重新制定的法律。除非双方同意独任

---

① Available at: https://www.bimco.org/Products/Shop/GENCON_94.aspx (Last visited on May 12, 2016).

仲裁员，否则各方应指定一名仲裁员，如此指定的仲裁员应指定第三名仲裁员，由此组成的三人仲裁庭或其中任何两个人的决定应为最终决定。在一方收到另一方仲裁员的书面提名后，该一方应在十四天内指定其仲裁员，否则，指定的单一仲裁员的决定应为最终决定。

......

(b) 本租船合同应受《美国法典》第九章和美国海事法管辖并按其解释，如因本租船合同引起任何争议，争议事项应提交在纽约的三位仲裁员，其中一名由双方当事人任命，第三名由如此选定的两人指定；他们或其中任何两人的决定为最终决定。为执行任何裁决，本协议可成为法院的规则。诉讼程序应按照海事仲裁员协会的规则进行。"

从上述例子可以看出，仲裁条款在各行业的格式合同中有着广泛的应用。然而，关于仲裁仍存在一些问题：什么是仲裁？仲裁中最重要的因素是什么？我们应该如何起草格式合同中的仲裁条款？在下几章中，我们将详细讨论这些问题。

one arbitrator shall be appointed by each party and the arbitrators so appointed shall appoint a third arbitrator, the decision of the three-man tribunal thus constituted or any two of them, shall be final. On the receipt by one party of the nomination in writing of the other party's arbitrator, that party shall appoint their arbitrator within fourteen days, failing which the decision of the single arbitrator appointed shall be final.

…

(b) This Charter Party shall be governed by and construed in accordance with Title 9 of the United States Code and the Maritime Law of the United States and should any dispute arise out of this Charter Party, the matter in dispute shall be referred to three persons at New York, one to be appointed by each of the parties hereto, and the third by the two so chosen; their decision or that of any two of them shall be final, and for purpose of enforcing any award, this agreement may be made a rule of the Court. The proceedings shall be conducted in accordance with the rules of the Society of Maritime Arbitrators, Inc."

From the examples mentioned above, it can be seen that arbitration clauses are widely used in standard form contracts in various industries. However, there are still some questions about arbitration: What is arbitration? What is the most important element in arbitration? How should we draft the arbitration clause in standard form contracts? In the next chapters, these questions will be discussed in detial.

Chapter II Introduction of Arbitration Agreement

1. The Concept and Characteristics of Arbitration

1.1 Concept of Arbitration

Generally, there are two kinds of arbitration. One is institutional arbitration and the other is *ad hoc* arbitration. Compared with "*ad hoc* arbitration", "institutional" arbitration is one that is administered by a specialist arbitral institution under its own rules of arbitration. There are many arbitration institutions, such as ICDR, IACAC, ICC and LCIA, as well as some regional arbitral institutions, such as those in Singapore and the Chambers of Commerce of Switzerland, Stockholm, and Vienna.[①]

The other kind of arbitration is ad hoc arbitration known as the "non-administered" arbitration. The ad hoc arbitration is conducted without the support of any arbitration institution.[②] The parties in the arbitration can choose an arbitrator or arbitrators to solve their disputes without the supervision of any arbitration institution. The applicable national arbitration legislation and national courts will, in general, be available for administering the procedural rules for the arbitration. And sometimes the parties can also choose a set of pre-existing designed procedural rules to govern ad hoc arbitration procedures. For instance, the parties can choose to use the UNCITRAL Arbitration Rules to govern their ad hoc arbitration.

---

① Redfern, A., Supra note 6, at 55-56.
② Born, G. (2010). *International Arbitration and Forum Selection Agreements: Drafting and Enforcing*. Kluwer Law International, at 63.

第二章 仲裁协议的介绍

一、仲裁的概念与特点

（一）仲裁的概念

仲裁一般有两种：一是机构仲裁，二是临时性仲裁。与"临时仲裁"相比，机构仲裁是由专业仲裁机构根据其自身的仲裁规则管理的机构。有许多仲裁机构，如ICDR、IACAC、ICC和LCIA，以及一些区域仲裁机构，如新加坡的仲裁机构和瑞士商会、斯德哥尔摩商会和维也纳商会。[①]

而临时仲裁则是被称为"不被行政管理"的仲裁形式。临时仲裁是在没有任何仲裁机构的支持下进行的。[②]仲裁当事人可以选择一位或多位仲裁员解决争议，无需仲裁机构监督。一般来说，临时仲裁程序中当事人可以选择适用的国家仲裁立法和国家法院来管理临时仲裁的程序。有时，当事人也可以选择一套预先设计好的的特别程序规则来管理临时仲裁程序。例如，当事人可以选择使用《联合国国际贸易法委员会（UNCITRAL）示范法》（以下简称示范法《UNCITRAL 仲裁示范法》）国际商事仲裁来管理他们的临时仲裁。

就仲裁的明确定义而言,《联合国国际贸易法委员会国际商事仲裁示范法》与大多数仲裁公约和国家法一样,没有明确的规则来定义"仲裁"的含义。①即便如此,在一些国家的仲裁法中也可以找到比示范法更详细的仲裁定义的好例子。

例如,埃及共和国的仲裁法第四条(1)规定,本法所称"仲裁",是指由双方自愿同意基于自己的自由意志解决争端的方式,当事人有权利选择将仲裁任务委托给一个永久的仲裁组织或中心。②

立陶宛还在其仲裁法第二条中提供了一个描述性的定义。立陶宛仲裁法第二条(a)规定,术语"仲裁"是指争端解决时自然人或法人经过协议,将争端提交或承诺提交至第三方,第三方由当事人选择协议或法律指定,而不是提交给国家法院审判。③

(二)仲裁的特点

仲裁在国际商业争端解决方面各有其优缺点。仲裁的优点如下所示。

第一,仲裁尊重双方当事人的自治权。仲裁只有在双方达成一致同意后才会开始。加里·博恩说,仲裁通常是双方自愿的,双方同意对他们的分歧进行仲裁。④仲裁协议是对当事人意图的陈述。当事人有权决定有关仲裁的一切事项,如仲裁所在地、仲裁庭的组成、仲裁程序等。

In terms of clear definition of arbitration, the UNCITRAL Model Law on International Commercial Arbitration, like most conventions and national laws on arbitration, does not have specific rules to define the meaning of "arbitration".① Even so, good examples of a more detailed arbitration definition than that in the Model Law can be found in some national arbitration laws.

For instance, Article 4(1) in the arbitration law of the Republic of Egypt states that for the purpose of this law, the term "arbitration" means voluntary arbitration agreed by two parties for dispute resolution based on their own free will, whether or not the chosen body to which the arbitral mission is entrusted by agreement of two parties is a permanent arbitral organization or center.②

Lithuania also provides a descriptive definition in the Article 2 of its arbitration law. The Article 2(a) of Lithuania Arbitration Law states that the term "arbitration" means dispute resolution when natural or legal persons subject to their agreement, submit or undertake to submit the claim to the third party or parties, chosen by them or appointed subject to the agreement or the law instead of submitting it to the state court.③

1.2 Characteristics of Arbitration

Arbitration has its own advantages and disadvantages when it comes to international commercial dispute resolution. The advantages of arbitration are listed below.

First, arbitration respects the autonomy of the parties. Arbitration starts only when both parties agree with it. Gary B. Born said arbitration is ordinarily consensual and the parties agree to arbitrate their differences.④ An arbitration agreement is the presentation of the parties' intention. The parties have rights to decide all matters concerning the arbitration, such as the seat of arbitration, the composition of the arbitral tribunal and the arbitration procedure, etc.

---

① Binder, P., & Sekolec, J. (2005). International Commercial Arbitration and Conciliation in UNCITRAL Model Law Jurisdictions. Sweet & Maxwell, at 33.

② Article 4 in the Arbitration Law of the Republic of Egypt.

③ Article 2 of Lithuania Arbitration Law.

④ Born, G. Supra note 35, at 2.

Second, arbitration is efficient because the procedure of arbitration is simpler than that of many other mechanisms of dispute resolution. For instance, in most countries arbitral awards are final, like Article 5 and Article 9 in China Arbitration Law, which state that if effective arbitration clauses exist, the award is final.[1]

Third, arbitration can protect the privacy of parties.[2] In most cases, arbitration is not open to the public. Therefore, this privacy safeguards the business reputation of the companies which are involved in cases. For instance，Article 20.7 on ICC Arbitration Rules regulates that the Arbitral Tribunal should take measures to protect trade secrets and confidential information.[3]

Fourth, arbitration has characteristics of being neutral. Arbitration is not disturbed by any individuals or organizations[4]. The parties can settle their disputes outside their jurisdiction and jurisdiction system, and the parties can choose arbitration institutions and the laws applicable to arbitration as they wish.[5]

It cannot be denied that arbitration is an efficient and flexible way in dispute resolution, but arbitration also has its limitation, because complete justice of the substantive law is not always ensured. For example, the parties have rights to choose arbitrators, but due to many factors, arbitrators may not be qualified enough to make the just award of arbitration. Furthermore, the arbitral awards may face the potential problems after arbitration proceedings, such as being set aside or refusal of recognition and enforcement.[6]

第二，仲裁具有终局性。因为仲裁程序比其他许多争议解决机制更简单。例如，大多数国家的仲裁裁决都是终局的，如《中国仲裁法》第五条和第九条，其中规定，如果存在有效的仲裁条款，则裁决是终局的。[1]

第三，仲裁可以保护当事人的隐私。[2]在大多数情况下，仲裁是不对公众开放的。因此，这种隐密性保护了企业的商业声誉。例如，《国际商会仲裁规则》第20.7条规定，仲裁庭应采取措施保护商业秘密和保密信息。[3]

第四，仲裁具有中立的特点。仲裁不受任何个人或组织的干扰，[4]当事人可以在其管辖范围和管辖制度之外解决争议，可以根据其意愿选择仲裁机构和适用于仲裁的法律。[5]

不可否认，仲裁是一种有效和灵活的争端解决方式，但仲裁也有其局限性，因为实体法的完全公正并不总是得到保证。例如，当事人有权选择仲裁员，但由于许多不可预判的因素，仲裁员可能没有足够的资格作出公正的仲裁裁决。此外，仲裁程序完成之后，仲裁裁决可能面临潜在的问题，例如仲裁裁决可能被撤销或被拒绝承认和执行。[6]

---

[1]　Article 5 and Article 9 in China Arbitration Law.
[2]　Collins, M. (1995). Privacy and Confidentiality in Arbitration Proceedings. Texas International Law Journal, 30(1), 121-134, at 122.
[3]　Article 20.7 on ICC Arbitration Rules.
[4]　Article 20.7 on ICC Arbitration Rules.
[5]　Id.
[6]　Sanders, P. (1979). A Twenty Years' Review of the Convention on the Recognition and Enforcement of Foreign Arbitral Awards. The International Lawyer, 269-287, at 275.

二、仲裁协议

（一）仲裁协议的概念

一些学者对仲裁协议的定义是：

法律上，国际仲裁协议是指双方或多方同意将当事人之间发生或可能发生的具有国际性质的争端应由一名或多名仲裁员裁决的协议。①

笔者认为仲裁协议是双方之间的一种合同，双方同意将其现有或未来的争议提交仲裁，并排除国家法院的管辖权。②一旦仲裁结束，仲裁裁决对双方当事人具有约束力，并与法院判决一样可被强制执行。

仲裁协议可能会对双方当事人产生一定的影响。第一点是，双方有义务根据仲裁协议提出争议。国际仲裁公约已经承认在存在仲裁协议时，仲裁是具有约束力的，当纠纷产生的时候当事人有义务将仲裁程序作为他们解决纠纷的首选。

例如，《中国仲裁法》③第五条明确规定，如果双方之间有有效的仲裁协议，双方有义务将争议提交仲裁。

2. Arbitration Agreement

2.1 Concept of Arbitration Agreement

Some scholars define the arbitration agreement as:

"In law, an international arbitration agreement is an agreement in which two or more parties agree that a dispute which has arisen or which may arise between them, and which has an international character, shall be resolved by one or more arbitrators."[1]

In my opinion, arbitration agreement is a contract between the parties where they agree to submit their existing or future disputes to arbitration and exclude the jurisdiction in national courts.[2] Once arbitration is concluded, the arbitral award is binding on the parties and as enforceable as a court judgment would be.

The arbitration agreement may have some effects on the parties. The first point is that the parties have an obligation to submit disputes based on the arbitration agreement. International conventions on arbitration have already recognized the binding nature of the obligation that when there is the existence of arbitration agreements, arbitration shall be the first choice for disputes resolution.

For example, Article 5 of Chinese Arbitration Law[3] clearly indicates that the parties are obliged to submit their disputes to arbitration if there is a valid arbitration agreement between them.

---

① Gaillard, E., & Savage, J. (Eds.). Fouchard Gaillard-Goldman on International Commercial Arbitration. Gaillard at 92.

② Zekos, G. I. (2008). International Commercial and Marine Arbitration. Routledge, at 301.

③ Article 5 of Chinese Arbitration Law provides that where the litigants have an arbitration agreement and one litigant brings a suit in the people's court, the people's court shall not accept it. However, exception is to be made when the arbitration agreement is invalid.

The second noteworthy point is that the arbitral tribunal has jurisdiction to hear all disputes covered by the arbitration agreement. The arbitration agreement empowers the arbitral tribunal to make a decision resolving the disputes between the parties. The arbitration agreement also determines which issues can be examined and decided by the arbitral tribunal. The arbitration agreement also has its negative effects. Namely, if the parties choose arbitration, it means that the courts lose jurisdiction to settle the disputes. Some support can be found from international conventions on arbitration, national legislation, etc.

Examples included Article II(3) of the New York Convention[①] and Article VIII of the UNCITRAL Model Law.[②] As for domestic law, some support can be found from China's Arbitration Law, which provides:

"Where the parties had agreed on an arbitration agreement, but one of the parties initiates an action before a people's court without stating the existence of the arbitration agreement, the people's court shall, unless the arbitration agreement is invalid, reject the action if the other party submits to the court the arbitration agreement before the first hearing of the case. If the other party fails to object to the hearing by the people's court before the first hearing, the arbitration agreement shall be considered to have been waived by the party and the people's court shall proceed with the hearing."[③]

However, national courts are still entitled to review the existence and validity of arbitration agreements. Furthermore, the parties can still get support or help from the courts in the process of arbitration, such as

第二个值得注意的问题是，仲裁庭有权审理仲裁协议中所约定的所有争端。仲裁协议授权仲裁庭作出解决双方当事人之间的争议的决定。仲裁协议还决定了哪些问题可以由仲裁庭审查和决定。仲裁协议也有其负面影响。也就是说，如果当事人选择仲裁，这就意味着法院失去了解决争议的管辖权。这种规定在国际仲裁公约、国家立法中都可以得到一些支持，

诸如《纽约公约》[①]第二条（3）和《UNCITRAL 仲裁示范法》[②]第八条。至于国内法，中国的《仲裁法》也有一些支持，其中第二十六条规定：

"当事人达成仲裁协议，一方向人民法院起诉未声明有仲裁协议，人民法院受理后，另一方在首次开庭前提交仲裁协议的，人民法院应当驳回起诉，但仲裁协议无效的除外；另一方在首次开庭前未对人民法院受理该案提出异议的，视为放弃仲裁协议，人民法院应当继续审理。"[③]

但是，国家法院仍然有权审查仲裁协议是否真实存在以及协议有效性。此外，当事人在仲裁过程中仍可获得法院的支持或帮助，如资产冻结、证据保

---

① The New York Convention Article II 3: The court of a Contracting State, when seized of an action in a matter in respect of which the parties have made an agreement within the meaning of this article, shall, at the request of one of the parties, refer the parties to arbitration, unless it finds that the said agreement is null and void, inoperative or incapable of being performed.

② The UNCITRAL Model Law Article 8(1): A court before which an action is brought in a matter which is the subject of an arbitration agreement shall, if a party so requests not later than when submitting his first statement on the substance of the dispute, refer the parties to arbitration unless it finds that the agreement is null and void, inoperative or incapable of being performed.

③ Article 26 of China Arbitration Law.

存等。[①]

例如,《UNCITRAL 仲裁示范法》第 9 条规定:

一方在仲裁程序之前或仲裁期间,要求法院采取临时保护措施,并要求法院批准该措施,这与仲裁协议并不相违背。

此外,《UNCITRAL 仲裁示范法》第 27 条规定了法院可以为寻找仲裁证据提供协助。[②]

(二)仲裁协议的类型

实际上,仲裁协议有两种类型。一是仲裁条款,主要是指双方承诺就该合同可能产生的争议提交仲裁的协议,仲裁条款通常包含在主合同中。另一种类型是仲裁协议书。仲裁协议书通常是在争议发生后形成的。[③]大多数国际商事仲裁是第一种类型,即根据商业合同中的仲裁条款进行。

一般来说,仲裁条款较短,而仲裁协议则较长。仲裁条款是对将来可能发生的纠纷的一种安排,因此仲裁条款没有详细的仲裁程序设计。

asset freezing, preservation of evidence, etc.[①]

For instance, Article 9 of the UNCITRAL Model Law on arbitration provides:

"It is not incompatible with an arbitration agreement for a party to request, before or during arbitral proceedings, from a court an interim measure of protection and for a court to grant such measure."

In addition, Article 27 of the UNCITRAL Model Law on arbitration regulates the court's assistance in offering evidence for arbitration.[②]

2.2 Types of Arbitration Agreement

In practice, there are two types of arbitration agreements. One is arbitration clause, defined as an agreement by which the parties undertake to submit to arbitration the disputes which may arise in regard to that contract. The other type is the submission agreement, usually formed after the dispute has arisen.[③] Most international commercial arbitrations take place following an arbitration clause in a commercial contract.

Generally speaking, arbitration clauses are short, while submission agreements are longer. An arbitration clause is an arrangement about disputes which may arise in the future, so it does not have terms in details.

---

① Hoellering, M. (1986). The UNCITRAL Model Law on International Commercial Arbitration. *The International Lawyer*, 20(1), 327-339, at 330.

② Article 27 of the UNCITRAL Model Law provides: The arbitral tribunal or a party with the approval of the arbitral tribunal may request from a competent court of this State assistance in taking evidence. The court may execute the request within its competence and according to its rules on taking evidence.

③ Alderman, R. (2001-2002). Pre-Dispute Mandatory Arbitration in Consumer Contracts: Call for Reform. Houston Law Review, 38(4), 1237-1268, at 1240.

Usually arbitration clauses may be inserted as a short model clause, recommended by an arbitral institution.

For example, the model arbitration clauses from ICC provides:

"All disputes arising out of or in connection with the present contract shall be finally settled under the Rules of Arbitration of the International Chamber of Commerce by one or more arbitrators appointed in accordance with the said Rules."[1] Or "Arbitration, if any, by I.C.C. Rules in London."[2]

On the contrary, a submission agreement, i.e. an arbitration agreement is concluded about a dispute that has already arisen. Arbitration agreement may be tailor-made to fit the particular dispute. Therefore, the arbitration agreement has terms in detail, like the place of arbitration, the applicable substantive law, the arbitrators, the rules of procedure to be applied, etc.

3. Potential Problems after Arbitration Proceedings

Once the arbitral award is made, the arbitration award shall be final and binding upon both parties.[3] Finality is a fundamental characteristic of arbitration and a key factor that attracts many parties to choose arbitration as a contractual dispute resolution mechanism.[4] The arbitral award is effective only when the parties have the ability and are willing to enforce it before a national court. However, there are some grounds for setting aside the arbitral awards or refusal of recognition and enforcement of arbitral awards. In this section, the potential problems after arbitration proceedings will be discussed.

---

① Standard ICC Arbitration Clauses, available at: http://www.iccwbo.org/products-and-services/arbitration-and-adr/arbitration/standard-icc-arbitration-clauses/ (Last visited on May 16, 2016).

② Id.

③ Siegel, T. M. (1995). Is Arbitration Final & (and) Binding—Public Policy Says, Not Necessarily—Exxon Shipping Company v. Exxon Seamen's Union. *J. Disp. Resol.*, 351-360, at 353.

④ Schmitz,A.(2002). Ending a Mud Bowl: Defining Arbitration's Finality Through Functional Analysis. *Ga. L. Rev.*, 37, 123-204, at 124.

通常，仲裁条款是仲裁机构推荐的格式条款，并且插入在商业合同中。

例如，ICC 提供了仲裁示范条款：

"因本合同而引起的或与本合同有关的所有争议，应根据国际商会仲裁的规则指定一名或多名仲裁员根据国际商会仲裁规则进行最终的解决。"① 或 "如果进行仲裁程序，使用伦敦 ICC 的规则进行仲裁。"②

相反，仲裁协议是就已经出现的争端达成的。仲裁协议可以根据特定的争议而量身定做。因此，仲裁协议有详细的条款，如仲裁地点、适用的实体法、仲裁员、要适用的程序规则等。

三、仲裁程序启动后的潜在问题

仲裁裁决一经作出，即为终局裁决，对双方均有约束力。③终局性是仲裁的一个基本特征，也是吸引许多当事人选择仲裁作为合同争议解决机制的一个关键因素。④仲裁裁决只有在当事人有能力并愿意在国家法院执行仲裁时才有效。但是，也有一些理由撤销仲裁裁决或拒绝承认和执行仲裁裁决。本节将讨论仲裁程序结束后可能出现的问题。

（一）仲裁裁决被撤销

仲裁庭作出仲裁裁决后，败诉方仍有可能对仲裁裁决提出质疑。例如，根据《UNCITRAL 国际商事仲裁示范法》，当裁决被"撤销"时，仲裁裁决可能面临危险的结果。这意味着仲裁裁决将不复存在，换句话说，法院的管辖权可以撤销该仲裁裁决，并宣布应全部或部分无视该裁决。[①] 这样，该仲裁裁决不可强制执行，在被撤销后将被视为无效。

由于仲裁中没有上诉程序的特点，仲裁败诉方可以援引有关法律对仲裁裁决提出质疑，如《示范法》第 34 条。[②] 一旦仲裁裁决被撤销，一方当事人可能会面临一定的风险，而仲裁裁决的有效性将不会处于一定的状态。这可能会导致一个更长的、更复杂的仲裁过程。

一个相当著名的例子是希尔马顿有限公司[③]诉法国全能估值有限公司案。该案件中，法国全能估值有限公司

3.1 Setting Aside

After the arbitral tribunal has made an arbitral award, the losing parties still have the possibility to challenge the arbitral awards. For instance, according to the UNCITRAL Model Law on International Commercial Arbitration, the arbitral awards may face a risky result when the award is "set aside". That means the arbitral awards would cease to exist— in other words, the jurisdiction of the courts may set the arbitral award aside and declare that the award should be disregarded in whole or in part.[①] If this is the case, The arbitral award is not enforceable and it would be considered invalid after being set aside.

An appeal procedure is not provided in abitration due to its features, so the losing party in arbitration may cite relevant laws to challenge the arbitral award, like Article 34 of the Model Law.[②] Once the arbitral award is set aside, the party may face certain risks, and the validity of arbitral award would not be in a certain status. It may lead to a longer and more complex process of arbitration.

The case *Société Hilmarton Ltd v. Société Omnium de traitement et de valorisation*[③] is quite a famous example of this. A French company, OTV

---

①   Redfern, A. Supra note 6, at 404.

②   Article 34 lists six grounds on which a court may set an award aside. The list of six grounds is exhaustive. The first group of four grounds appears in Article 34(2)(a) and must be raised and proved by the applicant. The second group of two grounds appears in Article 34(2)(b) and may be raised by the court on its own motion. The six grounds are: a. the incapacity of a party or invalidity of the arbitration agreement; b. a failure to notify the party making the application of the appointment of an arbitrator or initiation of proceedings; c. the award was beyond the scope of the arbitration agreement; d. invalid constitution of the arbitral tribunal; e. the subject matter was not arbitratable (not capable of resolution by arbitration); and f. violation of public policy.

③   Société Hilmarton Ltd v. Société Omnium de traitement et de valorisation, [1994] 92-15.137, Cour de Cassation, France, available at: http://www.newyorkconvention1958.org/index.php?lvl=notice_display&id=140&seule=1 (Last visited on May 12, 2016).

① entrusted an English company, Hilmarton with the task of providing advice and coordination for a bid to obtain and perform a contract for work in Algeria. Hilmarton used the ICC arbitration agreement in order to recover payment of the remaining balance of its fees. On August 19, 1988, the claim was dismissed and the arbitral award was declared enforceable in France even though it had been set aside in Switzerland. Hilmarton company challenged the decision of the Paris Court of Appeal which upheld the enforcement order.

After several years of long complex hearings, the Supreme Court affirmed the decision of the Paris Court of Appeal and dismissed the action. According to Article VII of the New York Convention, it can be found that the Paris Court of Appeal rightly held that OTV could avail itself of French rules pertaining to the recognition and enforcement of foreign awards in international arbitration. According to Article 1502 of the Code of Civil Procedure, there is not the same ground for refusal of recognition and enforcement of awards as set forth in Article V(1)(e) of the New York Convention. The Supreme Court in France added that the award rendered in Switzerland was an international award. An international arbitral award cannot be integrated into the legal order of a State. Therefore, the arbitral award continues to exist, even though it had been set aside, and could still be recognized in France.② Finally, the Supreme Court confirmed this approach in a decision of March 23, 1994.③

委托英国希尔马顿有限公司①为一个投标工作提供建议和斡旋,希望以此获得和履行在阿尔及利亚的工作合同。然而,希尔马顿有限公司利用国际商会的仲裁条款并进行仲裁,希望收回投标工作中剩余的费用。1988 年 8 月 19 日,仲裁庭作出了仲裁裁决,希尔马顿有限公司的索赔要求被驳回,仲裁裁决被宣布在法国可被强制执行,虽然该仲裁裁决在瑞士也已被撤销。希尔马顿公司对巴黎上诉法院维持执行命令的决定提出质疑。

经过几年漫长而复杂的庭审,最高法院维持了巴黎上诉法院的决定,并驳回了诉讼。根据《纽约公约》第七条,可以发现,巴黎上诉法院认为,法国全能估值有限公司可以利用法国有关在国际仲裁中承认和执行外国裁决的规则承认该仲裁裁决。但是根据法国《民事诉讼法典》第 1502 条,拒绝承认和执行裁决的理由与《纽约公约》第五条(1)(e) 中规定的不同法国最高法院补充说,在瑞士作出的裁决是一项国际裁决。一个国际仲裁裁决不能被纳入一个国家的法律秩序。因此,本案的仲裁裁决仍然存在,即使它已经被撤销,而且在法国仍然可以得到承认。②最后,最高法院在 1994 年 3 月 23 日的一项决定中证实了这一做法。③

---

① OTV is short for Omnium de traitement et de valorisation.
② The details about the facts and decisions are available at: http://www.newyorkconvention1958.org/index.php?lvl=notice_display&id=140&seule=1(Last visited on May 12, 2016).
③ Gaillard, E. (1999). The Enforcement of Awards Set Aside in the Country of Origin. *ICSID REVIEW*, 14, 16-45, at 20.

仲裁通常被认为是一种方便、更快、更便宜的纠纷解决方式,但希尔马顿案并没有明显地显示出这些特点。在希尔马顿案漫长的诉讼程序中,仲裁裁决的有效性自始至终均未确定。在这个过程中,双方花费了大量的金钱、时间和精力。因此,我们发现并不是每一个仲裁案件都会导致纠纷的迅速解决。如果仲裁裁决被撤销,强制执行是一个更加漫长和复杂的过程。

Arbitration is often said to be convenient, faster and cheaper, but the Hilmarton case didn't show these features evidently. In the long proceedings of the Hilmarton case, the validity of the arbitral award was pending from the beginning to the end. In the process, the parties consumed a lot of money, time and effort. Therefore, it is found that not every case using arbitration results in disputes being resolved rapidly. If the arbitral award is set aside, the enforcement is a prolonging and more complex process.

(二)拒绝承认和执行

3.2 Refusal of Recognition and Enforcement

仲裁裁决可以因国家法院的执行程序而强制执行。通常情况下,国际商事仲裁中的胜诉方希望该仲裁裁决立即得到承认和执行。《纽约公约》提供了仲裁裁决强制执行的法律框架。①《纽约公约》允许直接执行仲裁裁决,前提条件是该仲裁裁决是基于《纽约公约》任何缔约国合法承认的仲裁协议而作出的。众所周知,《纽约公约》"因受广泛认可而成为最成功的国际私法条约"。②下面将以《纽约公约》为例,介绍在国际商事仲裁中拒绝承认和执行的有关问题。

《纽约公约》第一条规定了对该公约的范围的限制,因为《纽约公约》只适用于要进行仲裁的国际商业协定。③

The arbitral award from a dispute can be forced into execution as a result of enforcement proceedings in a national court, and the prevailing party in an international commercial arbitration expects the award to be recognized and enforced without delay. The New York Convention provides the structure for award enforcement.① All that is needed is an arbitral award based on an arbitration agreement which is obtained by the court of any contracting states, and the convention allows the direct enforcement of an arbitral award. It is well known that the New York Convention is "the most successful private international law treaty on account of its widespread acceptance."② Next, the New York Convention will be taken as an example to introduce the issues about the refusal of recognition and enforcement in international commercial arbitration.

Article I of the New York Convention stipulate limitations on the scope of the convention, because the New York Convention only applies to international commercial agreements to arbitrate.③

---

① Id.

② Fry, J. D. (2009). Désordre Public International under the New York Convention: Wither Truly International Public Policy. *Chinese Journal of International Law*, 8(1), 81-134, at 81.

③ The New York Convention Article I (1): This convention shall apply to the recognition and enforcement of arbitral awards made in the territory of a State other than the State where the recognition and enforcement of such awards are sought, and arising out of differences between persons, whether physical or legal. It shall also apply to arbitral awards not considered as domestic awards in the State where their recognition and enforcement are sought.

Article II of the New York Convention provides various grounds for refusal of recognition and enforcement of an arbitral award, which are held as the standards to regulate the formal writing requirements with regard to this issue.[1]

Article III of the New York Convention requires each contracting state to recognize and enforce arbitral awards fairly.[2] There shall not be substantially more onerous conditions or higher fees or charges on the recognition or enforcement of arbitral awards to which this convention applies that are imposed on the recognition or enforcement of domestic arbitral awards.[3]

Article IV of the New York Convention provides that a party may obtain recognition and enforcement of

《纽约公约》第二条规定，当事人应当以书面协定的形式承认当事人彼此之间所发生或可能发生之一切或任何争议，如关涉可以仲裁解决事项之确定法律关系，不论为契约性质与否，应当提交仲裁时，各缔约国应承认此项协定。[1]

《纽约公约》第三条要求每个缔约国公平地承认和执行仲裁裁决。[2]承认或执行本公约适用的仲裁裁决，不应有此承认或执行国内仲裁裁决更严苛的条件或更高的费用或收费。[3]

《纽约公约》第四条规定，若仲裁裁决或仲裁协定所用文字非为裁决地所在国之正式文字，若需要申请仲裁裁决的

---

[1] The New York Convention Article II:
1. Each Contracting State shall recognize an agreement in writing under which the parties undertake to submit to arbitration all or any differences which have arisen or which may arise between them in respect of a defined legal relationship, whether contractual or not, concerning a subject matter capable of settlement by arbitration.
2. The term "agreement in writing" shall include an arbitral clause in a contract or an arbitration agreement, signed by the parties or contained in an exchange of letters or telegrams.
3. The court of a Contracting State, when seized of an action in a matter in respect of which the parties have made an agreement within the meaning of this article, shall, at the request of one of the parties, refer the parties to arbitration, unless it finds that the said agreement is null and void, inoperative or incapable of being performed.
[2] The New York Convention Article III:
Each Contracting State shall recognize arbitral awards as binding and enforce them in accordance with the rules of procedure of the territory where the award is relied upon, under the conditions laid down in the following articles. There shall not be imposed substantially more onerous conditions or higher fees or charges on the recognition or enforcement of arbitral awards to which this Convention applies than are imposed on the recognition or enforcement of domestic arbitral awards.
[3] Id.

承认及执行裁决时,应将这些文件翻译为该语言。①译本应由公设或宣誓之翻译员或外交或领事人员认证。

从第五条可以看出,《纽约公约》明确规定了拒绝承认和执行仲裁裁决的各种理由,这些理由被认为是关于这一问题的标准。根据《纽约公约》,外国仲裁裁决可以在缔约国得到承认和执行,除非《公约》第五条规定的理由发生。②

an arbitral award.① The parties should submit the dual certificates to the court. If the award or agreement is not made in an official language of the country in which the award is relied upon, a translation of these documents into such language shall be produced, and the translation shall be certified by an official or sworn translator or by a diplomatic or consular agent.

From Article V, it is found that New York Convention specifie various grounds for refusal of recognition and enforcement of an arbitral award, which are held as the standard regarding this issue. Under the New York Convention, a foreign award can be recognized and enforced in a contracting state unless there are some grounds as regulated in Article V of the Convention.②

---

① The New York Convention Article IV:

1. To obtain the recognition and enforcement mentioned in the preceding article, the party applying for recognition and enforcement shall, at the time of the application, supply:

(a) The duly authenticated original award or a duly certified copy thereof;

(b) The original agreement referred to in article II or a duly certified copy thereof.

2. If the said award or agreement is not made in an official language of the country in which the award is relied upon, the party applying for recognition and enforcement of the award shall produce a translation of these documents into such language. The translation shall be certified by an official or sworn translator or by a diplomatic or consular agent.

② The New York Convention Article V:

1. Recognition and enforcement of the award may be refused, at the request of the party against whom it is invoked, only if that party furnishes to the competent authority where the recognition and enforcement is sought, proof that:

(a) The parties to the agreement referred to in article II were, under the law applicable to them, under some incapacity, or the said agreement is not valid under the law to which the parties have subjected it or, failing any indication thereon, under the law of the country where the award was made; or (b) The party against whom the award is invoked was not given proper notice of the appointment of the arbitrator or of the arbitration proceedings or was otherwise unable to present his case; or (c) The award deals with a difference not contemplated by or not falling within the terms of the submission to arbitration, or it contains decisions on matters beyond the scope of the submission to arbitration, provided that, if the decisions on matters submitted to arbitration can be separated from those not so submitted, that part of the award which contains decisions on matters submitted to arbitration may be recognized and enforced; or (d) The composition of the arbitral authority or the arbitral procedure was not in accordance with the agreement of the parties, or, failing such agreement, was not in accordance with the law of the country where the arbitration took place; or (e) The award has not yet become binding on the parties, or has been set aside or suspended by a competent authority of the country in which, or under the law of which, that award was made.

2. Recognition and enforcement of an arbitral award may also be refused if the competent authority in the country where recognition and enforcement is sought finds that:

(a)The subject matter of the difference is not capable of settlement by arbitration under the law of that country; or (b) The recognition or enforcement of the award would be contrary to the public policy of that country.

Article V (l) provides that the defense may be raised by the parties to the recognition and enforcement of the award. Article V (2) maintains that the courts may have some reasons to deny recognition and enforcement of the award.[1]

The first ground for refusal of recognition and enforcement is the absence of a valid arbitration agreement. The reasons are listed below: one or both of the contracting parties lack the capacity of the arbitration agreement, or the agreement is invalid under the applicable law.[2]

The second ground provides that an arbitral award will be denied if the party is not given proper notice of either the appointment of the arbitrator or the proceedings,[3] or if the party was unable to present their case.[4] In other words, the lack of the due process would cause the refusal of recognition or enforcement.

The third ground is that the dispute, submitted by the parties, lacks arbitrability. If the dispute matters are not submitted or beyond the scope of the arbitration agreement, the arbitral award may be refused to be recognized and enforced.

The fourth ground for refusal of recognition and enforcement is the improper composition or procedure of the arbitral tribunal. If the composition of the arbitral authority or the arbitral procedure is not in accordance with the arbitration agreements or, the arbitral award does not conform to the law of the country where the arbitration takes place, the award may be refused to be recognized or enforced.

The fifth ground is the arbitration award is not binding or the award has been set aside or suspended by the national courts.[5]

第五条（1）规定，辩护可以由承认和执行裁决的当事人提出。第五条（2）认为，法院可能会拒绝承认和执行裁决。[1]

拒绝承认和执行的第一个理由是没有有效的仲裁协议。仲裁协议存在缺陷的原因如下：合同一方或双方缺乏仲裁协议的能力，或者该协议根据适用法律无效。[2]

第二项规定，如果当事人没有得到关于仲裁员的任命或诉讼程序的适当通知，[3]或者当事人不能陈述其案件，则仲裁裁决将被驳回。[4]由此可见，缺乏正当的仲裁程序将导致拒绝承认或执行。

第三种情况是由于双方提交的争议缺乏可仲裁性。如果争议事项没有提交或超出仲裁协议的范围，仲裁裁决可能会被拒绝承认和执行。

拒绝承认和执行的第四种情况是仲裁庭的组成或程序不当。仲裁机构的组成或仲裁程序不符合仲裁协议，或者仲裁裁决不符合仲裁发生国的法律的，可以拒绝承认或者执行。

第五种情况是，仲裁裁决不具有约束力，或者该裁决已被国家法院撤销或中止。[5]

---

① Id.
② Id.
③ Id.
④ Martinez, R. (1990). Recognition and Enforcement of International Arbitral Awards under the United Nations Convention of 1958: The "Refusal" Provisions. *The International Lawyer*, 487-518, at 499.
⑤ Id.

第六项情况是,有关该协定的标的物不能根据该国的法律通过仲裁来解决。①第七项情况是,如果该仲裁裁决违反了承认或执行该国法律的公共政策,则该仲裁裁决可能会受到质疑。

以上是《纽约公约》中仲裁裁决不予承认与执行的情况,在其他许多国际法或国家法律还有侧重于具体问题的不予承认与执行仲裁裁决的情况和理由。由于不同国家的法律文化不同,人们对《纽约公约》中的这些限制有不同的看法。

例如,中国是《纽约公约》的缔约国,但中国有两个保留,互惠保留和商业保留。互惠保留意味着中国只承认和执行在《纽约公约》②另一缔约国领土内作出的仲裁裁决。商业保留是指中国仅将《纽约公约》适用于执行因被认为是基于合同性质或非合同性质的商业法律关系的争议而引起的国际商事仲裁裁决,如货物销售、财产租赁、技术转让等。

这些规定,特别排除了外国投资者与东道国政府之间的争端。外国投资争端适用《解决其他国家与国民之间投资争端公约》。③此外,中国有自己的仲裁法,以及若干有关仲裁的司法解释和

The sixth ground is that the subject matter regarding the agreement is not capable of settlement by arbitration under the law of that country.① The seventh ground is that if the arbitral award is contrary to the public policy of the recognition or enforcement of the law of that country, the arbitral award may be challenged.

These grounds are from the New York Convention, and there are many other international laws or national laws that focus on the specific issue. There are different perceptions towards these grounds on the New York Convention because of different legal cultures in various countries.

For example, China is a Contracting State of the New York Convention, but China has two reservations, the reciprocity reservation and the commercial reservation. The reciprocity reservation means that China only recognizes and enforces the arbitral awards made within the territory of another Contracting State in the New York Convention.② The commercial reservation means that China only applies the New York Convention to the enforcement of international commercial arbitral awards arising from the disputes considered to be based on commercial legal relationships of a contractual nature or non-contractual nature, such as sale of goods, property leasing, technology transfer, etc.

Based on these regulations, the disputes between the foreign investors and governments of host countries are specifically excluded. Foreign investment disputes are covered by the Convention on the Settlement of Investment Disputes Between States and Nationals of Other States.③ In addition, China has its own arbitration law, some judicial interpretations of arbitration, and

① Id.
② See Notice of the Supreme People's Court on Implementing the Convention on the Recognition and Enforcement of Foreign Arbitral Awards Acceded to by China, available at: http://lawinfochina.com/display.aspx?lib=law&id=11873 (Last visited on May12, 2016).
③ Tao, J. (2008). *Arbitration Law and Practice in China.* Kluwer Law International, at 219.

Chinese Civil Procedure Law. These regulations all have provisions regarding arbitration. For instance, the Article 16 of Chinese Arbitration Law provides that the awards of ad hoc arbitration will not be recognized.[①]

《民事诉讼法》。这些规定都有有关仲裁的条款。例如，中国《仲裁法》第十六条规定，临时仲裁的裁决不被承认。[①]

3.3 Comments

From the above discussion, it can be found that some even after the proceedings of arbitration, some potential problems could still emerge. The main legal risks are that the award of arbitration may be set aside by national courts or may get a refusal of recognition and enforcement.

The New York Convention only has general terms. In addition, the regulations on arbitration in different countries may be different with the UNCITRAL Model Law on International Commercial Arbitration. Therefore, we should pay attention to the specific rules and laws of the countries on arbitration to ensure the recognition and enforcement of arbitral awards. Furthermore, from the New York Convention, it can be found that the main issue which leads to the set- aside and refusal of arbitral awards is the invalidity of the arbitration agreement. Thus, how to ensure the validity of the arbitration agreement is a key point which should be discussed in the design of arbitration clauses in standard form contracts.

（三）评论

从以上讨论可以发现，即使在仲裁程序之后，仍可能出现一些潜在的问题。主要的法律风险是，仲裁裁决可能被国家法院撤销，或者可能被拒绝承认和执行。

《纽约公约》只提供一般条款。此外，不同国家的仲裁规定可能与《UNCITRAL 国际商事仲裁示范法》有所不同。因此，我们应注意仲裁各国的具体规则和法律，以确保仲裁裁决被承认和执行。此外，从《纽约公约》中可以发现，导致撤销和拒绝仲裁裁决的主要问题是仲裁协议无效。因此，如何保证仲裁协议的有效性是格式合同仲裁条款设计中应讨论的关键。

---

① Article 16 of Chinese Arbitration Law: "An arbitration agreement shall include arbitration clauses stipulated in the contract and agreements of submission to arbitration that are concluded in other written forms before or after disputes arise. An arbitration agreement shall contain the following particulars: (1) an expression of intention to apply for arbitration; (2) matters for arbitration; and (3) a designated arbitration commission."

第三章 仲裁协议的效力

Chapter III Validity of the Arbitration Agreement

国际仲裁协议的存在和有效性对仲裁程序至关重要。仲裁协议是证明双方同意仲裁的基础，因此在没有有效和可执行的仲裁协议的情况下，不能进行仲裁。[①]正如前一章中讨论到的，缺少仲裁协议可能会导致仲裁裁决被质疑、拒绝承认和执行，如北京建龙重工集团诉黄金海洋集团有限公司，[②]以及皮亚诺股份有限公司诉亚夫里罗国际有限公司等案例[③]都说明了这些情况。

一些国际公约和区域性公约都对有效的国际仲裁协议作出了一些要求，并指出了仲裁协议的局限性。这些公约反映了一些国内仲裁法和国际商会、美国仲裁协会、伦敦国际仲裁庭等仲裁机构的实践中所存在的仲裁规则。

为了协调这些现代化的国际公约、国内的仲裁法和仲裁机构的规则，出现了非标准的《UNCITRAL 国际商事仲

The existence and validity of international arbitration agreements are critically important for the arbitral process. The arbitration agreement is the foundation of every consensual agreement, so there cannot be an arbitral reference in the absence of a valid and enforceable arbitration agreement.[①] As discussed in the previous chapter, the absence may cause challenge, refusal of recognition and enforcement of arbitration as seen in the case *Beijing Jianlong Heavy Industry Group v. Golden Ocean Group Ltd & Ors*,[②] as well as *Piallo GmbH v. Yafriro International Pte Ltd.*[③]

Some international conventions and regional conventions have provided some requirements for a valid international arbitration agreement and indicated the limitations of arbitration agreements. Some conventions reflect the provisions found in developed arbitration laws and in the practice of arbitral institutions such as the ICC, AAA, LCIA, etc.

To harmonize and modernize these international conventions, national arbitration laws, and the rules of arbitration institutions, the UNCITRAL Model Law on

---

[①] Onyema, E. (2010). International Commercial Arbitration and the Arbitrator's Contract. Routledge, at 9.

[②] Beijing Jianlong Heavy Industry Group v. Golden Ocean Group Ltd & Ors, [2013] EWHC 1063, King's Bench High Court, available at: http://www.cnarb.com/Item/5989.aspx (Last visited on May 12, 2016).

[③] Piallo GmbH v. Yafriro International Pte Ltd, [2013] SGHC 260, Singapore High Court, available at: http://www.singaporelaw.sg/sglaw/laws-of-singapore/case-law/free-law/high-court-judgments/15435-piallo-gmbh-v-yafriro-international-pte-ltd-2013-sghc-260 (Last visited on May 12, 2016).

International Commercial Arbitration appeared.[①] The UNCITRAL Model Law on International Commercial Arbitration plays a very important role in international arbitration. The Model Law was designed to promote the contracting states to reform and modernize their national arbitration. The Model Law reflects the worldwide consensus on key aspects of international arbitration practice, which have been accepted in various legal or economic systems around the world.[②]

Except the UNCITRAL Model Law, the New York Convention is another important reference in international commercial arbitration. By May 12, 2016 the New York Convention 1958 had been ratified by 153 countries around the world.[③] Article II and Article V of the New York Convention are the key provisions about the requirements of the validity of arbitration agreements.

1. Formal Validity

The formal validity of the arbitration agreement is an essential concern of arbitration. The issue of formal validity is very controversial in international commercial arbitration. In many international conventions and domestic laws, it is required that arbitration agreements should be in writing, as seen in Article 16 of the China Arbitration Law.[④] Other nations, such as Sweden and Japan do not require the arbitration agreement to be in writing.[⑤] In addtion, few countries allow oral arbitration agreements.[⑥] For international

---

① The Model Law is designed to assist States in reforming and modernizing their laws on arbitral procedure so as to take into account the particular features and needs of international commercial arbitration.

② Available at: http://www.uncitral.org/sites/uncitral. un.org/files/media-documents/uncitral/en/19-09955_e_ebook.pdf. (Last visited on May 12, 2016).

③ Available at: http://www.newyorkconvention.org/ list+of+contracting+states (Last visited on May12, 2016).

④ Article 16 of China Arbitration Law: "An arbitration agreement shall include the arbitration clauses provided in the contract and any other written form of agreement concluded before or after the disputes providing for submission to arbitration."

⑤ Kuang M.W. & Hong L.Y. (2013). *The Theories and the Development of the International Commercial Arbitration*, Hanlu Press, at 23.

⑥ In England, common law still recognizes an oral arbitration agreement, but it cannot be enforced under the Arbitration Act, see Article 27 of England Arbitration Act.

裁示范法》。[①]该示范法在国际仲裁中起着非常重要的作用,其旨在促进缔约国对其国家的仲裁法进行改革和现代化。该示范法反映了世界各地对国际仲裁实践的关键方面的共识,这些共识已被世界各地的各种法律或经济体系所接受。[②]

除上述示范法外,《纽约公约》是国际商事仲裁的另一个重要参考。截至2016年5月12日,世界上已有153个国家批准了《1958年纽约公约》。[③]《纽约公约》第二条和第五条是关于仲裁协议有效性要求的关键规定。

一、形式有效性

仲裁协议的形式要件有效性是仲裁过程中的一个重要问题,在国际商用仲裁中也存在争议。在许多国际公约和国内法律中,要求仲裁协议应采用书面形式,如《中国仲裁法》[④]第16条所述。也有不要求仲裁协议是书面形式[⑤]的国家,如瑞典、日本等。此外,极少有国家允许签订口头仲裁协议。[⑥]对于国际商事仲裁，也有一些关于口头仲裁协议的规定，包括《纽约公约》①第二条或《UNCITRAL 国际商事仲裁示范法》第七条。②

（一）书面协议

大多数国家仲裁法和国际公约要求"仲裁协议的形式必须是书面形式"或者"以书面形式书写"。③这些规定代表的意思是什么？

例如，《纽约公约》第二条规定：

"1. 当事人以书面协定承允彼此间所发生或可能发生之一切或任何争议，如关涉可以仲裁解决事项之确定法律关系，不论为契约性质与否，应提交仲裁时，各缔约国应承认此项协定。

2. "书面协议"一词应包括当事人所签订或在互换函电中所载明之契约仲裁条款或仲裁协定。

《UNCITRAL 仲裁示范法》第七条也有类似规定：

第七条　仲裁协议的定义和形式

（1）"仲裁协议"是指当事各方同意将在他们之间确定的不论是契约性或非契约性的法律关系上已经发生或可以

commercial arbitration, there are also some regulations regarding this issue. Some examples are included in Article II of the New York Convention,① or Article VII of the UNCITRAL Model Law on International Commercial Arbitration.②

1.1 Agreement in Writing

Most national arbitration law and international conventions require that "the form of arbitration agreements must be in writing".③ What is the meaning of "in writing?"

For instance, Article II of the New York Convention provides:

"1. Each Contracting State shall recognize an agreement in writing under which the parties undertake to submit to arbitration all or any differences which have arisen or which may arise between them in respect of a defined legal relationship, whether contractual or not, concerning a subject matter capable of settlement by arbitration.

2. The term 'agreement in writing' shall include an arbitral clause in a contract or an arbitration agreement, signed by the parties or contained in an exchange of letters or telegrams."

Article VII of the UNCITRAL Model Law also have a similar provision:

"The arbitration agreement shall be in writing. An agreement is in writing if it is contained in a document signed by the parties or in an exchange of letters, telex, telegrams or other means of telecommunication which provide a record of the agreement, or in an exchange statements of claim and

---

① Article II of the New York convention.
② Article VII of the UNCITRAL Model Law in International Commercial Arbitration.
③ Strong, S. I. (2012). What Constitutes an Agreement in Writing in International Commercial Arbitration? Conflicts Between the New York Convention and the Federal Arbitration Act. *Stanford Journal of International Law*, 47-75, at 48.

defense in which the existence of an agreement is alleged by one party and not denied by another. The reference in a contract to a document containing an arbitration clause constitutes an arbitration agreement provided that the contract is in writing and the reference is such as to make that clause part of the contract."

The provision of Article II of the New York Convention is stricter than Article VII of the UNCITRAL Model Law 2006. Article II requires the arbitration agreement to be valid either signed by the parties or contained in an exchange of letters or telegrams. However, Article VII has a broader scope of written forms covering other means of communication, such as electronic data interchange (EDI), fax, email and so on.[①]

Compared with the Model Law, the New York Convention was drafted during the 1950s, and the requirement of "arbitration agreement in writing" seems somewhat outdated.[②] There is a debate on Article II of the New York Convention as to whether the list of methods to meet the requirement of writing is exhaustive or non-exhaustive.[③]

发生的一切或某些争议提交仲裁的协议。仲裁协议可以采取合同中的仲裁条款形式或单独的协议形式。（2）仲裁协议应是书面的。协议如载于当事各方签字的文件中，或载于往来的书信、电传、电报或提供协议记录的其他电讯手段中，或在申诉书和答辩书的交换中当事一方声称有协议而当事他方不否认即为书面协议。在合同中提出参照载有仲裁条款的一项文件即构成仲裁协议，如果该合同是书面的而且这种参照足以使该仲裁条款构成该合同的一部分的话。

《纽约公约》第二条的规定比《UNCITRAL仲裁示范法》（2006年版）第七条更严格。第二条要求仲裁协议经当事人签署或交换信件、电报有效。但是，第七条的书面形式范围更广，包括其他通信方式，如电子数据交换（EDI）、传真、电子邮件等。[①]

与示范法相比，《纽约公约》是在20世纪50年代起草的，而"书面仲裁协议"的要求似乎有些过时。[②]关于《纽约公约》第二条书面形式的要求学术界是有争议的。[③]

---

① For instance, Article 178 of Switzerland's Federal Code on Private International Law (CPIL)and Article 7 of the UN-CITRAL Model Law regulate that the arbitration agreement shall be valid if it is made in writing, by telegram, telex, telecopier, or any other means of communication that establishes the terms of the agreement by a text.

② Kronke, H. (2010). *Recognition and Enforcement of Foreign Arbitral Awards: A Global Commentary on the New York Convention*. Kluwer Law International, at 75.

③ Kronke, H., Supra note 96, at 75-76.

为了解决这个问题，本书倾向于采用 UNCITRAL 的自由解释①，认为《纽约公约》第二条中所承认的"书面形式"并非详尽无遗。②

此外，《纽约公约》第七条（1）还规定：

"本公约之规定不影响缔约国间所订关于承认及执行仲裁裁决之多边或双边协定之效力，亦不剥夺任何利害关系人可依援引裁决地所在国之法律或条约所认许之方式，在其许可范围内，援用仲裁裁决之任何权利。"③

这表明，《纽约公约》的条款为国内法和法院留出了空间。国内法和法院可以根据国际贸易惯例或该裁决所依据的国家法律或条约作出不同解释。此外，世界上许多国家的立法趋势也给予了"书面形式"更多的解释空间。例如，在中国，CIETAC（中国国际经济贸易仲裁委员会）④的仲裁规则也作出了相似规定，承认新的通信方式作为"书面形式"的形式要件。

《CIETAC 仲裁规则》第五条规定：

"……如果仲裁协议包含合同、信函、电报、电传、传真、电子数据交换或电子邮件，则为书面形式。在交换仲裁请求和抗辩书中，一方主张存在，另一方不否认的，视为仲裁协议存在。"

In order to solve the problem, UNCITRAL provides a Recommendation① to expound the issue. The Recommendation tends to adopt a liberal approach for the issue of requirement of writing. The Recommendation holds the view that the circumstances described in Article II are not exhaustive.②

Also, Article VII (1) of the New York Convention clarifies:

"States nor deprive any interested party of any right he may have to avail himself of an arbitral award in the manner and to the extent allowed by the law or the treaties of the country where such award is sought to be relied upon."③

This indicates that articles of the New York Convention and the UNCITRAL Recommendation leave room for the national laws and courts. The national laws and courts can have a different explanation based on international trade practices or the law or the treaties of the country where such award is relied upon.

In addition, it is more practically significant to meet the legislative tendency of many countries in the world. For instance, in China, the CIETAC④ has also stipulated similar provisions to adopt the new methods of communications.

Article V of the CIETAC Arbitration Rules regulates:

"…An arbitration agreement is in writing if it is contained in the tangible form of a document such as a contract, letter, telegram, telex, fax, electronic data interchange, or email. An arbitration agreement shall be deemed to exist where its existence is asserted by one party and not denied by the other during the exchange of the Request for Arbitration and the Statement of Defense."

---

① Recommendation regarding the interpretation of article II, paragraph 2, and article VII, paragraph 1, of the Convention on the Recognition and Enforcement of Foreign Arbitral Awards, done in New York, 10 June 1958 (2006), available at: http://www.uncitral.org/uncitral/zh/uncitral_texts/arbitration/2006recommendation.html (Last visited on May12, 2016).

② Id.

③ Article VII (1) of the New York Convention.

④ CIETAC is short for China International Economic and Trade Arbitration Commission.

Another example, the case *Specht v. Netscape Communications Corporation*①, decided by the United States Court of Appeals for the Second Circuit, also proved that electronic data interchange could be recognized as "in writing". Hence, new methods of "writing" are recognized, allowing more convenience to the parties involved in the arbitration.

1.2 Signature Requirement

In Article II of the New York Convention, signing an arbitration agreement can be recognized as a way to reach "the agreement in writing". If the arbitration agreement is signed by the parties, most courts in the world would recognize it as satisfying the written form.② However, if the arbitration agreement has not been signed by the parties, the national courts have different opinions about this issue. Some courts may refuse to recognize the validity of an arbitration agreement without the signature, whereas some courts may take a liberal attitude towards this issue.

For instance, in China, most scholars believe that the signature is not a statutory requirement,③ but it does not mean that the signature is not important in Chinese practice. Many cases indicate that the signature can be a proof for concluding a contract. For example, for the case *Concordia Trading B.V. v. Nantong Gangde Oil Co., Ltd*,④ China Supreme Court held that the parties did not successfully conclude an arbitration agreement in writing because the arbitration agreement did not

另一个例子是斯佩克特诉网景通信公司案①。美国第二巡回上诉法院的裁决也证明了电子数据交换可以被承认为"书面形式"。因此,新的"书面形式"方法得到了承认,并为仲裁当事人提供了更多的便利。

(二)签名要求

《纽约公约》第二条中,签署仲裁协议可被视为达成"书面协议"的方式。如果仲裁协议是由双方签署的,世界上大多数法院都会承认它满足书面形式的要求。②但是,如果双方没有签署仲裁协议,国家法院对这个问题有不同的意见。有些法院可能会拒绝承认没有签字的仲裁协议的有效性,而有些法院可能会对这个问题采取自由的态度。

例如,在中国,大多数学者认为签名不是法定的要求,③但这并不意味着签名在中国的实践中并不重要。许多情况表明,签名可以作为签订合同的证据。例如,康科迪亚贸易公司诉南通港德石油有限公司案。④中国最高法院作出裁定认为,由于仲裁协议没有签字或

① Specht v. Netscape Communications Corporation, [2002] 306 F.3d 17, United States Court of Appeals for the Second Circuit, available at: http://www.casebriefs.com/blog/law/contracts/contracts-keyed-to-murphy/the-bargain-relationship/specht-v-netscape-communications-corporation/ (Last visited on May 12, 2016).
② Carbonneau, T. E. (2003). Exercise of Contract Freedom in the Making of Arbitration Agreement, *The Vand. J. Transnat'l L.*, 36, at 1205.
③ Tao, J. (2008). *Arbitration Law and Practice in China*. Kluwer Law International, at 49.
④ Concordia Trading B.V. v. Nantong Gangde Oil Co., Ltd, [2009] MinSiTaZi No. 22, China Supreme People's Court, available at: http://newyorkconvention1958.org/index.php?lvl=notice_display&id=1501&opac_view=2 (Last visited on May 12, 2016).

盖章，双方未能成功达成书面仲裁协议。当事人未提供真实签名或盖章的，法院可以拒绝执行仲裁协议。

在美国，法院将一些合同法原则应用于对非签署方具有约束力的仲裁协议，包括禁止反言、变更、代理和第三方受益人等情形。①巴黎法院还认为，法院对签名的要求并不严格。②

总之，大多数国家和国际公约放弃了签字的法定要求。③在目前的国际贸易惯例中，签名并不是签订仲裁协议的唯一手段。

（三）文件交换

除签字外，文件的交换也可被视为"书面协议"的另一种形式。仲裁协议产生于申请书和答辩书的交换，其中当事一方指称存在协议，而不被另一方否认，则认为存在仲裁协议。

目前，许多学者指出，通过交换文件而达成的仲裁协议不需要双方当事人签署。④但是，一些国家法院仍然要求在

have a signature or stamp. If the parties do not provide an authentic signature or stamp, the court can refuse to enforce the arbitration agreement.

In the United States, the courts apply some contract law principles to the arbitration agreement which is binding on the non-signatories, such as estoppel, alter-egos, agency and third parties' beneficiaries.① The Paris Court also has the opinion that the signature requirement is not strict.②

In summary, most countries and international conventions abandoned the statutory requirement of the signature.③ In current international trade practices, the signature is not the only means to enter into an arbitration agreement.

1.3 Exchange of Documents

Besides the signature, exchange of documents can also be recognized as another from of "the agreement in writing". The arbitration agreement emerges from the exchange of statements of claim and defense, in which one party claims that there is an agreement, and it is not denied by the other, and then the arbitration agreement is considered to exist.

Nowadays, many scholars point out that the arbitration agreement reached by the exchange of documents does not need the parties to sign it.④ However, some national courts still require the signature on

---

① Examples include, the case Kanematsu USA Inc. v. ATS- Advanced Telecommunications- Systems do Brasil Ltda., [2012] SEC 885, Brazil, Superior Tribunal de Justiça, available at: http://newyorkconvention1958.org/index.php?lvl=notice_display&id=1359 (Last visited on May 12, 2016), the case Javor v. Francoeur, [2003] BCSC 350, Canada, Supreme Court of British Columbia, available at: http://newyorkconvention1958.org/index. php? lvl=notice_display&id=957 (Last Visited on May 12, 2016).

② Hanotiau, B. (2005). *Complex Arbitrations: Multiparty, Multicontract, Multi-issue and Class Actions*. Kluwer Law International, at 122-123.

③ Examples include, Article VII of the UNCITRAL Model Law, Section V of the English Arbitration Act, etc.

④ Kronke, H., Supra note 96, at 81, Gaillard, E., &Savage, J.(Eds.) (1999). *Fouchard Gaillard Goldman on International Commercial Arbitration*. Kluwer Law International, at 619.

exchanged documents. For instance, the Brazilian court and Italian court have the opinion that the arbitration agreements are invalid if there is no signature from two parties.[1] In exchange of documents reciprocal documents transmission is required. The documents unilaterally sent from one party to the other party without the addressee cannot fulfill the requirement of mutuality.[2]

Like the above discussion, most countries today recognize the model means of exchange and give validity to them. More electronic methods have been adopted in international arbitration practices, like the United Nations Convention on the Use of Electronic Communications in International Contracts.[3]

The aim of the Electronic Communications Convention is to facilitate the use of electronic communications in international trade. Under the convention, the exchange of electronic communications can assure the conclusion of contracts and other communications exchanged electronically are as valid and enforceable as their traditional paper-based equivalents.[4] Therefore, more and more countries in the world recognize the electronic data exchange as a modern way of exchange of documents.

交换的文件上签字。例如，巴西法院和意大利法院认为，如果双方没有签字，仲裁协议就无效。[1]在文件交换中，需要相互传输文件。无收件人、单方面发送给另一方的文件不能满足相互性的要求。[2]

与上面的讨论一样，今天大多数国家都承认仲裁程序中的典型交换方式，并赋予它们有效性。在国际仲裁实践中采用了更多的电子方法，例如《联合国国际合同使用电子通信公约》。[3]

《电子通信公约》的目的是促进在国际贸易中使用电子通信。根据《电子通信公约》，电子通信的交换可以确保合同缔结和其他电子交换的通信同传统的纸质文件一样有效和可执行。[4]因此，世界上越来越多的国家承认电子数据交换是一种现代的文件交换方式。

① Van D. B. (1996). *Yearbook Commercial Arbitration.* Vol XXXI. Kluwer Law International, at 690.
② Poudret, J. F., & Besson, S. (2007). *Comparative Law of International Arbitration.* Sweet & Maxwell, at 153-154.
③ United Nations Convention on the Use of Electronic Communications in International Contracts, available at: http://www.uncitral.org/uncitral/en/uncitral_texts/electronic_commerce/2005Convention.html (Last visited on May 12, 2016).
④ Id.

（四）口头和默许的仲裁协议

在国际商业惯例中，双方可以同意仲裁，但仲裁协议可能尚未签署或交换。仲裁协议可能是口头的或默认的。[①]口头和默许通常有三种形式可得到承认：（1）由双方参照书面仲裁协议口头订立；(2) 收到仲裁条款的合同或包含仲裁条款的合同或文件；(3) 前一系列包含仲裁条款的合同已以书面形式订立，但产生争议的合同中没有仲裁条款。[②]

1.4 Oral and Tacit Arbitration Agreement

In international commercial practice, the parties may consent to arbitration, but the arbitration agreement may not have been signed or exchanged. The arbitration agreement may be oral or tacit.[①] The oral and tacit acceptance can usually be recognized in three forms: (i) the agreement is orally concluded by the parties referring to a written arbitration agreement; (ii) a contract or a document containing arbitration clauses is sent to the addressee who accepts it orally or tacitly; (iii) previous series of contracts containing arbitration clause have been concluded in written forms, but the contract on dispute is not.[②]

---

① For instance, Article 4 of the English Arbitration Act provides: (1) The mandatory provisions of this Part are listed in Schedule 1 and have effect notwithstanding any agreement to the contrary. (2) The other provisions of this Part (the "non-mandatory provisions") allow the parties to make their own arrangements by agreement but provide rules which apply in the absence of such agreement. (3) The parties may make such arrangements by agreeing to the application of institutional rules or providing any other means by which a matter may be decided. (4) It is immaterial whether or not the law applicable to the parties' agreement is the law of England and Wales or, as the case may be, Northern Ireland. (5) The choice of a law other than the law of England and Wales or Northern Ireland as the applicable law in respect of a matter provided for by a non-mandatory provision of this Part is equivalent to an agreement making provision about that matter. For this purpose, an applicable law determined in accordance with the parties' agreement, or which is objectively determined in the absence of any express or implied choice, shall be treated as chosen by the parties.

Article 5 of the English Arbitration Act provides: (1) The provisions of this Part apply only where the arbitration agreement is in writing, and any other agreement between the parties as to any matter is effective for the purposes of this Part only if in writing. The expressions "agreement", "agree" and "agreed" shall be construed accordingly. (2) There is an agreement in writing—(a) if the agreement is made in writing (whether or not it is signed by the parties), (b) if the agreement is made by exchange of communications in writing, or (c) if the agreement is evidenced in writing. (3) Where parties agree otherwise than in writing by reference to terms which are in writing, they make an agreement in writing. (4) An agreement is evidenced in writing if an agreement made otherwise than in writing is recorded by one of the parties, or by a third party, with the authority of the parties to the agreement. (5) An exchange of written submissions in arbitral or legal proceedings in which the existence of an agreement otherwise than in writing is alleged by one party against another party and not denied by the other party in his response constitutes as between those parties an agreement in writing to the effect alleged. (6) References in this Part to anything being written or in writing include its being recorded by any means.

② Poudret, J. F., & Besson, S., Supra note111, at 165-166.

In the New York Convention, only signed contracts and exchanged documents can satisfy the formal requirement, while the oral and tacit acceptance cannot. Some national laws also hold the same opinion. However, there are still some countries that recognize the oral and tacit acceptance as a valid arbitration agreement.

在《纽约公约》中，只有已签署的合同和已交换的文件才能满足正式要求，而口头和默许则不能满足正式要求。一些国家的法律也持有同样的观点。然而，仍有一些国家承认口头和默许是有效的仲裁协议。

For example, Section 1031 of German Law also extends the "in writing" requirements in some aspects. Section 1031 of German Law[①] provides:

例如，1998 年《德国民事诉讼法典》第 1031 条也在某些方面扩展了"书面形式"的要求。1998 年《德国民事诉讼法典》[①]第 1031 条规定：

"(2) The form requirement of subsection 1 shall be deemed to have been complied with if the arbitration agreement is contained in a document transmitted from one party to the other party or by a third party to both parties and—if no objection was timely raised the contents of such document are considered to be part of the contract in accordance with common usage."

"根据 1998 年《德国民事诉讼法》第 1031 条："如仲裁协议已经包括在一方传递给另一方或则第三方传递给双方的文件中，并且（如果在有效期内并没有被提出异议）其内容根据惯例被视为合同的一部分，则应认为已经符合书面形式要求，在仲裁程序中对争议实体进行讨论即可弥补任何形式要件上的缺陷。"

---

① Section 1031 of German Law provides: "(1) The arbitration agreement shall be contained either in a document signed by the parties or in an exchange of letters, telefaxes, telegrams or other means of telecommunication which provide a record of the agreement. (2) The form requirement of subsection 1 shall be deemed to have been complied with if the arbitration agreement is contained in a document transmitted from one party to the other party or by a third party to both parties and—if no objection was timely raised—the contents of such document are considered to be part of the contract in accordance with common usage. (3) The reference in a contract complying with the form requirements of subsection 1 or 2 to a document containing an arbitration clause constitutes an arbitration agreement provided that the reference is such as to make that clause part of the contract···". In these modern arbitration laws, there has in effect been a victory of substance over form. As long as there is some written evidence of an agreement to arbitrate, the form in which that agreement is recorded is now largely irrelevant.

从该条款中我们可以发现，德国法律中并不需要得到双方当事人的书面同意。在某些情况下，没有反对意见可以被认为是一种默许。①除了德国以外，《英国仲裁法》（1996 年版）、《瑞士联邦国际私法法典》第 178 条（1）也有类似的规定。这些国家法律对严格的书面形式有一定程度的放松。在国际层面上，人们试图对"书面协议"进行自由的解释。如上所述，《示范法》第七条放弃了签署和文件交换的要求，接受口头和默认，UNCITRAL 的建议进一步说明《纽约公约》第二条中的"书面形式"不是确认仲裁协议有效的唯一条件。

（五）评论

总而言之，仲裁协议的"书面形式要件"的问题与当事人是否真的同意仲裁的意志有关。②对于"书面形式要件"的有效性问题，国际上目前没有统一的解释和意见。一些国家对仲裁协议的形式持开放的态度，仲裁协议的形式可以是灵活的，更接近国际惯例。但是，一些国家仍然认为，仲裁协议应遵循传统的书面形式。严格的形式要求可以更严格，以证明当事人的意图和同意仲裁。

From the provision we can find that German Law does not require a written assent by the parties. In certain circumstances, the absence of objection can be recognized as a tacit consent.[①] In addition to Germany, the English Arbitration Act 1996 and Article 178(1) of Swiss PIL also have similar regulations. These national laws have a certain degree of relaxation to the rigid written form. At international level, there is an attempt to have the liberal interpretation of "agreement in writing". As it is discussed above, the Article VII of UNCITRAL Model Law, the UNCITRAL Recommendation abandon the requirements of signature and exchange of documents and accept the oral and tacit acceptance, and the UNCITRAL Recommendation further provides that the written forms in Article II of the New York Convention are non-exhaustive.

1.5 Comments

To make a summary, the issue of formal validity is related to the consent to arbitration by the parties.[②] There are no uniform interpretations and opinions about the issue of formal validity. Some countries have open attitudes to the forms of arbitration agreements. The forms of arbitration agreements can be flexible and closer to the international practices. However, some countries still hold the opinion that the arbitration agreement should follow the traditional written forms. The strict form requirements can be more rigorous to prove the parties' intention and consent to arbitration.

---

① Lew, J. D., Mistelis, L. A., & Kröll, S., Supra note 7, at 134.

② Lew, J. D., Mistelis, L. A., & Kröll, S., Supra note 7, at 130.

From my perspective, the aim of the writing requirements is to prove the two parties, consent to have arbitration. There are two reasons for supplying formal validity requirements. The first point is that it would be provided as proof that the parties actually agreed with the arbitration agreement. The formal requirements are intended to ensure that the existence of such an agreement is clearly established. Second, the written agreement can be a record for the content of the arbitration agreement in subsequent proceedings.

In modern arbitration laws, there has been a victory of substance over form. As long as there is some written evidence of an arbitration agreement, the form in which that agreement is recorded is now largely irrelevant. There is also a trend that more and more national and international laws have the arbitration-favorable rules. They tend to have liberal interpretation of the formal validity.

In addition, the liberal interpretation of "writing requirement" can cater to the business practice to some extent. For instance, in some industries, the parties often rely on oral agreements or some tacit agreements. If the oral or tacit agreement can be defeated easily, it would be another kind of unfairness. The existence of the agreement would be ambiguous. Essentially, it would not be good for the conclusion of business, and it may even run counter to some business practices.

在笔者看来,"书面形式要件"的目的是证明双方同意进行仲裁。提供正式"书面形式要件"有两个原因。第一点是,"书面形式要件"可以作为证明双方真实同意仲裁协议的证据。"书面形式要件"的目的是确保协议的存在。第二,书面协议可以作为后续诉讼中仲裁协议内容的记录。

在现代仲裁法中,有一种实质胜过形式的胜利。只要有充分的有关"仲裁协议"的书面证据,该协议的形式现在基本上无关紧要了。还有一种趋势是,越来越多的国家法律和国际法律拥有有利于仲裁的规则。他们倾向于对正式的有效性有自由的解释。

此外,对"书面要求"的自由解释在一定程度上可以迎合商业实践。例如,在一些行业中,双方往往依赖于口头协议或一些默契。如果口头或隐性的协议很容易被击败,那将是另一种不公平。口头协议的存在将被认为是模棱两可的。从本质上说,它不利于交易的成交,甚至可能与某些商业实践相违背。

二、实质有效性

仲裁协议的实质效力所涉及的主要问题包括：仲裁当事人的同意、当事人订立仲裁协议的能力、仲裁协议的解释、仲裁协议的范围、仲裁条款的可分性等。①简而言之，有许多方面可以影响仲裁协议的实质有效性。下面将提供一些例子，介绍一些涉及仲裁协议实质有效性的主要问题。

（一）双方当事人的法律行为能力

大多数国家的仲裁法律规定，自然人或法人应具有订立仲裁协议的法律能力。仲裁协议要求当事人具有法律行为能力，因为这是当事人解决纠纷的合同。仲裁当事人的范围可以包括个人、合伙企业、公司等。

当事人不具备订立仲裁协议的法律能力的情况下，其他的当事人可以在仲裁程序一开始便提出质疑。请求方可以请求法院或者仲裁庭终止仲裁。例如在乌克兰诉挪威海德鲁铝业公司一案中②，法院认为未持有必需的外贸许可。因此，乌克兰被告被认为缺乏签订仲裁协议的能力。此外，我们还得到了《纽约公约》第五条（1）的支持，③该条规

2. Substantive Validity

The main issues involved in the substantive validity of an arbitration agreement include the consent of parties to arbitration, the capacity of parties to enter into an arbitration agreement, the interpretation of an arbitration agreement, the scope of an arbitration agreement, the separability of arbitration clauses, etc.① In short, there are many aspects that can affect the substantive validity of an arbitration agreement. I will provide examples to introduce some main issues involving the substantive validity of arbitration agreements below.

2.1 Legal Capacity of Parties

Most national arbitration laws mandate that the natural or legal person should have the legal capacity to enter into an arbitration agreement. An arbitration agreement requires parties to have legal capacity because it is a contract through which they solve their disputes. The scope of the parties in arbitration may include individuals, partnerships, corporations, etc.

If the parties do not have the legal capacity to enter into an arbitration agreement, they may be challenged at the beginning. The requesting party may ask the court or the arbitral tribunal to terminate the arbitration. For example, we can examine the results of the case *State of Ukraine v. Norsk Hydro ASA*.② The court held the opinion that the Ukrainian defendant did not have the required foreign trade permission. Therefore, the Ukrainian defendant lacked the capacity to enter into the arbitration agreement.③

---

① Kronke, H., Supra note 96, at 52-53.
② State of Ukraine v. Norsk Hydro ASA, Svea Hovrätt, [2007] T 3108-06, Swedish Supreme Court, available at: http://www.jus.uio.no/ifp/english/research/projects/choice-of-law/events/2009/presentations/article_cordero_moss.pdf (Last visited on 12 May, 2016).
③ Lew, J. D., Mistelis, L. A., & Kröll, S., Supra note 7, at 141.

Also, we find support from the New York Convention in Article V(1), which mandates that parties that lack legal capacity cannot enter into an arbitration agreement.[①]

2.2 A Defined Legal Relationship

The parties should have a defined legal relationship in arbitration, or the agreement may be invalid. The New York Convention and the Model Law corroborates this. Whether the parties conclude a contract or not, legal relationships should be identified.

Article II of the New York Convention prescribes that the parties shall be in "a defined legal relationship, whether contractual or not."[②]

Also, Article VII of the Model Law states that "'Arbitration agreement' is an agreement by the parties to submit to arbitration all or certain disputes which have arisen or which may arise between them in respect of a defined legal relationship, whether contractual or not."

In the practice, most commercial arbitration cases show that there will be an agreement that relates to a written contract between the parties, and the requirements of Article II of the New York Convention will easily be satisfied.[③] That is to say, almost all international commercial arbitration cases are derived from contractual relationships between the involved parties.

定，缺乏法律行为能力的各方不能签订仲裁协议。[①]

（二）确定的法律关系

当事人在仲裁中应有明确的法律关系，否则协议可能无效。《纽约公约》和示范法也证实了这一点。无论双方是否签订合同，都应有确定法律关系。

《纽约公约》第二条亦有阐述认为，当事人之间需要存在"一种确定的法律关系，无论当事人之间是否为合同关系"。[②]

此外，《UNCITRAL 仲裁示范法》第七条规定："'仲裁协议'是双方就确定的法律关系发生的所有或某些争议提交仲裁的协议，无论当事人之间是否存在合同关系。"

在实践中，大多数商事仲裁案件表明，双方之间通常拥有书面的合同协议。因此《纽约公约》中第二条的要求很容易得到满足。也就是说，大部分的国际商事仲裁是基于合同关系的。

---

① Article V(1) of the New York Convention regulates: 1. Recognition and enforcement of the award may be refused, at the request of the party against whom it is invoked, only if that party furnishes to the competent authority where the recognition and enforcement is sought, proof that: (a) The parties to the agreement referred to in article II were, under the law applicable to them, under some incapacity, or the said agreement is not valid under the law to which the parties have subjected it or, failing any indication thereon, under the law of the country where the award was made.

② Article II of the New York Convention.

③ Redfern, A., Supra note 6, at 161.

但是,《纽约公约》第二条是开放条款。①根据该条款,无论是基于合同关系或非合同关系的争议均可以被仲裁。②根据《纽约公约》,仲裁协议的裁决原则上可强制执行。但是,如果仲裁条款过于模糊,那么仲裁条款可能不被接受。③例如,如果双方起草仲裁协议,包含类似"他们之间可能出现的任何争议"的措辞,那么这一仲裁条款可能会被认为是有问题的。

此外,如果非合同类型的纠纷通过提交协议提交仲裁,则提交协议应当足够精确,以避免产生质疑。仲裁协议是仲裁员管辖权的基础。如果仲裁协议中的条款不明确,则可能会出现解释问题。仲裁庭必须考虑争议,然后从仲裁协议中引出双方是否有意通过仲裁来解决现有的冲突。

(三)进行仲裁的真实意图

仲裁的有效性是建立在双方都有通过仲裁解决争议的意图之上的。④如果仲裁协议不是基于当事人的真实意图,则仲裁条款的有效性可能面临质疑。

However, Article II of the New York Convention may exclude an open-ended agreement.[1] On the contrary, the terms "whether contractual or not" in this article would appear to confirm that "non-contractual" claims[2] may be arbitrated. The awards of arbitration agreements are enforceable under the New York Convention in principle.[3] Yet if the arbitration clauses are too ambiguous, then the arbitration clauses may not be accepted. For example, if the parties draft an arbitration agreement that contains wording like (d) "any dispute that could arise between them," then this arbitration clause could be considered questionable.

In addition, if non-contractual disputes are submitted to arbitration by means of a submission agreement, then the submission agreement should be precise enough to avoid doubts. The arbitration agreement is the basis of the arbitrators' jurisdiction. If the terms in an arbitration agreement are not definite, then interpretation issues may arise. The arbitral tribunal must consider the disputes and then elicit from the arbitration agreement whether or not the parties intend the conflict at hand to be resolved by arbitration.

2.3 True Intention to Arbitrate

The validity of arbitration is built on the idea that both parties have the intention of solving their disputes through arbitration.[4] If the arbitration agreement is not based on the true intentions of the parties, then the validity of the arbitration clause may face challenges.

---

① For example, A and B agree to arbitrate any dispute which may arise between them.

② For example, tort, competition, and other public law claims, etc.

③ Born, G., Supra note 35, at 155.

④ Byrnes, J., Pollman, E. (2003). Arbitration, Consent and Contractual Theory: The Implications of EEOC v. Waffle House. *Harvard Negotiation Law Review*, 8, 289-312, at 289.

For example, Article 2 of the UNCITRAL Model Law on International Commercial Arbitration[1] stipulates that "the arbitration should come from the true intention from the two parties." It also requires the parties to "undertake to submit to arbitration" in regard to their disputes. Article 2 can be divided into various meanings. First, the agreement should depend on the autonomy of the parties. Second, the agreement must provide for arbitration, rather than other ways of dispute resolution. Third, the agreement must have originated from the parties' free will.

Therefore, if a party is fraudulent or forces the other party to sign the arbitration agreement contrary to the true intention of the other party, then the arbitration agreement may be invalid. Furthermore, claims may arise due to one party not knowing that the contract contains the arbitration clauses. Usually, the arbitration clause is included in general conditions. There are normally clear instructions when the arbitration clauses are on the reverse side of a document. The arbitration will be hindered if there are not clear instructions.

The situation can be more complex when the general conditions and the arbitration agreement are separate. For instance, in the case *Progressive Casualty Insurance Co v. C.A. Reaseguradora Nacional De Venezuela.*[2] the general conditions and the arbitration agreement are separate. Finally, the court held the view that the document was available to parties at the time when the valid arbitration agreement was formulated. The separate arbitration agreement reflected the true intentions of both parties. Therefore, the court determined that the arbitration agreement was valid.

It is important to ensure that the wording adopted in an arbitration agreement is adequate to represent the intentions of the parties. Subsequently, the arbitration agreement should be drafted in broad, inclusionary terms rather than referring only to certain categories of dispute arbitration and leaving others to the jurisdiction of national courts.

例如,《UNCITRAL 国际商事仲裁示范法》[1]第 2 条规定:"仲裁应来自双方的真实意图。"它还要求双方就其争议"承诺提交仲裁"。第二条可分为多种含义。第一,该协议应取决于双方当事人的自主权。第二,该协议必须规定仲裁,而不是其他解决争端的方式。第三,该协议必须起源于双方的自由意志。

因此,如果一方存在欺诈行为或强迫另一方违背另一方的真实意图签署仲裁协议,则该仲裁协议可能无效。此外,一方可能因不知道合同中包含仲裁条款而产生索赔。通常,仲裁条款也包括在一般条件中。当仲裁条款出现在文件的背面时,通常会有明确的指示。如果没有明确的指示,仲裁将会受阻。

当合同一般条款和仲裁协议分开时,情况可能会更加复杂。例如,进步保险公司诉委内瑞拉国际保险公司案[2]。该案件中合同普通条款和仲裁协议是分开的。最后法院认为,双方在自愿制定有效的仲裁协议时,当事各方同意将纠纷交付仲裁程序。单独的仲裁协议反映了双方的真实意图。因此,法院裁定该仲裁协议是有效的。

仲裁协议中所采用的措辞足以代表双方的真实意图,这是很重要的。进一步说,仲裁协议起草时应当注意使用更具包容性的措辞,而不是只提及将某些类别的争议提交仲裁,这将导致适用仲裁程序的排除和国家法院管辖的介入。

---

[1] Article 2 of the UNCITRAL Model Law on International Commercial Arbitration.

[2] Progressive Casualty Insurance Co v. C.A. Reaseguradora Nacional De Venezuela, [1993]991F.2d.42, United States Court of Appeals Second Circuit, available at: http://openjurist. org/991/f2d/42/progressive-casualty-insurance-co-v-ca-reaseguradora-nacional-de-venezuela (Last visited on May 12, 2016).

（四）瑕疵仲裁协议

含有瑕疵的仲裁条款的问题也是影响仲裁协议实质有效性的一个重要问题。当事人可以根据其自主权起草仲裁协议。有时由于双方都不是仲裁领域的专家，因此，双方当事人在起草和订立仲裁协议时，不可避免地会出现一些仲裁条款的瑕疵。这将导致对于仲裁协议是否有效，甚至是否存在的问题，争议极有可能发生。由于不能穷尽列出各种瑕疵仲裁协议的情形，所以在下面介绍常见的瑕疵仲裁协议。

1. 同时约定仲裁或法院管辖

当事人既约定适用仲裁程序又约定通过诉讼的方式来解决争端的协议可以被视为具有瑕疵的仲裁协议。根据大多数国家的法律实践，双方不能同时选择仲裁和诉讼来解决其争端。

例如，《最高人民法院关于适用〈中华人民共和国仲裁法若干问题的解释〉》第 7 条规定，当事人同时选择仲裁和诉讼作为其代理解决方式的，仲裁协议无效。另一个例子是武钢集团国际经济贸易总公司诉福州天恒船务有限公司、财富国际船务有限公司案。①该案中，当事人之间的争议解决协议约定："仲裁，如果需要在香港解决争议，则适用英国法律解决。"法院认为该协议无效，因为这份仲裁协议不能确定仲裁是解决争端的唯一方法。

2.4 Pathological Arbitration Agreement

The issue of pathological arbitration clauses is also an important factor for the substantive validity of an arbitration agreement. Parties can draft arbitration agreements based on their autonomy. Sometimes, the parties are not the experts in the arbitration area. Therefore, it is inevitable that the parties may make some faults when drafting and concluding an arbitration agreement. It is very likely for disputes to arise regarding the validity or even the existence of an arbitration agreement. It is impossible to list all kinds of pathological arbitration agreements, so I will introduce the main kinds of pathological arbitration agreements below.

(a) Reference of Disputes to Arbitration as Well as Courts

An agreement that provides for arbitration mixed with litigation may be recognized as a pathological arbitration agreement. Most countries mandate that the parties cannot choose arbitration and litigation for their disputes resolution at the same time.

For instance, in Article 7 of the Interpretation of the Supreme People's Court Concerning Some Issues on the Application of the Arbitration Law of the People's Republic of China, it is stated that an arbitration agreement is invalid if the parties choose both arbitration and litigation as their ways of dispute resolution. Another example is the case of International Economic & Trading Corporation WISCO v. Fuzhou Tianheng Shipping Co., Ltd. and Caifu International Shipping Co.① The dispute resolution agreement between the parties states that "arbitration, if any to be

①　International Economic & Trading Corporation WISCO v. Fuzhou Tianheng Shipping Co., Ltd. and Caifu International Shipping Co. [2009] Civil 4 Others No.36, Chinese Supreme Court, available at: http://www.lawinfochina.com/display.aspx?lib=law&id=13352&CGid=&EncodingName=big5 (Last visited on May 12, 2016).

settled in Hong Kong with English Law to apply." The court found that the agreement was invalid because it was uncertain whether arbitration was the exclusive method with which to resolve disputes.

(b) Uncertainty

In some circumstances, uncertain arbitration clauses may be recognized as pathological. Some vague and imprecise expressions lack certainty.

The first example is the following: "In the event of any unresolved dispute, the matter will be referred to the International Chamber of Commerce."[①]

In the first example, the arbitration clause does not clearly stipulate whether the "unresolved dispute" will be settled by arbitration or other ways of dispute resolution. The reference of the arbitration clause is too broad.

The second example is the following: "All disputes arising in connection with the present agreement shall be submitted in the first instance to arbitration. The arbitrator shall be a well-known chamber of commerce (like the ICC) designated by mutual agreement between the parties."[②]

In the second example, the drafters did not select an arbitral tribunal. In addition, people may also be confused about the expression of "well-known chamber of commerce". How can "well-known chamber of commerce" be defined? Which chambers are considered to be "well-known?"

These examples all have the problem of uncertainty. This kind of arbitration agreement may cause ambiguous expression. It is difficult to make sense of these arbitration agreements. Also, it may cause arguments among parties.

(c) Non-existent Arbitral Institutions or Rules

In some cases, the parties, the arbitral institutions, or the rules in their arbitration clauses refer to arbitral institutions that are non-existent. For example, the

① Derains, Y., & Schwartz, E. A. (2005). *A Guide to the ICC Rules of Arbitration*. Kluwer Law International, at 180.
② Redfern, A., Supra note 6, at 166.

2. 仲裁协议具有不确定性

某些情况下，不确定的仲裁条款可能被认为是具有瑕疵的。一些模糊和不精确的条款表述是缺乏确定性的。

第一个例子是："如果有任何未解决的争端，该事项将提交给国际商会。"[①]

在第一个例子中，仲裁条款并没有明确规定"未解决的争议"是通过仲裁还是其他争议解决方式来解决。这样的仲裁条款设置得太过宽泛，会导致缺乏"确定性"。

第二个例子如下："与本协议有关的所有争议应首先提交仲裁。仲裁员应为由双方相互协议指定的知名商会（如国际商会）。"[②]

在第二个例子中，起草者没有选择一个仲裁庭。此外，人们也可能会对"知名商会"的表达感到困惑。如何定义"知名商会"？哪些商会被认为是"知名的"？

这些例子都有不确定性的问题。这种仲裁协议可能会引起含糊的表达。人们很难理解这些仲裁协议。此外，也可能会引起双方之间的争论。

3. 约定不存在的仲裁机构或仲裁规则

某些情况下，当事人、仲裁机构或其仲裁条款中的规则指的是不存在的仲裁机构。例如，双方同意选择新加坡商会作为其仲裁机构，但法院发现该商会并不存在。在印度国际旅社[1]诉拉胡尔客车私人有限公司一案中[2]，仲裁条款规定，仲裁应根据"1956年印度公司法"或"根据国际贸易法"进行。然而，进行仲裁所需的规则实际上并不存在，因此这样的仲裁协议也是无效的。

4. 仲裁程序无法进行

《纽约公约》第二条规定，如果当事各方发现该协议本身"无效"、"无法执行"或"无法履行"，他们可以拒绝仲裁。例如，仲裁协议的错误约定导致仲裁庭不能根据当事人的仲裁协议而成立。另一个例子是 ACC 有限公司诉环球水泥有限公司案。[3]在该案中，仲裁条款约定由两名特定仲裁员中的任一名进行仲裁。然而，当开始仲裁解决争议纠纷时，两名仲裁员都已经死亡，因此仲裁程序无法进行。

（五）关于瑕疵仲裁协议的不同处理方法

法院有不同的方式来处理有瑕疵的仲裁条款。一些法院认为，有瑕疵的仲裁条款可能会产生潜在的不利影响。有瑕疵的仲裁条款由于条款的模糊性而无效或无法执行。然而实践中，一些法院支持仲裁条款的可执行性。这些法院可以试图采用一种有利于仲裁条款生效

parties agreed to choose the Singapore Chamber of Commerce as their arbitral institution, but the court found that the chamber was not existent.[1] In another case, *International Agencies v. Rahul Coach Builders Pvt. Ltd.*,[2] the arbitration clause stipulates that the arbitration should occur under "the laws of Indian Company's Act 1956" or "as per International Trade Laws." The rules under which the arbitration had to be conducted did not exist.

(d) Inoperability

Article II of the New York Convention regulates that the parties can refuse arbitration if they find the agreement itself is "null and void," "inoperable," or "incapable of being performed." For example, an arbitral tribunal cannot be established on the basis of one arbitration agreement. Another example is the case *ACC Limited v. Global Cements Ltd.*[3] The arbitration clause provided for arbitration by either of two specific arbitrators. However, the two arbitrators were dead when disputes arose.

2.5 Different Approaches on Pathological Arbitration Agreements

Courts have different ways to deal with pathological arbitration clauses. Some courts hold that the pathological clauses could potentially have adverse

---

① Srinivasan, B. (2015). Defective Arbitration Clauses: An Overview. Indian Institute of Quantity Surveyors Annual Insight. at 52-53.

② International Agencies v. Rahul Coach Builders Pvt. Ltd., 2015 (2) TMI 822, the Supreme Court of India, available at: https://indiankanoon.org/doc/68847411/ (Last visited on May 12, 2016).

③ ACC Limited v. Global Cements Ltd., [2012] 7 SCC 71, the Supreme Court of India, available at: http://www.cnica.org/images/cnica18.pdf (Last visited on May 12, 2016).

effects. A pathological arbitration clause is invalid or unenforceable due to vagueness. However, some courts are in favor of the enforceability of these arbitration clauses. These courts may try to adopt an interpretation that is in favor of giving effect to the arbitration clauses. The court may enforce the valid part of the arbitration clause, or the court may rewrite the defective part of the arbitration clause by supplying meaning that is most reasonable in the context of the arbitration clause.

Although some pathological arbitration clauses can avoid the fate of becoming invalid, in such cases, it costs time and effort in the court to determine whether the arbitration clause is valid or not. Also, some parties may challenge the validity of an arbitration clause in a country other than the one chosen by the parties in the agreement.[①] This may lead to multiple proceedings in different jurisdictions.[②] It may lead to inconsistent decisions about the enforceability of the arbitration clause in different jurisdictions. This can make the process of the arbitration more complex.

2.6 Comments

The parties can oppose the enforcement of arbitration awards that are based on invalid arbitration agreements.[③] Mostly, parties object to the enforcement of arbitration awards on the basis of formal validity issues. The substantive invalidity of an arbitration agreement by virtue of the New York Convention is seldom invoked.[④]

Also, the New York Convention does not have explicit terms with which to stipulate substantive validity of an arbitration agreement. The convention just has some choice-law rules for the applicable law in such issues. Usually, an arbitration agreement's substantive validity is determined according to the law that is applicable to the disputes.[⑤]

---

① Srinivasan, B. (2015). Defective Arbitration Clauses: An Overview. Indian Institute of Quantity Surveyors Annual Insight, 52-53.
② Id.
③ For instance, Article V of the New York Convention, Article 17 of Chinese Arbitration Law.
④ Kronke, H., Supra note 96, at 282.
⑤ Zuberbühler, T. (2008). Non-signatories and the Consensus to Arbitrate. ASA Bulletin, 26(1), 18-34, at 18.

的解释。法院可以强制执行仲裁条款的有效部分，或者法院可以通过提供仲裁条款中最合理的含义来重写仲裁条款中有缺陷的部分。

虽然一些有瑕疵的仲裁条款可以避免在这种情况下成为无效仲裁协议，但在法庭上确定仲裁条款是否有效却需要当事人花费时间和精力。[①]此外，一些当事方可能会对仲裁协议中双方选定的国家以外的国家的有效性提出质疑。[②]这可能会使仲裁过程在不同的法域下显得更加复杂。

（六）评论

基于无效仲裁协议的仲裁裁决，当事人可以反对执行。[③]通常情况下，当事人通常因为仲裁协议的形式要件不符合规范而反对仲裁裁决的执行。而根据《纽约公约》认定的仲裁协议实质性无效的情况则较少被提及。[④]

并且，《纽约公约》也没有明确的条款来规定仲裁协议的实质性效力。该公约只是对此类问题的适用法有一些选择规则。通常，仲裁协议的实质有效性是根据适用于争议的法律来确定的。[⑤]

此外，仲裁协议还应当符合作为合同的一般要求。[1]因此，根据合同法[2]，仲裁协议可能因错误、欺诈、不公平、弃权等问题而在实质上无效。

问题是，适用于主合同的法律是否可以适用于仲裁协议。适用的法律、主合同与仲裁协议的适用法律之间的关系是什么？具体情况见第三章第三节的讨论。

三、"仲裁庭自裁管辖原则"和可分离性

仲裁庭在裁决争议的实质性问题之前，应当具有管辖权。仲裁庭的管辖权是基于合同因素和管辖权因素的结合。仲裁庭的管辖权可能与当事人的意愿或适用于仲裁协议的不同法律有关。

许多格式合同都包含仲裁条款。由于某些原因，主合同可能会无效或终止。这就对基于主合同的仲裁条款的有效性提出了质疑。"仲裁可分性"和"仲裁庭自裁管辖"的原则可以解决这些问题。这两种学说通常被称为国际商事仲裁的基石。[3]

它们是不同的，但经常联系在一起，就像一只手和一只手套的关系一般。[4]这两种原则具有相同的功能——防止在仲裁过程中的早期司法干预，并最大限度地提高仲裁作为解决国际商业争端的有效手段的有效性。[5]

In addition, an arbitration agreement should meet the ordinary requirements of a contract.[1] Therefore, an arbitration agreement may be substantively invalid according to contract law[2] due to issues such as mistakes, fraud, unconscionability, waivers.

The question is whether the law applicable to the main contract can apply to the arbitration agreement. What is the relation between the applicable law, the main contract, and the law governing the arbitration agreement? The details are discussed in Section 3, Chapter III.

3. "Competence-Competence" and Sparability

Before an arbitral tribunal determines the substantive issues of disputes, it should have jurisdiction. The jurisdiction of an arbitral tribunal is based on a complex mixture of contractual and jurisdictional elements. The jurisdiction of the arbitral tribunal may be related to the will of the parties or the different laws that are applicable to the arbitration agreement.

Many standard contracts contain arbitration clauses. For some reasons, the main contract may be void or terminated. This calls into question the validity of an arbitration clause based on the main contract. The doctrines of "separability" and "competence-competence" may solve these problems. These two doctrines are often called the cornerstones of international commercial arbitration.[3]

They are different, but often linked, like a hand and a glove.[4] These two doctrines share the same function—to prevent early judicial intervention in the arbitration process and maximize the effectiveness of arbitration as an efficient means of resolving international commercial disputes.[5]

---

[1]　Lew, J. D., Mistelis, L. A., & Kröll, S., Supra note 6, at 141.

[2]　Poudret, J. F., & Besson, S., Supra note111, at 263.

[3]　Graves, J. M., & Davydan, Y. (2011). "Competence-Competence and Separability—American Style", published as Chapter 8 in International Arbitration and International Commercial Law: Synergy, Convergence and Evolution, 157-178, at 158.

[4]　Barcelo III, J. J. (2003). Who Decides the Arbitrators' Jurisdiction? Separability and Competence-Competence in Transnational Perspective Vand. J. Transnat'l L., 36, 1115-1202, at 1116.

[5]　Graves, J. M., & Davydan, Y., Supra note149, at 158.

3.1 "Competence-Competence"

The principle of competence-competence empowers the tribunal to decide on its own jurisdiction,[1] avoiding the need to wait for a court determination of an issue. The doctrine means that the arbitral tribunal can move expeditiously to decide the merits of the parties' disputes. The doctrine is accepted by many countries nowadays.[2] It is also a foundational principle of the modern law of arbitration.[3]

For instance, Section 17(1) of the Ontario Arbitration Act states that the arbitral tribunal may rule on its own jurisdiction to conduct the arbitration and rule on objections with respect to the existence or validity of the arbitration agreement.[4] Also, at international level, we can find similar provisions. For instance, Article 16 (1) of the UNCITRAL Model Law on International Commercial Arbitration states the following:

"The arbitral tribunal may rule on its own jurisdiction, including any objections with respect to the existence or validity of the arbitration agreement. For that purpose, an arbitration clause which forms part of a contract shall be treated as an agreement independent of the other terms of the contract. A decision by the arbitral tribunal that the contract is null and void shall not entail ipso jure the invalidity of the arbitration clause."

Article 23(1) of the UNCITRAL Arbitration Rules 2010 reads as follows:

---

① Lew, J. D., Mistelis, L. A., & Kröll, S. (2003). *Comparative International Commercial Arbitration*. Kluwer Law International, at 102.
② Barcelo III, J. J., Supra note145, at 1165.
③ Thomas G. (2012). What are the Limits of Competence-Competence for Arbitral Tribunals? Available at www.heintzmanadr.com (Last visited on May 12, 2016).
④ Id.

（一）"仲裁庭自裁管辖原则"

仲裁庭自裁管辖原则是指：仲裁庭能够根据自己的管辖权作出决定，①而不必等待法院对问题作出决定。该原则意味着仲裁庭可以迅速裁决当事人争议的是非曲直。这一学说如今已被许多国家所接受。②这也是现代仲裁法的一个基本原则。③

例如，《安大略仲裁法》第17条（1）规定，仲裁庭可根据自己的管辖权进行仲裁裁决，并就仲裁协议的存在或有效性的异议作出裁决。④此外，在国际层面，我们也可以找到类似的规定。例如，《UNCITRAL 国际商事仲裁示范法》第16条规定如下：

"仲裁庭可以根据自己的管辖权作出裁决，包括对仲裁协议的存在或有效性提出的任何异议。为此目的，构成合同一部分的仲裁条款应被视为独立于该合同其他条款的协议。仲裁庭关于该合同无效的决定，并不意味着该仲裁条款无效。"

《UNCITRAL 仲裁规则》（2010年版）第23条（1）规定如下：

"仲裁庭有权就其自身的管辖权作出裁决，包括对该仲裁协议的存在或有效性提出的任何异议。为此目的，构成合同一部分的仲裁条款应被视为独立于该合同其他条款的协议。仲裁庭裁定合同无效，不导致仲裁条款无效。"

即使没有这种规定，仲裁法庭传统上也有权对按其自身管辖权管辖的案件作出裁决。例如，在德士古海外石油公司诉阿拉伯利比亚共和国政府的案件中[1]，仲裁庭根据习惯规则决定了管辖权。[2]德博伊斯森还指出，由仲裁条款的有效性衍生出来的仲裁庭自裁管辖原则本身就是一种"习惯规则"。[3]

（二）评论

仲裁庭自裁管辖原则的基础在于当事各方的假定意愿，即将当事人所有的争议交予仲裁员进行裁决，包括管辖权。[4]该原则可以避免法院司法程序的早期干预以确定仲裁协议的有效性而造成的拖延。当事人之间的实质性纠纷可以由仲裁庭及时解决。

"The arbitral tribunal shall have the power to rule on its own jurisdiction, including any objections with respect to the existence or validity of the arbitration agreement. For that purpose, an arbitration clause that forms part of a contract shall be treated as an agreement independent of the other terms of the contract. A decision by the arbitral tribunal that the contract is null shall not entail automatically the invalidity of the arbitration clause."

Even if such provisions did not exist, arbitral tribunals have traditionally entitled to have rights to rule on cases on their own jurisdiction. For instance, in the case of *Texaco Overseas Petroleum Company v. The Government of the Libyan Arab Republic*,[1] the arbitral tribunal determined jurisdiction on the basis of a customary rule.[2] De Boisséson also points out that the competence-competence principle that is derived from the validity of an arbitration clause is itself a "customary rule."[3]

3.2 Comments

The foundation of the competence-competence principle lies in the presumed will of the parties to give all aspects of their disputes to the arbitrators, including jurisdiction.[4] The principle can avoid delay because of the early intervention of the judicial processes of courts to determine the validity of the arbitration agreement. The substantive disputes between the parties can be solved by arbitral tribunals in time.

---

[1]　Texaco Overseas Petroleum Company v. The Government of the Libyan Arab Republic, YCA 1979, at 177 et sq., available at: http://www.trans-lex.org/261700#toc_0 (Last visited on May 12, 2016).

[2]　Lew, J. D., Mistelis, L. A., & Kröll, S., Supra note 7, at 14-18.

[3]　Steingruber, A. M. (2012). *Consent in International Arbitration*. OUP Oxford, at 98.

[4]　Id.

However, the competence-competence principle is only efficient when the arbitral tribunal has real priority over the courts.[①] If the country does not recognize the competence-competence principle, then the power of the arbitral tribunal to rule on its own jurisdiction may be affected by the courts' control to some degree.[②]

As for the recognition of the competence-competence principle, different countries hold different opinions. France[③] and Article VI(3) of the European Convention on International Commercial Arbitration[④] completely prohibit the control of the courts. Countries like Germany, Italy, and England allow for control from the courts, but the control may be argued on time and reasons.[⑤] However, there are still some countries that do not recognize the competence-competence principle. China is an example. Article 5 of Chinese Arbitration Law[⑥] and the Reply of the Supreme People's Court Regarding Several Issues Relating the Validity of Arbitration Agreements regulates that if courts find that the arbitration agreement between parties may be invalid, then the arbitration proceedings should be suspended until the court makes a decision.

---

① Poudret, J. F., & Besson, S., Supra note111, at 458.

② Gaillard, E., & Savage, J. (Eds.). *Fouchard Gaillard-Goldman on International Commercial Arbitration*. Gaillard, at 675-676.

③ For instance, Article 1458 of the French Code of Civil Procedure provides: Where a dispute, referred to an arbitral tribunal pursuant to an arbitration agreement, is brought before a court of law of the State, the latter must decline jurisdiction. Where the case has not yet been brought before the arbitral tribunal, the court must also decline jurisdiction save where the arbitration agreement is manifestly null. In both cases, the court may not raise sua sponte its lack of jurisdiction.

④ Article VI(3) of the European Convention on International Commercial Arbitration: Where either party to an arbitration agreement has initiated arbitration proceedings before any resort is had to a court, courts of Contracting States subsequently asked to deal with the same subject-matter between the same parties or with the question whether the arbitration agreement was non-existent or null and void or had lapsed, shall stay their ruling on the arbitrator's jurisdiction until the arbitral award is made, unless they have good and substantial reasons to the contrary.

⑤ Poudret, J. F., & Besson, S., Supra note116, at 410-413. Examples also include some provisions from Article 819(b)(3) of Italian ICCP 2006, Article 1032 of German ZPO, Article 32 and Article 72 of the English Arbitration Act etc.

⑥ Article 5 of Chinese Arbitration Law: "A people's court shall not accept an action initiated by one of the parties if the parties have concluded an arbitration agreement, unless the arbitration agreement is invalid."

然而，只有在仲裁庭真正优先于法院时，仲裁庭自裁管辖原则才有效。[①]如果国家不承认仲裁庭自裁管辖原则，那么仲裁庭基于自身管辖权作出裁决的权力可能在一定程度上受到法院的控制的影响。[②]

对于承认仲裁庭自裁管辖原则，不同的国家有不同的意见。法国[③]和《欧洲国际商事仲裁公约》[④]第六条（3）完全禁止法院的控制。德国、意大利和英国等国家允许从法院获得控制权，但控制权可以根据时间和理由进行辩论。[⑤]但是，仍有一些国家不承认仲裁庭自裁管辖原则。中国就是一个例子。中国《仲裁法》[⑥]和《最高人民法院关于确认第五条仲裁协议效力几个问题的批复》规定，法院认定当事人之间的仲裁协议可能无效的，应当中止仲裁程序，直至法院作出决定为止。

综上所述，大多数法律制度都承认仲裁庭自裁管辖原则。仲裁法庭有权确定仲裁协议的有效性。然而，根据一些国家法律，法院和仲裁法庭之间存在着复杂的关系，法院可以介入仲裁程序。在这种情况下，法院可能有管辖权对仲裁协议的有效性作出裁决。

In summary, most legal systems recognize the competence-competence principle. Arbitral tribunals have rights to determine the validity of arbitration agreements. However, based on some national laws, there is a complex interaction between the courts and arbitral tribunals. The courts can intervene in arbitration proceedings. In these circumstances, the courts may have jurisdiction to rule on the validity of the arbitration agreement.

（三）仲裁的可分离性

仲裁"可分性"原则规定，基础合同的无效对仲裁条款没有影响。同样，仲裁条款的无效也不会使标的合同无效。[①]

仲裁条款是独立的、不同于主合同的。司法机关或者仲裁庭可以根据有效的仲裁条款为争议当事人作出仲裁裁决。

仲裁协议与主合同的可分性原则可能会产生两种法律后果。

第一，主合同的地位并不影响仲裁协议。换句话说，仲裁协议的有效性并不取决于主合同。有关主合同的和解并不一定会终止仲裁协议。[②]

第二，仲裁协议可以受不同于主合同管辖法律的法律管辖。[③]仲裁协议的自主权可能还会导致仲裁协议中所适用

3.3 Separability

The doctrine of "separability" provides that the invalidity of the underlying contract will not have an influence on the arbitration clause. In the same way, the invalidity of the arbitration clause will not render the underlying contract invalid.[①]

Arbitration clauses are separate, independent, and distinct from main contracts. The judicial authorities or the arbitral panel can make the arbitration award for the disputing parties on the basis of valid arbitration clauses.

The doctrine of the separability of the arbitration agreement from the main contract may have two legal consequences.

First, the status of the main contract does not affect the arbitration agreement. In other words, the validity of the arbitration agreement does not depend on the main contract. The settlement relating to the main contract will not necessarily terminate the arbitration agreement.[②]

Second, the arbitration agreement may be governed by a law that is different from the law that governs the main contract.[③] The autonomy of the arbitration agreement also reflects that the law governing the arbitration agreement will not necessarily

---

[①]　Mustafayeva, A. (2015). Doctrine of Separability in International Commercial Arbitration. *Baku State University Law Review*, 1, at 93.

[②]　Lew, J. D., Mistelis, L. A., & Kröll, S., Supra note 6, at 102.

[③]　Poudret, J. F., & Besson, S., Supra note111, at 178.

be administered by rules of the same nature and origin as those that govern the main contract.

The doctrine of separability protects the integrity of the agreement to arbitrate.[①] It also plays an important role in ensuring that parties' intentions to submit their disputes to arbitration are not easily defeated.[②]

Nowadays, most countries and many international conventions and international documents widely use the doctrine of separability of the arbitration clause in international commercial arbitration. For instance, Article 15(2) of the International Arbitration Rules of the American Arbitration Association[③] states the following:

"The tribunal shall have the power to determine the existence or validity of a contract of which an arbitration clause forms a part. Such an arbitration clause shall be treated as an agreement independent of the other terms of the contract. A decision by the tribunal that the contract is null and void shall not for that reason alone render invalid the arbitration clause."

Additionally, Article 7 of the Arbitration Act 1996 of England,[④] Article 178 of Switzerland's Federal Code on Private International Law 1987,[⑤] and Article 1040

的法律不一定是由与管辖主合同的规则具有相同性质和来源的规则来管理的。

可分性原则保护了仲裁协议的完整性。[①]在确保当事人将争端提交仲裁的意图不会轻易被对方破坏方面，它也发挥着重要作用。[②]

目前，大多数国家和许多国际公约和国际文件在国际商事仲裁中广泛使用仲裁条款的可分性原则。例如，美国仲裁协会的国际仲裁规则[③]的第 15 条说明了以下内容：

"对于仲裁条款构成其一部分的合同，仲裁庭有权确定该合同的存在或效力。该仲裁条款应被视为独立于本合同其他条款的协议。仲裁庭裁定该合同无效，不得仅因此而使仲裁条款无效。"

此外，1996 年《英国仲裁法》[④]第 7 条、1987 年《瑞士联邦国际私法》[⑤]

---

① Lew, J. D., Mistelis, L. A., & Kröll, S., Supra note6, at 102.

② Id.

③ Article 15 of the International Arbitration Rules of the American Arbitration Association.

④ Article 7 in the Arbitration Act 1996 of England regulates: "Unless otherwise agreed by the parties, an arbitration agreement which forms or was intended to form part of another agreement (whether or not in writing) shall not be regarded as invalid, non-existent or ineffective because that other agreement is invalid, or did not come into existence or has become ineffective, and it shall for that purpose be treated as a distinct agreement."

⑤ Article 178(3) of the Switzerland's Federal Code on Private International Law 1987 regulates: "the validity of an arbitration agreement may not be contested on the grounds that the principal contract is invalid or that the arbitration agreement concerns a dispute which has not yet arisen."

第 178 条和《德国民事诉讼法典》^①第 1040 条也接受了这一原则。此外，一些国际公约和国际仲裁文件也支持这一原则，如 1961 年《欧洲国际商事仲裁公约》^②第 5 条（1）、《UNCITRAL 国际商事仲裁示范法》^③第 16 条和 2010 年《UNCITRAL 仲裁规则》^④第 23 条。

of the German Code of Civil Procedure[①] accept this doctrine. Moreover, some international conventions and international documents of arbitration also support this doctrine, such as Article 5(1) of the 1961 European Convention on International Commercial Arbitration,[②] Article 16 of the UNCITRAL Model Law on International Commercial Arbitration,[③] and Article 23 of the UNCITRAL Arbitration Rules 2010.[④]

---

① Section 1040 (1) of the Germany Code of Civil Procedure regulates: "The arbitral tribunal may decide on its own competence, and in this context also regarding the existence or the validity of the arbitration agreement. In this context, an arbitration clause is to be treated as an agreement independent of the other provisions of the agreement."

② Article 5(1) of the 1961 European Convention on International Commercial Arbitration regulates: "The party which intends to raise a plea as to the arbitrator's jurisdiction based on the fact that the arbitration agreement was either non-existent or null and void or had lapsed shall do so during the arbitration proceedings, not later than the delivery of its statement of claim or defense relating to the substance of the dispute; those based on the fact that an arbitrator has exceeded his terms of reference shall be raised during the arbitration proceedings as soon as the question on which the arbitrator is alleged to have no jurisdiction is raised during the arbitral procedure. Where the delay in raising the plea is due to a cause which the arbitrator deems justified, the arbitrator shall declare the plea admissible."

③ Article 16 (1) of the UNCITRAL Model Law on International Commercial Arbitration: "The arbitral tribunal may rule on its own jurisdiction, including any objections with respect to the existence or validity of the arbitration agreement. For that purpose, an arbitration clause which forms part of a contract shall be treated as an agreement independent of the other terms of the contract. A decision by the arbitral tribunal that the contract is null and void shall not entail ipso jure the invalidity of the arbitration clause."

④ Article 23 (1) of the UNCITRAL Arbitration Rules regulates: "The arbitral tribunal shall have the power to rule on its own jurisdiction, including any objections with respect to the existence or validity of the arbitration agreement. For that purpose, an arbitration clause that forms part of a contract shall be treated as an agreement independent of the other terms of the contract. A decision by the arbitral tribunal that the contract is null shall not entail automatically the invalidity of the arbitration clause."

3.4 Comments

(a) Do Arbitration Clauses and Main Contracts Share the Same Fate

In my opinion, the standards concerning the validity of arbitration agreements have different results in different jurisdictions. However, the application of the doctrine of separability is the international trend in most legal systems. Many courts in many countries support this doctrine. The courts believe that the consent to arbitration should be treated separately from the consent to the other terms of the contract.[①] Whether there was ever a contract will not even affect the existence of an arbitration agreement.

In addition, the doctrine of separability is limited to preventing the fate of the main contract from automatically affecting the arbitration agreement. Under the doctrine of separability, disputes can be determined by arbitration based on parties' own consent. This leaves space for parties to choose the applicable law. There are some examples below:

An example is offered by the U.S. Supreme Court case of *Prima Paint Corp. v. Flood & Conklin Mfg. Co.*[②] The basis of the case pointed out that, according to the principles of the federal law, the party did not assert that the arbitration agreement in the contract was made as a result of fraud. Therefore, the arbitration agreement can be separated from the main contract, and the two parties can solve their disputes on the basis of the arbitration agreement.

---

① Steingruber, A. M. (2012). *Consent in International Arbitration*. OUP Oxford, at 105.

② Prima Paint Corp. v. Flood & Conklin Mfg. Co., [1967] Co. 388 U.S. 395, United States Supreme Court, available at: https://supreme.justia.com/cases/federal/us/388/395/case.html (Last visited on May 12, 2016).

（四）评论

1. 仲裁条款和主合同会有相同的命运吗

有关仲裁协议有效性的标准在不同的司法管辖范围中有不同的结果，但可分性原则的适用是大多数法律制度中的国际趋势。许多国家的许多法院都支持这一原则。法院认为，同意接受仲裁应与同意接受本合同的其他条款分开对待。[①]是否真实存在合同，甚至不会影响仲裁协议的存在。

此外，仲裁可分性原则仅限于防止主合同的命运影响仲裁协议。仲裁可分性原则下，争议可以通过基于当事人自己同意的仲裁来确定。这就为当事人选择适用的法律留下了空间。下面有几个例子：

普林玛油漆公司诉富劳德康克林制造公司案中[②]，美国最高法院指出，根据联邦法律的原则，当事各方并没有声称该合同中的仲裁协议是由于欺诈行为而产生的。因此，仲裁协议可以与主合同分开，双方可以根据仲裁协议解决纠纷。

在另一个例子中，原告港口保险有限公司诉堪萨通用国际保险有限公司。①当事人认为带有仲裁协议的合同无效，因此，仲裁协议无效。法院持有不同的意见，即合同最初的非法性不能对仲裁条款本身提出质疑。②合同中的仲裁条款可以作为包含双方相互承诺的记录。而在菲奥娜信托公司诉普里瓦洛夫案中，③上诉法院的结论是，关于合同是否可以被撤销的争议不会破坏仲裁协议作为一项明确协议的有效性。④

2. 适用于主合同的法律是否也适用于其仲裁条款

在提交协议中，当事人通常会选择一条适用于主合同的法律。被选择的法律可以决定合同的解释和有效性、当事人的权利和义务、履行方式和违约的后果。

这可能会引起一场关于适用于主合同的法律是否与仲裁条款的适用法律不同的争论。关于这个问题，有两种主要的观点。

一些人认为，适用于主合同的法律应与适用于仲裁条款的法律相同。因

In another example, the plaintiff in the case of *Harbor Assurance Co. Ltd. v. Kansa General International Insurance Co. Ltd.*① argued that the contract with the arbitration agreement was null and void and that, therefore, the arbitration agreement was invalid. The court held a different opinion—that the initial illegality of the contract cannot impeach the arbitration clause itself.② The arbitration clauses in contracts can be seen as records that contain the mutual promises between the parties. In the case of *Fiona Trust v. Privalov*,③ the Court of Appeal concluded that a dispute regarding whether a contract could be set aside would not undermine the validity of the arbitration agreement as a distinct agreement.④

(b) Is the Law that Is Applicable to a Main Contract Also Applicable to Its Arbitration Clause

In a submission agreement, parties usually choose a law that is applicable to the main contract. The law controls the interpretation and validity of the contract, the rights and obligations of the parties, the mode of performance, and the consequences of breaches of contract.

This may cause a debate about whether the law that is applicable to a main contract may be different from the law governing the arbitration clause. There are two main views on this issue.

Some argue that the law that is applicable to the main contract should be the same as the law governing the arbitration clause. Thus, the law that is applicable

---

① Harbor Assurance Co. Ltd. v. Kansa General International Insurance Co. Ltd., [1993] 1 Lloyd's Rep. 455, House of Lords, available at: http://translex.uni-koeln.de/302700 (Last visited on May 12, 2016).

② Hober, K., & Magnusson, A. (2008). The Special Status of Agreements to Arbitrate: The Separability Doctrine, Mandatory Stay of Litigation, The. Disp. Resol. Int'l, 2, 56.

③ Fiona Trust v. Privalov, [2015] EWHC 527, High Court of England and Wales, available at: http://hsfnotes.com/arbitration/2015/03/19/fiona-trust-v-privalov-in-the-high-court/ (Last visited on May 12, 2016).

④ Hober, K., & Magnusson, A., Supra note118, at 65.

to the main contract can automatically apply to the arbitration clause.

For instance, in the cases *Union of India v. McDonnell Douglas Corporation*[①] and *Sonatrach Petroleum Corporation (BVI) v. Ferrell International Limited*,[②] both courts held that the law governing the arbitration clauses would be the same as the law applicable to the main contract. They believe that the separability of arbitration clauses does not mean that the arbitration clauses are totally independent of the main contract. The commitment of the law that is applicable to contracts means the commitment to the law applicable to arbitration agreements. There is no need to choose another law for an arbitration clause.

From a different perspective, some argue that the law that is applicable to the main contract can be different from the law governing the arbitration clause. The French case *Etablissements Raymond Gosset v. Socitété Carapelli*[③] is representative of this view.[④] In the Gosset case, the French Court de Cassation held that the separability of arbitration was unaffected by invalid contracts.[⑤]

此，适用于主合同的法律可以自动适用于仲裁条款。

例如，在印度联邦诉麦道公司[①]和索纳特拉奇石油公司诉法雷尔国际有限公司案中[②]，两家法院都认为，适用于仲裁条款的法律将与适用于主合同的法律相同。他们认为，仲裁条款的可分性并不意味着仲裁条款完全独立于主合同。适用于合同的法律的承诺，是指对适用于仲裁协议的法律的承诺。没有必要为仲裁条款选择另一种法律。

从不同的角度来看，一些人认为，适用于主合同的法律可能不同于管理仲裁条款的法律。法国戈塞特案[③]是这一观点的代表。[④]在戈塞特案中，法国最高法院认为，仲裁的可分性不受无效合同的影响。[⑤]

---

① Union of India v. McDonnell Douglas Corporation, [1993] 2 Lloyd's Rep. 48, Queen's Bench Division Commercial Court, available at: https://www.i-law.com/ilaw/doc/view.htm?id=149987 (Last visited on May 12, 2016).

② Sonatrach Petroleum Corporation (BVI) v. Ferrell International Limited, [2001] APP.L.R. 10/04, High Court of England and Wales, available at: http://www.nadr.co.uk/articles/published/ArbLR/Sonatrach%2 (Last visited on May 12, 2016).

③ Etablissements Raymond Gosset v. Socitété Carapelli, [1963] Rev. crit. dr. int. prive 615, ICC Court, available at: http://lawjournal.mcgill.ca/userfiles/other/5414892-07.pdf (Last visited on May 12, 2016).

④ Gravel, S., & Peterson, P. (1991). French Law and Arbitration Clauses—Distinguishng Scope from Validity: Comment on ICC Case No. 6519 Final Award. McGill LJ, 37, 510, at 512.

⑤ Marful-Sau, S. (2009). Can International Commercial Arbitration Be Effective Without National Courts? A Perspective of Courts Involvement in International Commercial Arbitration,11, at 14.

《阿塞拜疆民法典》第 352 条也支持可分性原则。[①]合同的任何部分的无效都不影响仲裁条款的效力。主合同的实体法不一定与仲裁协议的实体法相同。

在笔者看来，如果当事人选择适用可分性原则，那么适用于主合同的法律就可以不同于适用于仲裁条款的法律。然而，这并不意味着适用于主合同的法律不能与管辖仲裁条款的法律相同。有时，主合同和仲裁条款选择相同的法律最方便。这是因为对主合同和仲裁条款适用不同的法律可能会给仲裁庭带来额外的任务，仲裁员们要裁决案件可能会花费更多的时间。仲裁程序可能会延长。此外，当事人可能不熟悉许多不同国家的法律。当事人可能对外国法律的适用提出质疑，这可能因对不同法律不熟悉而引起争议。

如上所述，双方可以自由选择适用于其协议的法律。他们还可以决定是否适用可分性原则。在某些特殊情况下，当事各方可能对适用的法律没有选择。适用于确定仲裁协议的有效性的方法有很多，如适用于包含该条款的主合同的法律，适用于仲裁的程序法，或由当事人选择的实体法。[②]这是一个与许多因素有关的复杂问题。笔者将在下一部分中详细介绍这些细节。

Article 352 of the Civil Code of Azerbaijan also supports the doctrine of separability.[①] The invalidation of any part of a contract would not affect the validity of the arbitration clause. The substantive law of the main contract should not necessarily be the same as that of the arbitration agreement.

In my opinion, if the parties choose to apply the separability doctrine, then the law that is applicable to the main contract can be different from the law governing the arbitration clause. However, this does not mean that the law that is applicable to the main contract cannot be the same as the law governing the arbitration clause. Sometimes, it is the most convenient to choose the same law for the main contract and the arbitration clause. This is because applying different laws to the main contract and arbitration clause may create additional tasks for the arbitral tribunal. It may cost more time for the arbitrators to make decisions about cases. It may prolong the process of arbitration. Besides, the parties may not be familiar with many different national laws. The parties may question the application of a foreign law, which may cause some disputes due to the lack of familiarity with different laws.

As stated above, parties are free to choose the laws that are applicable to their agreements. They can also decide whether to apply the separability doctrine. In some particular cases, parties may not have the choice regarding the governing law. There are many approaches that are applicable to the determination of the validity of an arbitration agreement, such as the law that is applicable to the main contract containing the clause, the procedural law that is applicable to the arbitration, or the substantive law that was chosen by the parties.[②] It is a complex issue that is related to many factors. I will introduce the details in the next part.

[①]　Article 352 of the Civil Code of Azerbaijan specifies the invalidity of part of a transaction does not result in invalidity of the other parts of the contract if the contract could be concluded without including the invalid part into the transaction.

[②]　Redfern, A., Supra note 6, at 52.

4. Applicable Laws in International Commercial Arbitration

In international commercial arbitration, the applicable laws play important roles and have significant impacts on the arbitral proceedings and awards. If the parties want to predict the outcomes of the arbitration, such expectations may be easily achieved if a valid choice of the applicable law is made by the parties themselves.

In addition, the choice of the applicable law is critical in the stage of recognition or enforcement of the arbitral awards. An award made by an arbitrator who failed to observe or respect the parties' favored law can be successfully challenged by the losing party, and most courts will refuse to enforce such an award.

In general, there are two kinds of laws that are applicable to arbitration clauses in contracts. They are *lex arbitri* and the law governing the arbitration agreement.[①] I will introduce the details below.

4.1. *Lex Arbitri*

4.1.1 Concepts of *Lex Arbitri*

Some people argue that the *lex arbitri* is the procedural law of arbitration. In my opinion, *lex arbitri* is not simply a matter of procedure. *Lex arbitri* is composed of a set of laws and rules. It is mainly comprised of the laws chosen by the parties, the arbitration rules, and the national or international procedural laws adopted by the parties or arbitrators.[②] *Lex arbitri* can affect the jurisdiction of arbitral tribunals, the substantive laws that are applicable to arbitration, and the laws governing the procedure of arbitration. English scholars define *lex arbitri* as "a set

---

① Chukwumerije, O. (1994). Applicable Substantive Law in International Commercial Arbitration. *Anglo-American Law Review*, 23(3), 265-310, at 265.

② Id.

四、国际商事仲裁中的适用法律

国际商事仲裁中，适用的法律发挥着重要的作用，对仲裁程序和裁决产生了重要的影响。当事人想要预测仲裁结果时，如果当事人自己对适用的法律作出了有效的选择，这种预期就很容易实现。

此外，在承认或执行仲裁裁决的阶段，适用法律的选择也至关重要。仲裁员若不遵守或不尊重当事人所选择的法律而作出裁决，可以被败诉一方成功地提出质疑，大多数法院将拒绝执行该裁决。

一般情况下，合同中的仲裁条款有两种法律可以适用，即仲裁法和管辖仲裁协议的法律。[①]笔者将在下面介绍这些细节。

（一）仲裁法

1. lex arbitri 的概念

有些人认为，Lex Arbitri 是仲裁的程序法。在笔者看来，Lex Arbitri 并不仅仅是一个程序法问题。Lex Arbitri 是由一套法律和规则组成的。它主要由当事人所选择的法律、仲裁规则以及当事人或仲裁员所采用的国家或国际程序法组成。[②]仲裁可以影响仲裁法庭的管辖权、适用于仲裁的实体法以及管理仲裁程序的法律。英国学者将仲裁法定义为

"适用于在仲裁所在地进行的仲裁的一套强制性法律规则"。① 它也可以被定义为"仲裁的司法所在地"。简而言之，Lex Arbitri 控制仲裁的全过程，并"决定仲裁庭与国家法院之间的关系"。②

Lex Arbitri 的功能可以分为两个方面。一个方面是内部仲裁法，另一个方面是外部的仲裁法。③内部仲裁法控制着仲裁的过程。它与仲裁的结构和程序有关，如仲裁庭的组成、仲裁程序的进行以及当事人的权利和义务等。④

内部仲裁法要求当事人在陈述案件时应受到平等对待。对于外部仲裁法，它支配着仲裁的外部问题。它包括司法援助、监督国家法院的仲裁程序等。⑤外部仲裁法还根据国家法律或强制性国际规则和公共政策来确定可仲裁性。⑥应当注意的是，外部仲裁法可以用来对仲裁裁决提出质疑。仲裁裁决可以因不同的理由而被拒绝。

2. 本座理论和离域理论

如上所述，我们可以发现 Lex Arbitri 在国际商事仲裁中起着重要的作用。根据仲裁的自愿性原则，当事人有

of mandatory rules of law applicable to the arbitration at the seat of the arbitration."① It can also be defined as "the juridical seat of arbitration." In brief, *lex arbitri* controls the process of arbitration and "determines the relationship between the arbitral tribunal and national courts."②

The function of *lex arbitri* can be divided into two aspects. One is internal *lex arbitri*, and the other is external *lex arbitri*.③ Internal *lex arbitri* controls the process of arbitration. It is related to the structure and procedure of arbitration, such as the constitution of the arbitral tribunal, the conduct of the arbitration proceedings, and the rights and obligations of parties.④

Internal *lex arbitri* requires the parties to be treated equally when they present their cases. As for external *lex arbitri*, it governs the external issues of arbitration. It includes judicial assistance, the supervision of national courts over arbitration proceedings, and so on.⑤ External *lex arbitri* also determines arbitrability based on national laws or mandatory international rules and public policy.⑥ It should be noted that external *lex arbitri* can be used to challenge the arbitral awards. Arbitral awards may be refused on different grounds.

4.1.2 Seat Theory and Delocalized Theory

As stated above, we can find that *lex arbitri* plays a significant role in international commercial arbitration. On the basis of the autonomy principle of arbitration,

---

① Tweeddale, A., & Tweeddale, K. (2005). *Arbitration of Commercial Disputes: International and English Law and Practice*. Oxford University Press, at 29.

② Reisman, W. M. (1997). *International Commercial Arbitration: Cases, Materials and Notes on the Resolution of International Business Disputes*. Foundation Press, at 691.

③ Mistelis, L. (2006). Reality Test: Current State of Affairs in Theory and Practice Relating to "Lex Arbitri,". *Am. Rev. Int'l Arb.*, 17, 1001-1021, at 1010.

④ Id.

⑤ Id.

⑥ Id.

parties have the rights to choose the laws they prefer as the *lex arbitri*, such as those in accordance with the laws of Switzerland, Hong Kong, or other places.

However, questions may be raised when the people do not have a choice of *lex arbitri*. There are two main theories related to this issue. They are seat theory and delocalized theory.

(a) Seat Theory

The seat theory holds that the *lex arbitri* is the *lex loci arbitri*. Thus, the arbitrators should follow the mandatory norms of the arbitration seat.[①] For instance, if the place of arbitration is China, then the arbitration process will be subject to the national arbitration law of China.

The famous supporter of the seat theory, F. A. Mann,[②] points out that international arbitration is in fact national arbitration. It is impossible for the arbitral proceedings to ultimately detach from a national legal system. This is because the arbitration awards must be enforced by some jurisdiction and the enforcement of the award will be subject to the law of that jurisdiction. Hence, there is a factual connection between arbitral proceedings and the *lex arbitri*.

Several institutional rules and legal systems also underline the importance of this geographical link between the place of arbitration and the law governing that arbitration.[③] For instance, the Swiss Arbitration Act provides, "The provisions of this Chapter shall apply to any arbitration if the seat of the arbitral tribunal is in

权选择自己喜欢的仲裁适用法，如当事人可以选择瑞士、香港或其他地方的法律。

然而，当事人没有选择仲裁适用法时，可能会出现法律适用问题。有两种主要的理论与这个问题有关：本座理论和离域理论。

(a) 本座理论

本座理论认为，仲裁程序所适用的法律应当是仲裁所在地的法律。因此，仲裁员应遵循仲裁所在地的强制性规范。[①]例如，如果仲裁地点是中国，那么仲裁程序将受中国的国家仲裁法的管辖。

本座理论的著名支持者曼恩[②]指出，国际仲裁实际上是一种国家仲裁。仲裁程序脱离仲裁所在地的国家法律系统是不可能的。这是因为仲裁裁决必须由某个具有管辖权的法院强制执行，而裁决的执行将服从该管辖权的法律约束。因此，在仲裁程序和仲裁法之间存在着事实联系。

一些制度规则和法律制度也强调了仲裁地点和管辖仲裁的法律之间的这种地理联系的重要性。[③]例如，《瑞士仲裁法》规定："如果仲裁庭所在地在瑞士，

---

① Park, W. W. (1983). The Lex Loci Arbitri and International Commercial Arbitration. *International and Comparative Law Quarterly*, 32(1), at 32.

② Kjos, H. E. (2013). *Applicable Law in Investor-State Arbitration*. Oxford University Press, at 62.

③ For instance, Article VII (2) of the New York Convention, Article 1(2) of the UNCITRAL Model Law, Artcle 176 (1) in Chapter 12 of Switzerland's Federal Code on Private International Law 1987, and Section 2 of the English Arbitration Act 1996.

本章的规定适用于任何仲裁……"①《中国仲裁法》第 58 条还规定, 国家法院有权对仲裁裁决进行审查。②

然而, 一些人批评本座理论可能会限制当事人的意思自治。如果国家法院不停止对仲裁过程的干预, 那么自治将是空话。此外, 马苏德提到, 国内法院对顺利的仲裁程序不是必要的。同时, 当事人也可以自行避免仲裁裁决的无效。③

(b) 离域理论

目前离域理论的概念还没有得到精确的阐明。④奥拉塔瓦拉教授指出, 离域仲裁可能是一种国际仲裁, 它不是基于某一国内法律秩序而产生的。⑤这似乎是一种独立于任何国家法律秩序的仲裁形式。⑥此外, 自治权也是仲裁的基础。当事人可以选择他们喜欢的任何法律。离域仲裁可以脱离仲裁地点的程序规则、任何特定国家法律的程序规则、仲裁地点的实体法、任何具有特定管辖权的国家实体法等。⑦

Switzerland..."① Article 58 of Chinese Arbitration Law also mandates that the national court has the right to examine the awards of arbitration.②

However, some people criticize that seat theory may limit party autonomy. If the national courts do not stop interference in the process of arbitration, then the autonomy would be a myth. Furthermore, Masood A. mentions that the national court is not necessary for smooth arbitral proceedings. Also, the parties can avoid the invalidity of the arbitration awards by themselves.③

(b) Delocalized Theory

The concept of the delocalized theory has not been precisely articulated.④ Professor Olatawura points out that the delocalized arbitration may be a kind of international arbitration that is not derived from or based on a national legal order.⑤ It seems a form of arbitration independent of any national legal order.⑥ Also, autonomy is the foundation of arbitration. The parties can choose whatever law they prefer. Delocalized arbitration can be detached from the procedural rules of the place of arbitration, the procedural rules of any specific national law, the substantive law of the place of arbitration, the national substantive law of any specific jurisdiction, etc.⑦

---

① Chapter 12 of Switzerland's Federal Code on Private International Law Act 1987.

② Article 58 of Chinese Arbitration Law regulates, "The parties may apply to the intermediate people's court at the place where the arbitration commission is located for cancellation of an award if they provide evidence proving that the award involves one of the following circumstances…"

③ Masood, A. (2011). The Influence of the Delocalization and Seat Theories Upon Judicial Attitudes Towards International Commercial Arbitration.The Journal of the chartered Institute of Arbitrators,77, at 123.

④ Redfern, A., Supra note 6, at 88-90.

⑤ Olatawura, O. O. (2003). Delocalized Arbitration under the English Arbitration Act 1996: An Evolution or a Revolution. Syracuse J. Int'l L. & Com., 30, at 49.

⑥ Janićijević, D. (2005). Delocalization in International Commercial Arbitration. FACTA UNIVERSITATIS-Law and Politics, 9, at 64.

⑦ Id.

Delocalized theory stresses that commercial arbitration should be free from the constraints of national laws. The process of arbitration should not be affected or controlled by national laws.[①] The case *General National Maritime Transport Company v. Société Gotaverken Arendal A.B.*[②] is a famous case to support this. The judge in the case explains that the choice of the place of the arbitral proceedings is done only to assure neutrality. It does not mean that the parties are willing to be subject to the law of the place of arbitration. They hold the opinion that the arbitral award has an "international" nature, and therefore, the Paris court does not have jurisdiction. This case encouraged the supporters of the delocalized theory at that time. However, this case also raises the question of who has the power to finally determine the case. This question may cause uncertainty in commercial arbitration.

Another case, *Société Hilmarton Ltd v. Société Omnium de traitement et de valorisation (OTV)*,[③] was very important in bringing out the impractical nature of the delocalized theory. The court held that the arbitral award remained in existence, even though it had been set aside in Switzerland. Because the arbitral award was not integrated in the legal system of Switzerland, the arbitral award could be recognized in France. The case reflects that international arbitration could, perhaps, deal with the floating awards. It may degrade the integrity of the arbitration process, the validity of the arbitration process, or the enforceability of the arbitral award, which would still have an uncertain status. It may prolong the process of arbitration, going against the reasons why parties choose arbitration to settle their disputes—find a fast, convenient, and economic method of dispute resolution.

---

① Habib, S. (2013). Delocalized Arbitration Myth or Reality? Analyzing the Interplay of the Delocalization Theory in Different Legal Systems. Available at: http://bspace.buid.ac.ae/bitstream/1234/361/1/100149.pdf (Last Visited on May 12, 2016).

② General National Maritime Transport Company v. Société Gotaverken Arendal A.B., [1980] Cour d'appel de Paris, available at:http://newyorkconvention1958.org/index.php?lvl=notice_display&id=111(Last Visited on May 12, 2016).

③ Société Hilmarton Ltd v. Société Omnium de traitement et de valorisation, [1994] 92-15.137, Cour de Cassation, France, available at: http://www.newyorkconvention1958.org/index.php?lvl=notice_display&id=140&seule=1 (Last visited on May 12, 2016).

离域理论强调，商事仲裁应不受国家法律的约束。仲裁程序不应受到国内法律的影响或控制。[①]通用国家海运公司诉法国阿伦达尔银行案[②]是一个支持这一观点的著名案例。该案件的法官解释说，选择仲裁程序的地点只是为了确保中立性。这并不意味着双方都愿意受仲裁地法律的约束。他们认为，仲裁裁决具有"国际"性质，因此，巴黎法院没有管辖权。这个案例鼓励了当时离域理论的支持者。然而，这个案件也提出了一个问题，即谁有权力最终裁决这个案件？这个问题可能会导致商事仲裁裁决的不确定性。

另一个案件是希尔马顿有限公司诉法国全能估值有限公司案[③]。这个案件认为离域理论的实践性是有待考量的。法院认为，该案件的仲裁裁决仍然存在，尽管它已在瑞士被撤销。由于仲裁裁决未纳入瑞士法律体系，因此它在法国可以得到承认。该案反映出国际仲裁或许存在流动性。适用离域理论可能会降低仲裁程序的完整性、仲裁程序的有效性或仲裁裁决的可执行性，这些仍然具有不确定性。适用离域理论可能会延长仲裁过程，违背当事人选择仲裁解决纠纷的原因——找到一种快速、方便、经济的争议解决方法。

3. 评论

离域理论似乎是强大而又有说服力的。首先，仲裁地点的法律并不一定会影响所有的国际仲裁程序。有些争议可以由双方商定的或由仲裁法庭提供的其他法律来确定。此外，有时仲裁程序也可以由一个仲裁机构来管理。这样的机构可以接管各国国内法庭的职能。[①]因此，支持者认为，仲裁程序不需要与当地法律或当地法院进行互动。[②]其次，当今国际间仲裁法的日益协调是一个不可否认的趋势。从这个意义上说，个别国家法律的影响就会减少，[③]不同国家之间的仲裁法律的差异会减弱。最后，离域理论支持者认为充分尊重当事人的自治是很重要的，仲裁案件中的当事人可以选择任何他们喜欢的法律，这可以充分发挥商事仲裁的灵活性。

实际上的情况是什么？在实践中，依据本座理论而产生的仲裁裁决比采用离域理论而产生的仲裁裁决更具有可执行性。如今，并没有特别多的国家完全支持离域理论。大多数国家认为，国家法院对仲裁程序的有效性的判断是必不可少的。[④]

4.1.3 Comments

It seems that delocalization theory is powerful and eloquent. Firstly, the law of the place of arbitration does not necessarily affect all international arbitration proceedings. Some disputes may be determined by other laws that are agreed upon by the parties or provided by the arbitral tribunals. Besides, sometimes the arbitration may be administered by an arbitral institution, like ICC. Such an institution can take over the regulatory functions of states.[①] Therefore, the supporters argue that there is no need for the arbitration proceedings to interact with the local law or the local courts.[②] Secondly, there is an undeniable trend that the arbitration laws nowadays are increasingly harmonized. In this sense, the impact of individual national laws decreases.[③] Differences in the application of different methods are weakening. Thirdly, the supporters believe that delocalized theory fully respects the autonomy of parties: they can choose any laws they prefer. It can give full play to the flexibility of commercial arbitration.

What is the reality of it actually happening? In practice, the seat theory is more likely to produce an enforceable award than the delocalized theory. Nowadays, not many countries fully support the delocalized theory. Most countries hold the opinion that the national courts are indispensable to the effectiveness of the arbitral process.[④]

[①]　Redfern, A., Supra note 6, at 91.

[②]　Tetsuya N. (2000). The Place of Arbitration – Its Fictitious Nature and Lex Arbitri, *Mealey's International Arbitration Report*,15(10), at 23-29.

[③]　Kaufmann-Kohler, G. (2003). Globalization of Arbitral Procedure. *Vand. J. Transnat'l L.*, 36, at 1320.

[④]　Simões, F. D., Supra note 27.

Firstly, there is a natural connection between the arbitration and the arbitration seat. The arbitration cannot completely avoid help from national courts. The courts can give some support and assistance in arbitration, such as freezing assets and property and preserving evidence. Also, the recognition and enforcement of the arbitral awards still requires the support of national courts. It seems unrealistic for a country to only recognize and enforce the arbitral awards without the supervision of the process. If the court does not examine the process of arbitration, then how can it decide if the award is legal? It may put international commercial arbitration into a legal vacuum.

Secondly, the practice shows that most countries want to exercise some control over domestic arbitration, and it is impossible to abolish the sovereign rights of states over arbitration in their territories. In most countries' arbitration laws, the validity of the arbitration itself depends on whether the arbitral tribunal complies with the mandatory provisions of the *lex loci arbitri*. If the arbitral tribunal does not comply with the provisions, the arbitral awards may face the risks of being challenged, or the courts may refuse to enforce the award decision.

首先，仲裁与仲裁地之间存在着一种自然的联系。仲裁不能完全避免来自仲裁地国内法院的帮助。法院可以在仲裁的过程中提供一些支持和协助，如冻结资产和财产以及保存证据。此外，对仲裁裁决的承认和执行仍然需要国家法院的支持。在没有国家监督仲裁程序的情况下去承认和执行仲裁裁决似乎是不现实的。如果法院不审查仲裁程序，那么它如何才能决定该裁决是否合法呢？这可能会使国际商事仲裁陷入法律真空。

其次，采用本座理论表明大多数国家希望对国内仲裁行使一些控制权，而且不可能废除国家在其领土上对仲裁行使司法主权。在大多数国家的仲裁法中，仲裁本身的有效性取决于仲裁庭是否遵守仲裁，若仲裁庭所作出的仲裁裁决未遵守的强制性规定。若仲裁庭所作出的仲裁裁决未遵守，裁决可能面临被法院质疑的风险，或者法院可能拒绝执行裁决决定。

B.P. 勘探（利比亚）有限公司诉阿拉伯利比亚共和国政府案件[①]中的仲裁员持有类似的意见，即大多数仲裁员会选择一个有效、可靠、方便的仲裁规则来适用于案件。如果允许仲裁庭无视仲裁地法律的强制性规定，则双方当事人可能无法获得双方所设想的可强制执行的仲裁裁决。

最后，仲裁地点的选择意味着当事人或仲裁员熟悉仲裁所在地的法律。将仲裁所在地的法律作为其仲裁法，对双方和仲裁员都很方便。特别是对于格式合同而言，适用离域理论会产生不确定性。在实践中，格式合同被多次使用。为使合同顺利进行，仲裁条款应起草得清晰、优质。如果仲裁适用法不确定，或者仲裁裁决的执行存在不确定性，那么可能会给双方造成更多的争议。因此，在笔者看来，如果当事人没有关于仲裁法的选择，那么本座理论将是一个明智的选择。

（二）有关仲裁协议的法律

达成后的仲裁协议具有法律效力，并为当事人创造合法的权利和义务。处理争议的过程中不可能存在法律的真空，必须有一个旨在处理争议的法域管辖仲裁协议。例如，需要某个特定的法域去处理仲裁协议的有效性和解释合同。然而，国际商事仲裁与国内仲裁不同，国际商事仲裁中通常涉及不止一种

The arbitrator in the case *B.P. Exploration Company (Libya) Limited v. Government of the Libyan Arab Republic*[①] holds a similar opinion that most arbitrators would choose a valid, reliable, convenient *lex arbitri* to apply to the case. If the arbitral tribunal is allowed to disregard or ignore the mandatory provisions, then the parties may not be able to obtain the enforceable arbitral award that they envisaged.

Lastly, in my view, the choice of the place of arbitration implies that the parties or the arbitrators are familiar with the law of the arbitration seat. Applying the law of the arbitration seat as their *lex arbitri* may be convenient for both the parties and the arbitrators. Especially for standard form contracts, the delocalized theory will create uncertainty. In practice, standard form contracts are used many times. In order to make the contracts work smoothly, the arbitration terms should be drafted clearly and well. If the application law is uncertain, or there is uncertainty about whether the arbitral award can be enforced, then this may cause more disputes for the parties. Thus, in my opinion, if the parties do not have a choice of *lex arbitri*, then the seat theory would be a wise choice.

4.2 The Law Governing Arbitration Agreements

Arbitration agreements are intended to have legal effects and create legal rights and duties for the involved parties. They cannot exist in a vacuum and must have a legal system designed to deal with issues, such as the validity of arbitration agreements and the interpretation of contracts. However, international commercial arbitration, unlike its domestic counterpart, usually involve more than one system of law or legal

---

① B.P. Exploration Company (Libya) Limited v. Government of the Libyan Arab Republic. (1973) 53 I.L.R. 297, Lagergren, Sole Arbitrator. Available at: https://zh.scribd.com/document/190391346/BP-Exploration-v-Libyan-Arab-Republic-53-I-L-R-297-1973 (Last Visited on May 12, 2016).

rules,[1] which may have serious implications for the parties who are engaged in arbitration battles.

The issue of the governing law of an arbitration agreement is important[2] because the governing law of arbitration can determine the validity of the arbitration agreement. If the parties express choice of the governing law of the arbitration agreement, then no problems wiu arise. However, if the parties do not make a choice, then the law that is applicable to the arbitration clause may go through some tests.[3] For example, some courts may decide to adopt the law of the arbitration seat as the governing law while others may apply the close connection principle to this issue.[4] The close connection principle may be related to many factors, for instance, the chosen arbitration rules and the seat of arbitration.

In the following section, I will introduce the main international trends and opinions about this issue and use examples to illustrate different approaches.

4.2.1 The Law Applicable at the Seat of Arbitration

As stated above, the seat of arbitration is an important element in arbitration. Sometimes, the parties may choose a law that is applicable in the seat of arbitration as the law that is applicable to their arbitration agreement.

(a) England

England is a famous country that supports this opinion. For example, the new arbitration rules of the London Court of International Arbitration (LCIA) assert the following:

---

① Moses, M. L. (2012). *The Principles and Practice of International Commercial Arbitration.* Cambridge University Press, at 5-9.

② Mustafayeva, A. (2015). Doctrine of Separability in International Commercial Arbitration. *Baku St. UL Rev., 1,* at 97.

③ Id.

④ Gaillard, E., & Savage, J. (Eds.). *Fouchard Gaillard-Goldman on International Commercial Arbitration.* Gaillard at 92. at 170.

法域或法律规则,[1]这可能对仲裁程序中的各方产生较大的影响。

仲裁协议的适用法律问题是重要的[2],因为适用仲裁法律可以决定仲裁协议的有效性。如果当事人对仲裁协议的适用法律有明确的选择,那么就不会出现任何问题。但是,如果当事人没有作出选择,那么适用于仲裁条款的法律可能要经过一些检验。[3]例如,一些法院可能决定将仲裁所在地的法律作为管辖法律,而另一些法院可能将密切联系原则适用于这个问题。[4]密切联系原则可能与许多因素有关,例如所选择的仲裁规则和仲裁所在地。

下一节中将介绍关于这个问题的主要国际趋势和意见,并使用例子来说明不同的方法。

1. 在仲裁机构所在地适用的法律

如上所述,仲裁所在地是仲裁中的一个重要因素。有时,当事人可以选择适用于仲裁所在地的法律作为适用于其仲裁协议的法律。

（a）英格兰

英国是支持这一观点的著名国家。例如,伦敦国际仲裁院 (LCIA) 的新仲裁规则主张如下:

"除以下第 16.5 条另有规定外，仲裁协议和仲裁的准据法应为仲裁所在地适用的法律，除非双方书面同意应用其他法律或法律规则，并且当事人同意的事项不违背仲裁所在地的强制性法律。"①

伦敦国际仲裁院的规则已用于一些仲裁案件。例如，伦敦皇家法院②的一个案件裁决如下：

"当事人决定选择英格兰作为仲裁所在地，意味着双方明确（或暗示）同意适用英国的法律，任何试图攻击或撤销仲裁裁决的诉讼只能是被英国法律允许的。"③

另一个例子是，阿萨诺维亚有限公司诉克鲁斯市毛里求斯控股公司案，④双方选择印度法律作为格式合同的适用法律。与此同时，双方都选择了伦敦作为仲裁中心。在这种情况下，争论的焦点是哪种法律应该适用于仲裁协议（伦敦法律或印度法律）。最后，最高法院认为印度的法律应该适用。为加快确定准据法，一些仲裁机构亦认为仲裁适用法应当以格式合同中约定的法律为准则。

（b）香港地区

香港是以国际化闻名的专业仲裁

"Subject to Article 16.5 below, the law applicable to the Arbitration Agreement and the arbitration shall be the law applicable at the seat of the arbitration, unless and to the extent that the parties have agreed in writing on the application of other laws or rules of law and such agreement is not prohibited by the law applicable at the arbitral seat."①

The rule of LCIA has been used in some arbitration cases. For example, a case of the Royal Court of London② was ruled as follows:

"The choice of England as the seat of the arbitration was determinative of the matter as much as the parties had, by that agreement, expressly (or perhaps impliedly) agreed that any proceedings seeking to attack or set aside the Partial Award would only be those permitted by English law."③

For another example, in the case *Arsanovia Ltd & Ors v. Cruz City Mauritius Holdings*,④ the parties chose Indian law as the governing law for the underlying contract. At the same time, the parties chose London as the seat of arbitration. In this case, the debate was which law should apply to the arbitration agreement (London law or Indian law). Finally, the court found that Indian law should apply. To expedite the determination of the governing law, some arbitral institutions have stated that the applicable law of arbitration should be the same as the law agreed on in the standard from contract.

(b) Hong Kong

Hong Kong has a friendly disposition toward arbitration due to its international, cultural, and professional arbitration institutions, such as the Hong

---

① Article 16.4 of LCIA.

② C v. D, [2007] EWCA Civ 1282, England and Wales Court of Appeal, available at: http://www.bailii.org/ew/cases/EWCA/Civ/2007/1282.html (Last visited on 12 May, 2016).

③ Id.

④ Arsanovia Ltd & Ors v. Cruz City Mauritius Holdings, [2012] EWHC 3702 (Comm), High Court of England and Wales, available at: http://hsfnotes.com/arbitration/2013/03/01/high-court-applies-sulamerica-test-in-arsanovia-and-gives-rise-to-unexpected-results/ (Last visited on 12 May, 2016).

Kong International Arbitration Center,[1] and is the chosen location for many disputes. In Hong Kong, there are no strict rules for the issue of the governing law of an arbitration agreement. Even so, we still can find that the courts are inclined to treat the law of the arbitration seat as the governing law of the arbitration agreement.

For instance, the case *Klöckner Pentaplast Gmbh & Co Kg v. Advance Technology (H.K.) Company Limited*[2] stated the following:

"There is no doubt that the proper law of the contract and the *Lex arbitri* of the arbitration may be different. There is no doubt too, that practical difficulties may arise when the *lex arbitri* is different from that of the seat of the arbitration, but there is no rule that the *lex arbitri* must be the law of the seat of the arbitration. That is especially so where the law is chosen by the parties."

In this case, the court finally concluded that the governing law of the arbitration agreement should be the law of the arbitration seat. The court also explains that only when there are no expressed terms about the governing law of arbitration agreements in contracts, the law of the arbitration seat will be the governing law.

4.2.2 *Lex Fori*

Lex fori is a Latin expression. It means the laws of a forum. There are some countries that believe that *lex fori* is a very important law, especially in some civil law countries. Civil law countries often stress judicial sovereignty. If there is an absence of the

之地，对仲裁态度友好，许多争议当事人会选择香港作为仲裁地。[1]例如，香港国际仲裁中心就是一家国际化、有文化底蕴且专业的仲裁机构。在香港，有关仲裁协议的适用法律，并没有严格的规则。即便如此，我们仍然可以发现，香港法院倾向于将仲裁所在地的法律视为仲裁协议所适用的法律。

例如，科佩有限公司诉先进技术（香港）股份有限公司案[2]中的声明如下：

"毫无疑问，合同适用的法律和仲裁协议适用的法律可能有所不同。当当事人选择的仲裁适用法与仲裁所在地的法律不同时，可能会出现实际困难，但没有规定仲裁适用法必须是仲裁所在地的法律，特别是在由当事人自由选择仲裁适用法的时候就会出现这种情形。"

在该案中，法院最终得出结论，仲裁协议的适用法律应是仲裁所在地的法律。法院还解释说，只有在合同中对仲裁协议的适用法律没有明确的条款时，仲裁地的法律才将成为仲裁适用法。

2. 法院地法

lex fori 是一组用拉丁语表达的法律词汇，通常被解释为"法院地法"。很多国家认为"法院地法"是一项非常重要的法律，特别是在一些大陆法系国家。大陆法系国家经常强调司法主权。如果

---

① Klöckner Pentaplast Gmbh & Co Kg v. Advance Technology (H.K.) Company Limited, [2010] HCA1526, available at: http://www.hkiac.org (Last visited on May12, 2016).

② Id.

当事人在仲裁协议中没有适用法律的选择，那么该国的法院将使用本国现行法律作为仲裁协议的适用法律。在下文，将以中国为例来解释这个问题。

中国的仲裁法对仲裁协议的适用法律没有明确的规定。但是，我们可以在最高人民法院的司法解释中找到一些线索。在我国，最高人民法院的司法解释与国家法律具有同等的法律效力。《最高人民法院关于适用〈中华人民共和国仲裁法〉若干问题的解释》①第十六条规定，当事人未选择法律，但约定了仲裁地点的，适用仲裁地点所在地的法律。如果他们没有就适用的法律或地点达成一致，则应适用法律地法。

上述司法解释第十六条的规定也适用于实践中的许多情况。例如，浙江逸盛石化有限公司诉卢森堡英威达技术有限公司的案件中②，双方对合同的履行存在争议。法院认为，当事人双方的合意仅适用于主合同的法律，而不适用于仲裁条款的法律。根据《最高人民法院关于适用〈中华人民共和国仲裁法〉若干问题的解释》第十六条，中国最高法院认为该仲裁协议应当适用中国法律。另一个案件，沧州东鸿包装材料

choice of law, then the national courts will use *lex fori* as the governing law of an arbitration agreement. Next, I will offer China as an example to explain the issue.

Chinese Arbitration Law has no clear regulation about the governing law of an arbitration agreement. However, we can find some clues in the judicial interpretation by the Supreme People's Court. In China, the judicial interpretation by the Supreme People's Court has the same legal force as national laws. Article 16[1] of the Interpretation of the Supreme People's Court Concerning Some Issues on the Application of the Arbitration Law of the Peoples's Republic of China regulates that if the parties do not choose the law, but the place of arbitration has been agreed, then the law of that place shall apply. If they have not agreed on the applicable law or the location, then the *lex fori* shall apply.

Article 16 also applies to many cases in practice. One case that supports this claim is *Zhe jiang Yisheng Petrochemical Co. Ltd. v. Luxembourg INVISTA Technologies Co. Ltd.*,[2] in which the parties had disputes over performance of the contract. The court held that the parties only agreed on the law that was applicable to the main contract and not the law that was applicable to the arbitration clause. According to Article 16 of the Interpretation of the Supreme People's Court Concerning Some Issues on the Application of the Arbitration Law of the People's Republic of China, the court applied Chinese law to the arbitration agreement. Another case is *Cangzhou Donghong Packing Material Co. v.*

---

[1] Article 16 of the Interpretation of the Supreme People's Court Concerning Some Issues on the Application of the Arbitration Law of the People's Republic of China, regulates that "The applicable law agreed by the parties shall apply to the determination of the validity of a foreign-related arbitration agreement. Where no applicable law has been chosen but the place of arbitration has been agreed, the law of that place shall apply. Where the parties have not agreed on the applicable law and the place of arbitration has not been agreed, or not clearly agreed, the *lex fori* shall apply."

[2] Zhe jiang Yisheng Petrochemical Co. Ltd. v. Luxembourg INVISTA Technologies Co. Ltd., Zhe jiang Intermediate People's Court, Arbitration Case No.4 (2012). Available at: http://www.vccoo.com/v/128bfe (Last visited on May 12, 2016)

France DMT company,[1] in which the court applied Chinese law as the law applicable to the arbitration clause because the parties did not initially agree on the applicable law.

4.2.3 The Law that Has the Closest and Most Real Connection to the Arbitration Agreement

The use of the law that has the closest and most real connection to the arbitration agreement as the applicable law to an arbitration agreement has generally been recognized in international commercial arbitration legislation and practice. For instance, this notion is applied in the New York Convention, the European Convention on International Commercial Arbitration, and the Inter-American Convention on International Commercial Arbitration.[2] Similar decisions have also appeared in the United Kingdom, Germany, Egypt, Belgium, Switzerland, Japan, and other countries in their domestic courts.[3]

However, which law has the closest and most real connection to the arbitration agreement? Different scholars have contrary opinions. For instance, Marc Blessing held that there are nine laws that can be applicable to arbitration agreements, *locus regit formam actus*, the law of the seat of the arbitral tribunal, *lex arbitri*, the law of the place that enforces the award of arbitration, ect.[4]

We can also find some support from the Royal Court of London in the case *Sulamerica CIA Nacional de Seguros SA and Others v. Enesa Engenharia SA and Others*.[5] In this case, the Court

有限公司诉法国 DMT 公司合同纠纷案中，[1]中国法院采用中国的法律作为仲裁适用法，因为双方当事人在一开始便未在仲裁协议中达成仲裁程序适用法的合意。

3. 最密切联系说

使用与仲裁协议具有最密切和最真实联系的法律作为仲裁协议的适用法律，在国际商事仲裁的立法领域和实践中已普遍得到承认。例如，这一概念适用于《纽约公约》《欧洲国际商事仲裁公约》和《美洲国际商事仲裁公约》。[2]英国、德国、埃及、比利时、瑞士、日本和其他国家的国内法院也出现了类似的判决。[3]

然而，哪条法律与仲裁协议有最接近和最真实的联系呢？不同的学者有不同的观点。例如，马克·布莱新认为有九项法律可以适用于仲裁协议、仲裁协议、仲裁庭所在地法、仲裁法、执行仲裁裁决的地方法等。[4]

我们还可以在伦敦皇家法院那里找到一些支持。例如，南非国民保险公司诉恩内萨工程有限公司案。[5]在本案

---

① Cangzhou Donghong Packing Material Co. v. France DMT Company, Supreme People's Court of the People's Republic of China, Civil Other Case No.6 (2006). Available at: http://www.110.com/ziliao/article-577916.html (Last Visited on May 12, 2016).

② Article 5(1) of the New York Convention, Article 6(2) of the European Convention, Article 5(1) of the American Convention.

③ Rubino-Sammartano, M. (2001). *International Arbitration Law.* Kluwer Law International, at 132.

④ See Blessing M. (1998) The Law Applicable to the Arbitration Clause. ICCA Congress series, at 168.

⑤ Sulamerica CIA Nacional de Seguros SA and Others v. Enesa Engenharia SA and Others, [2012] EWHC 42 (Comm), High Court of England and Wales, available at: https://www.cliffordchance.com/briefings/2014/06/singapore_high_courtfindsthat-partiesar.html (Last visited on May 12, 2016).

中,上诉法院指出,选择适用的法律主要有三种方式。第一种情况是,适用的法律将是由双方共同选择的法律。第二项规定是适用法律是当事人的默示选择。第三种情况,如果没有选择或迹象表明适用的法律,那么将选择与仲裁协议有最接近和最真实的联系的法律。①

在实践中,法院地法、仲裁所在地法和执行裁决地点的法律被认为是与仲裁协议有最密切和最真实联系的法律。它们是仲裁中最常用的法律。

4. 主合同中适用的法律

由于仲裁的可分性,仲裁协议被视为独立于主合同的安排。因此,适用于仲裁协议的法律不一定与管辖合同的法律相同。但是,这并不意味着适用的仲裁协议法律必须与合同适用的法律不同,如果当事人没有在仲裁条款中明确规定适用的法律,那么可以使用适用的合同法律来裁决争议。

例如,学者 S. Jarvin 和 Y. Derains 发表观点认为:"人们普遍认为在没有具体规定的情况下,适用于主合同的法律选择也默认了仲裁条款的情况。"②在这种情况下,双方假定或打算将仲裁协议与主合同适用相同的法律。

新加坡也是支持这一观点的国家。

of Appeal stated that there were three main ways to choose the applicable law. The first circumstance was that the applicable law would be the law chosen by both parties. The second stipulation was that the applicable law would be the implied choice from the parties. Finally, if there was no choice or indication of the applicable law, then the applicable law would be the one that had the closest and most real connection to the arbitration agreement.①

In practice, the law of a forum, the law of the seat of arbitration, and the law of the place that enforces the award are considered as the laws that have the closest and most real connections to arbitration agreements. They are the most commonly used laws in arbitration.

4.2.4 The Governing Law of the Parties' Underlying Contract

As a result of the separability of arbitration, an arbitration agreement is treated as a separate arrangement that is independent from the main contract. Therefore, the law that is applicable to the arbitration agreement does not have to be the same as the law that governs the contract. However, it does not mean that the applicable law of the arbitration agreement must be different from the governing law of the contract. If the parties do not specify the applicable law in an arbitration clause, then the governing law of the contract can be used to adjudicate the dispute.

For instance, S. Jarvin and Y. Derains held the following view about an arbitration case: "It is commonly accepted that the choice of law applicable to the principal contract also tacitly governs the situation of the arbitration clause, in the absence of a specific provision."② In this case, the parties assumed or intended the arbitration agreement to be subject to the same law as the main contract.

Singapore is also a country in support of this opinion. For example, in the case of *First Link Investments Corp Ltd v. GT Payment Pte Ltd and*

---

① The details and facts about the case are available at: http://www.kwm.com/en/hk/knowledge/insights/arbitration-agreements-which-lawapplies-20140929 (Last visited on May 12, 2016).

② Jarvin, S., & Derains, Y. (1990). *Collection of ICC Arbitral Awards* (Vol. 1). ICC Publishing, at 316.

Others,[①] the court stated the following[②]:

"… It cannot always be assumed that commercial parties want the same system of law to govern their relationship of performing the substantive obligations under the contract, and the quite separate (and often unhappy) relationship of resolving disputes when problems arise.

…

In fact, a more commercially sensible viewpoint would be that the latter relationship often only comes into play when the former relationship has already broken down irretrievably. There can therefore be no natural inference that commercial parties would want the same system of law to govern these two distinct relationships. The natural inference would instead be to the contrary. When commercial relationships break down and parties descend into the realm of dispute resolution, parties' desire for neutrality comes to the fore; the law governing the performance of substantive contractual obligations prior to the breakdown of the relationship takes a backseat at this moment (it would take the main role subsequently when the time comes to determining the merits of the dispute), and primacy is accorded to the neutral law selected by parties to govern the proceedings of dispute resolution."[③]

例如，在第一链接投资有限公司[①]诉 GT 支付有限公司案[②]中法院陈述如下：

"……不能总是假定商业当事人希望用同样的法律体系来管理他们履行合同项下的实质性义务的关系，以及在出现问题时解决争端的完全独立（且往往是不愉快）的关系。

……

事实上，在商业实践中更明智的观点是，往往只有在前一种关系已经不可挽回地破裂时，后一种关系才会发挥作用。因此，不可能有任何自然而然的推论，即商业双方会希望用同样的法律体系来管理这两种不同的关系。自然的推论将是相反的。当商业关系破裂，当事人双方产生争议，此时双方通常渴望得到中立。在当事人双方的商业关系破裂之前，管理实质性合同义务履行的法律处于次要地位（随后，当确定争端的是非曲直时，它将发挥主要作用），当事人为管辖争端解决程序而选择的中立法律被赋予优先权。"[③]

---

① First Link Investments Corp Ltd v. GT Payment Pte Ltd and Others, [2014] SGHCR 12, Singapore High Court, available at: https://www.cliffordchance.com/briefings/2014/06/singapore_high_courtfindsthatpartiesar.html (Last visited on 12 May, 2016).

② The facts and details about the case are available at: http://www.singaporelaw.sg/sglaw/laws-of-singapore/case-law/free-law/high-court-judgments/15620-firstlink-investments-corp-ltd-v-gt-payment-pte-ltd-and-others-2014-sghcr-12 (Last visited on 12 May, 2016).

③ Id.

在这里,新加坡法院的观点与英国和中国的观点不同。新加坡法院认为,采用默示的方式确定最终合适的法律是存在不确定性的问题的。它可能导致仲裁适用法律的不确定性。不确定性不利于解决争端。因此,在新加坡,如果双方没有选择适用于其仲裁协议的法律,则法院将采用主合同的法律作为仲裁协议的适用法。

5. 示范条款

许多国家和地区对仲裁协议的管理问题没有明确的规定或强制性规则。为避免适用法律选择缺失的问题,采用推荐的示范仲裁条款是一个新的好方法。

香港是世界著名的仲裁中心,在国际仲裁方面保持着领先地位。香港国际仲裁中心(HKIAC)为各方提供示范条款①。HKIAC 仲裁规则建议如下:

"以下签字各方,同意将因(简单描述已出现或可能引起的争议、纠纷、分歧或索赔的合同)引起的或与之相关的任何争议、纠纷、分歧或索赔(包括任何有关非合同性义务的争议),提交香港国际仲裁中心,按照《香港国际仲裁中心机构仲裁规则》进行机构仲裁。

本仲裁协议适用的法律应为……(香港法律)。

仲裁地点应为……(香港)。

仲裁员的人数应为……(一名或三名)。仲裁程序应以……(选择语言)进行。"

Here, the court in Singapore held a different view from that of England and China. The Singapore Court holds the opinion that the determination of the implied proper law ultimately remains a question of construction. It may cause uncertainty regarding the applicable law of arbitration. Uncertainty is not good for dispute resolution. Therefore, in Singapore, if the parties have not chosen the law that is applicable to their arbitration agreement, then the court will adopt the law of the main contract as the law of the arbitration agreement.

4.2.5 Model Clause

Many countries and regions do not have clear provisions or mandatory rules regarding the issue of the governing of an arbitration agreement. To avoid the problem of the absence of the choice of applicable law, using the recommended model arbitration clause is a new good way.

Hong Kong is a world-famous arbitration center and maintains a forefront position in international arbitration. The Hong Kong International Arbitration Center (HKIAC) provides model clauses for parties. The HKIAC Arbitration Rules[①] recommends the following:

"We, the undersigned, agree to refer to arbitration administered by the Hong Kong International Arbitration Center (HKIAC) under the HKIAC Administered Arbitration Rules any dispute, controversy, difference or claim (including any dispute regarding non-contractual obligations) arising out of or relating to:

(Brief description of contract under which disputes, controversies, differences or claims have arisen or may arise).

The law of this arbitration agreement shall be … (Hong Kong law).

The seat of arbitration shall be … (Hong Kong).

The number of arbitrators shall be … (one or three). The arbitration proceedings shall be conducted

---

① Available at: http://www.hkiac.org/arbitration/model-clauses (Last visited on May 12, 2016).

in … (insert language)
…"

The model clause from HKIAC has significant effects in practice. The model clause is also supported by the Hong Kong courts. It is a good way to solve the problem of the absence of a choice of arbitration law in an arbitration agreement. This approach is appreciated by many famous scholars.

Royal Queen's Counsel Julian Lew commented that "HKIAC arbitration clause added in terms of its choice of law provisions in the Model initiatives can be described as ingenious, and coinciding with the timing."

The lawyer Promod Nair also highly appreciates the HKIAC model provisions. He said that in some recent cases where the parties did not choose the law applicable to the arbitration agreement, substantive law should apply to the main contract, or other legal disputes may come under the different jurisdictions of the arbitration agreement. He believes that "the parties can simply use HKIAC model clauses to avoid these problems."[①]

4.2.6 Comments

For the issue of the law that is applicable to the arbitration agreement, most countries respect the parties' autonomy at first. The parties' expressed or implied choice will be supported by the arbitral tribunal or national courts. If there is no expressed or implied law in a contract, then there may be different answers, depending upon the regulations of different countries. The common choices include the law applicable at the seat of arbitration, *lex fori*, the law that has the closest and most real connection to the arbitration agreement, and the governing law of the parties' underlying contract.

HKIAC 中的示范仲裁条款在实践中具有显著的效果。该示范条款也得到了香港法院的支持。这是解决仲裁协议中没有选择仲裁法的一个好方法。这种方法受到了许多著名学者的赞赏。

皇室法律顾问朱利安·卢称："香港国际仲裁中心在示范协议中加入仲裁条款，在其法律选择条款方面可谓匠心独运，恰逢其时。"

律师普罗莫德·奈尔也非常赞赏 HKIAC 使用示范条款的规定。他说，在最近的一些案件中，当事人没有选择适用于仲裁协议的法律时，主合同应当适用实体法，否则可能由于仲裁协议的不同管辖范围而引发其他法律纠纷。他认为，"当事人可以使用 HKIAC 示范条款来避免这些问题。"[①]

6. 评论

对于适用于仲裁协议的法律问题，大多数国家首先尊重当事人的自主权。双方明示或暗示的选择将得到仲裁庭或国家法院的支持。如果在合同中没有明示或默示的法律，那么可能会有不同的答案，这取决于不同国家的规定。常见的选择包括适用于仲裁所在地的法律、法院地法、与仲裁协议有最密切和最真实联系的法律，以及当事人基础合同所适用的法律。

---

① Id.

尽管有许多替代的法律选择来管理仲裁协议，但由于缺乏明确的选择，仍然可能存在争议。这可能导致不确定性和长期的管辖权问题。此外，它还可能导致仲裁程序的延迟。

（三）适用于实质问题的法律

适用于仲裁中的实质性问题的法律是指一种特定的法律制度。它意味着当事人的纠纷将由某一特定国家法律的实体法规则来解决。它控制着合同的解释和有效性、当事人的权利和义务、履行方式以及违约的后果。

在国际商事仲裁中，可能有多个国家法律可以作为合同中的实体法。此外，这些不同的法律也有可能在某一特定问题上有相互矛盾的法律规则。这可能会对相关各方造成法律风险。因此，有必要讨论适用于仲裁中实质性问题的法律的选择。

1. 当事人的自治权

关于适用于仲裁中实质性问题的法律问题，几乎每个国家都尊重自治原则。当事人可以选择就适用的法律达成一致。此外，我们还可以在许多国际公约中找到支持。例如，《华盛顿公约》第42条、《示范规则》第33条和（《国际商会仲裁规则》第17条）。少数适用仲裁协议的国家的仲裁法有特殊规定，但这些规定是基于当事人自主原则，如瑞

Even though there are many alternative choices of laws to govern arbitration agreements, there can still be disputes due to the lack of expressed choice. It may lead to uncertainty and protracted jurisdictional challenges. Also, it may lead to the delay of the arbitration process.

4.3 The Law Applicable to the Substantive Issues

The parties' disputes will be solved by the rules of substantive law of a particular national law. The law applicable to substantive issues in arbitration denotes a particular system of law. It controls the interpretation and validity of the contract, the rights and obligations of the parties, the mode of performance, and the consequences for breaches of contract.

In international commercial arbitration, there may be more than one national laws that can be the substantive law in a contract. Besides, there is a possibility that these different laws may have contradictory rules of law on a particular issue. This may cause legal risks for the involved parties. Therefore, there is a need to discuss the choice of the law that is applicable to the substantive issues in arbitration.

4.3.1 Autonomy of the Parties

Concerning the issue of the law that is applicable to the substantive issues in arbitration, almost every country respects the autonomy principle. The parties can choose to agree on the applicable law. Also, we can find support in many international conventions, for example, Article 42 of the Washington Convention, Article 33 of the Model Rules, and Article 17 of the ICC Arbitration Rules. Few national arbitration laws that are applicable to arbitration agreements have special provisions, but these provisions are based on the principle of party autonomy, such as the Swedish Arbitration Act, Portugal Arbitration Act and UK

Arbitration Act are the relevant provisions.[①]

4.3.2 The Range of Possible Options

(a) Substantive Laws or Conflict Laws Rules

There is no doubt that parties can choose a substantive law as the law that is applicable to the substantive issue at hand. However, some authors point out that this methodology is a rigid "single-aspect methodology."[②] They suggest that the conflict laws rules can be the applicable law would be a question. In my view, the choice of substantive law is better than the choice of conflict law rules.

Firstly, choosing a substantive law as the applicable law is the mainstream viewpoint. Most countries hold the opinion that the choice of the laws of a country shall refer to the substantive laws of that country and not its conflict of laws rules. Only when the parties do not have any choice of laws can an arbitral tribunal make a choice based on the conflict of laws rules. We can find some support from national laws and international conventions. For instance, Article 7(1) of the European Convention on International Commercial Arbitration[③] provides the following:

"The parties shall be free to determine, by agreement, the law to be applied by the arbitrators to the substance of the dispute. Failing any indication by the parties as to the applicable law, the arbitrators shall apply the proper law under the rule of conflict that the

典《仲裁法》、《葡萄牙仲裁法》和《英国仲裁法》等相关规定。[①]

2. 可选的范围

(a) 实体法或冲突法规则

毫无疑问，当事各方可以选择一种实体法作为适用于解决争议实质性问题的法律。然而，一些作者指出，这种方法是一种严格的"单方面的方法"。[②]他们认为，也可以选择合适的冲突法规则进行法律的指引。笔者认为，实体法的选择比冲突法规则的选择要好。

第一，选择实体法作为适用法是主流观点。大多数国家认为，一个国家的法律的选择应参照该国的实体法，而不是其法律的冲突规则。只有在当事人没有任何法律选择时，仲裁庭才能根据法律冲突规则作出选择。我们可以从国家法律和国际公约中找到一些支持。例如，《欧洲国际商事仲裁公约》[③]第 7 条（1）规定：

"当事人可自由通过协议决定仲裁员适用于争议实质的法律。如果当事人对适用的法律没有任何指示，仲裁员应根据仲裁员认为适用的冲突规则适用适

---

① Liu X., (2004). The Law Applicable to International Commercial Arbitration Agreement, *Law Magazine*, 93-97, at 96.

② Croff, C. (1982). The Applicable Law in an International Commercial Arbitration: Is It Still a Conflict of Laws Problem? *The International Lawyer*, 16 (4), 613-645, at 628.

③ Article 7(1) of the European Convention on International Commercial Arbitration provides: "The parties shall be free to determine, by agreement, the law to be applied by the arbitrators to the substance of the dispute. Failing any indication by the parties as to the applicable law, the arbitrators shall apply the proper law under the rule of conflict that the arbitrators deem applicable. In both cases the arbitrators shall take account of the terms of the contract and trade usages."

当的法律……"

另一个例子是，1996年《英国仲裁法》第46条（2）和（3）规定如下：

"为此目的，当事人选择某一个国家的法律应被理解为参照该国的实体法，而不是其法律冲突规则。

如果没有这种选择或协议，法庭应适用其认为适用的因相互冲突的法律规则而确定的法律。"

第二，当事人选择指定国家的实体法作为其适用法律的主要原因是他们熟悉该法律。如果他们选择了法律冲突的规则，可能会导致反致。法院可就出现的任何法律冲突采用另一外国管辖权的规则。但是，当事人可能不熟悉这个外国司法管辖辖区的法律，因此，这可能违反了当事人选择指定国家的实体法的初衷。

第三，法律冲突规则的选择可能会导致漫长而复杂的仲裁过程。法律冲突规则不是实质性的法律，它们不能直接适用于一个案件。仲裁庭或法院需要一段时间才能找到合适的实体法来适用于该案。此外，对于最终哪一个实体法能适用该案件，可能会引起一些争议。

(b) 国家法律或非国家法律

大多数情况下，双方会选择某一国家法律作为其争端的适用法律。[①]但是有时，当事人可能选择非国家标准，因为某一国家法律可能不涵盖争议的所有问题。因此，各方需要一套非国家规

arbitrators deem applicable…"

As another example, Article 46 (2) and (3) of the English Arbitration Act 1996 provides the following:

"For this purpose the choice of the laws of a country shall be understood to refer to the substantive laws of that country and not its conflict of laws rules.

If or to the extent that there is no such choice or agreement, the tribunal shall apply the law determined by the conflict of laws rules which it considers applicable."

Secondly, the main reasons for which parties choose a substantive law in a designated country as their applicable law is that they are familiar with the law. If they choose the conflict of laws rules, it may cause *renvoi*. The court may adopt the rules of another foreign jurisdiction with respect to any conflict of laws that arises. However, the parties may not be familiar with the law of this foreign jurisdiction. Therefore, it may violate the original intention of the parties to choose the substantive law of the designated country.

Thirdly, the choice of conflict of laws rules may cause a long, complex process of arbitration. Conflict of laws rules are not substantive laws. They cannot be directly applied in a case. It takes time for the arbitral tribunal or the courts to find a suitable substantive law to apply to the case. Also, it would be likely to cause some disputes due to the issue of which substantive law can finally be applied in the case.

(b) National Law or Non-national Law

In most cases, the parties would choose a national law as the applicable law for their disputes.[①] However, sometimes, the parties may select a non-national standard because a national law may not cover all the matters of a dispute. Therefore, the parties need a set of non-national rules to fill the gaps. These non-national standards

---

① Redfern, A., Supra note 6, at 111-114.

include international customs or usages, transnational law, supranational law, *lex mercatoria*, and so on.[1] They are a set of rules that are developed to regulate international trade in the merchants' community. Below, I offer *lex mercatoria* as an example with which to discuss the application of non-national rules.

Lex mercatoria is Latin for "merchant law." In the early time, the fulcrum of commerce lies in customs, not law.[2] In the Middle Ages, European and Eastern merchants developed customs and usages to regulate their trade. They called these customs and usages as *lex mercatoria*. The *lex mercatoria* was developed and accepted by the various trade areas and as rules for merchants.[3] The *lex mercatoria* is not based on the national laws but evolved customs and business practices. The *lex mercatoria* that was handed down by merchants continues to be used today.

There are various opinions about the sources of *lex mercatoria*. Professor O. Lando believes that the relevant sources of *lex mercatoria* are public international law, general principles of law, uniform laws, rules of international organizations, customs and usages, standard form contracts, and the of arbitral awards.[4] The famous scholar Schmitthoff thinks that the sources of *lex mercatoria* are international legislation and international commercial customs and usages.[5] Although the sources of the *lex mercatoria*

则来填补空白。这些非国家标准包括国际习俗或惯例、跨国法、超国家法、商人法等。[1]它们是一套为规范商人群体的国际贸易而制定的规则。下面，笔者以"商人法"为例来讨论非国家规则的应用。

lex mercatoria 在拉丁语中是"商人法"的意思。在早期，习惯法是商业中重要的部分，而不是法律。[2]在中世纪，欧洲和东方的商人发展了习俗和惯例来规范他们的贸易。他们把这些习俗和习惯称为 lex mercatoria。该法是被各种贸易区发展并接受的，是商人的规则。[3]该法不是基于国家法律，而是不断发展的习俗和商业惯例，一直流传并使用至今。

关于商人法的渊源，兰多教授认为，商人法的来源是国际公法、一般法律原则、统一法律、国际组织规则、风俗习惯、格式合同和仲裁裁决。[4]著名学者施密托夫认为，该法的来源是国际立法和国际商业惯例。[5]虽然如上所述，商人法法律渊源尚未完全商定，但一般观点认为商人法的来源是：法律的一般

---

① Croff, C. (1982). The Applicable Law in an International Commercial Arbitration: Is It Still a Conflict of Laws Problem? *The International Lawyer*, 16 (4), 613-645 at 623.

② Trakman, L. E. (1983). *The Law Merchant: The Evolution of Commercial Law*. Littleton, CO: FB Rothman, at 7.

③ Goldring, J. (1976). Australian Law and International Commercial Arbitration. *Columbia Journal of Transnational Law*, 15(2), 265-310, at 271.

④ Lando, O. (1985). The Lex Mercatoria in International Commercial Arbitration. ICLQ, 34(4), 747-768, at 749-752.

⑤ Schmitthoff, C. M. (1981). *Commercial Law in a Changing Economic Climate* (Vol. 20). London: Sweet & Maxwell, at 22-23.

原则、习惯、惯例和国际贸易统一法以及仲裁法学。①

使用商人法具有自身的优势。它可以打破国家法律的地区限制。双方可以根据从事国际贸易的所有或大多数国家所共有的惯例和习惯来解决其争端。②此外，商人法是基于商业传统而发展起来的。当事人双方将更熟悉特定行业的惯例和风俗习惯。

的确，大多数国家都支持自治原则。双方可以选择他们喜欢的任何适用的法律。但是，笔者不建议仲裁方选择商人法作为其仲裁协议的适用法律。

首先，商人法的范围太宽泛，当事人无法解决争议。正如笔者在前几段中所讨论到的，它没有一个权威的定义和范围，这可能会导致仲裁员在试图应用该法时造成混淆。正如雷西曼所说，商人法的不精确和抽象使其应用"危险地近似于赌博"。③

其次，另一个问题是规范的层次结构。商人法有各种各样的渊源来源。如果不同的来源存在冲突，那么应该采用哪一种？这些问题会使得仲裁裁决不可预测。

are not wholly agreed upon, as demonstrated above, the sources of *lex mercatoria* are commonly agreed to be the following: general principles of law, customs, usages, uniform laws of international trade, and arbitral jurisprudence.①

The use of *lex mercatoria* indeed has advantages. It can break the regional limits of national laws. The parties can solve their disputes on the basis of the usages and customs that are common to all or most of the states engaged in international trade.② Furthermore, the *lex mercatoria* is developed based on business traditions. The parties would be more familiar with the usages and customs in specific industries.

It is true that most countries support the autonomy principle. The parties can choose whatever applicable they prefer. However, I do not recommend the arbitrating parties to choose *lex mercatoria* as the applicable law for their arbitration agreements.

Firstly, the scope of *lex mercatoria* is too broad and too general for parties to solve their disputes. As I have discussed in previous paragraphs, there is not an authoritative definition and scope for *lex mercatoria*. This may cause the confusion for arbitrators when they try to apply *lex mercatoria*. As M. Resiman mentions, the imprecision and abstraction of the *lex mercatoria* make its application "perilously close to a crapshoot"③

Secondly, the other problem is the hierarchy of norms. There are various sources of *lex mercatoria*. If there is a conflict regarding the different sources of *lex mercatoria*, then which one should be applied? This makes arbitration awards unpredictable.

---

① Goldring, J., Supra note 245, at 273.
② Lando, O. (1985). The Lex Mercatoria in International Commercial Arbitration. *ICLQ*, 34(4), 747-768, at 745.
③ Chukwumerije, O. (1994). Applicable Substantive Law in International Commercial Arbitration. *Anglo-Am ericanlaw Review*, 23(3), 265-310, at 279.

Thirdly, few countries accept the arbitral awards that are based on non-state laws.[①] Michaels believes that the *lex mercatoria* is an emerging global commercial law that freely combines elements from national and non-national law.[②] However, in practice, the awards of arbitration based on the *lex mercatoria* may face the risks of being set aside and the refusal of recognition and enforcement by courts due to the uncertain nationalities of the law.

(c) Determination by Arbitrators

If the parties to a contract do not include the "choice of law" clause, then the arbitrators have the duty to determine the applicable law for the depute. There are some different opinions regarding this.

One of the famous opinions is to choose the law of the arbitration seat. This is also called the territorial theory, which emphasizes the close relationship between the place of arbitration and the applicable law of arbitration. Professor Sauser[③] maintains that when parties do not select a law applicable to their contract, then the conflict of laws rule of the country where the arbitral tribunal has its place will apply. His opinion is supported by Mann. In Mann's view,[④] an arbitration clause, like any other contract terms between parties, cannot be suspended in the air. The arbitration clause must draw its authority from a national law provision. Therefore, the country of the seat of arbitration is the only country that can control arbitration.

This opinion is also approved in China. Article 18 of Law of the People's Republic of China on Choice of Law for Foreign-Related Civil Relationships stipulates the following:

最后，极少数国家接受基于非国家法律的仲裁裁决。[①]有学者认为，商人法是一种新兴的全球商法，它自由地结合了国家法和非国家法的要素。[②]但是，在实践中，基于法律依据的仲裁裁决可能面临由于法律国籍不确定而被撤销及被法院拒绝承认和执行的风险。

（c）仲裁员的决定

如果当事人的合同不包括"法律选择"条款，那么仲裁员以及其代理人有义务帮助当事人确定适用的法律。对此不同学者有一些不同的看法。

其中一个著名的观点是选择仲裁地的法律，这也被称为领土理论，它强调仲裁地点与适用的仲裁法之间的密切关系。索瑟教授[③]认为，当事人没有选择适用于其合同的法律时，那么仲裁庭所在国家的法律冲突规则将被适用。他的观点得到了曼恩的支持。在曼恩[④]看来，仲裁条款就像当事人之间的其他合同条款一样，不能如空气般被无视。仲裁条款必须从国家法律的规定中获得其权威。因此，仲裁所在地的国家法律是唯一可以控制仲裁的法律。

这一意见在中国的法律中也得到了认同。《中华人民共和国涉外民事关系法律适用法》第十八条规定：

---

① Croff, C. (1982). The Applicable Law in an International Commercial Arbitration: Is It Still a Conflict of Laws Problem? *The International Lawyer*, 16(4), 613-645, at 623.

② Michaels, R. (2007). The True Lex Mercatoria: Law Beyond the State. *Indiana Journal of Global Legal Studies*, 14(2), at 468.

③ Croff, C., Supra note 251.

④ Mann, F. A. (1984). England Rejects "Delocalised" Contracts and Arbitration. *International and Comparative Law Quarterly*, 33(1), at 195.

当事人可以协议商选择仲裁协议适用的法律。当事人没有选择的，适用仲裁机构所在地法律或者仲裁地法律。"

然而，这一观点却受到了许多作者的质疑。[①]有些人指出，实践中可能很难确定仲裁的地点。例如，仲裁庭可能在两个或两个以上的不同国家举行，或者有时仲裁可以通过当事人和仲裁员之间的信件交换来进行。在这些案件中，哪个国家是仲裁地点将是一个问题。另一种批评则认为，仲裁地的选择可能是偶然的。该选择可能与双方或合同没有任何联系。例如，假定双方分别来自中国和日本，并且出于经济原因，他们决定在两国之间的韩国进行仲裁。在这种情况下，韩国与合同或双方没有任何关系。

除了领土理论之外，去领土化理论也很有名。去领土化理论强调，对适用法律的范围的选择不受国家领土的限制，它可以是国际性的。去领土化理论打破了国家的边界。仲裁员可以根据自己的需要来选择实体法或法律冲突规则。有许多国际资源可以成为适用的法律，如国际私法、国际法律冲突制度等。

"The parties concerned may choose the laws applicable to arbitral agreement by agreement. If the parties do not choose, the laws at the locality of the arbitral authority or of the arbitration shall apply."

However, this opinion has been challenged by many authors.[①] Some people point out that it may be difficult to identify the place of arbitration. For instance, the hearings may be held in two or more different countries, or sometimes, arbitration may be conducted by an exchange of letters between the parties and the arbitrator. Which country is the place of arbitration would be a question in these cases. Another criticism maintains that the selection of the seat may be a fortuity. The choice may not have any link with the parties or the contract. For instance, assume that the two parties are from China and Japan respectively, and for economic reasons, they decide that the arbitration shall sit halfway, in Korea. In this case, Korea has no connection to the contract or the parties.

Apart from the territorial theory, the denationalization theory is also famous. The denationalization theory stresses that the choice of the scope of the applicable law is not limited by national territory— it can be international. The denationalization theory breaks the boundaries of countries. The arbitrators can choose the substantive law or the conflicts of laws rules based on their needs. There are many international resources that can be the applicable laws, such as international private law, the international conflicts of laws system, and so on.

---

① Lew, J. D. (1997). Determination of Applicable Substantive Law. *Int'l Bus. Law., 25*, at 157.

In my view, the arbitrators have the right to choose an applicable law that has no connection to the place of arbitration. Particularly when the law is well-developed and natural, it can easily be used to solve the disputes between parties. Also, in some special cases, such as electronic commerce cases, the disputes take place in the virtual space. If the law of the physical place is applied compulsorily, it may easily lead to more controversies. Lastly, harmonization is the international trend for arbitration.[①] Nowadays, many countries have adopted a policy of support for arbitration, and countries have phased out many unnecessary restrictions on arbitration.

在笔者看来，仲裁员有权选择与仲裁地点无关的适用法律。特别是在法律健全而自然的情况下，它可以很容易地用来解决当事人之间的纠纷。此外，在某些特殊情况下，如电子商务案例中，纠纷可能发生在虚拟空间。如果现实地理位置的法律被强制适用，可能容易引起更多的纠纷。最后，仲裁法的协调统一是当今的国际趋势。如今，许多国家已经采用了支持仲裁的政策，各国已经逐步取消了对仲裁的许多不必要的限制。

---

① Simões, F. D., Supra note 27.

第四章　格式条款的适用法律

Chapter IV Law Applicable to Standard Terms

在前文,笔者探讨了仲裁的有效性和法律适用的问题。但是,如果我们想确保具有仲裁条款的格式合同是有效的,我们也应该知道格式合同中条款有效性的要求。

从国际层面分析,关于这个问题的国际公约或条约极少。即使在《联合国国际货物销售合同公约》中,我们也找不到关于合同或格式合同中标准条款有效性的相关规定。然而,我们可以在《国际统一私法协会国际商事合同通则》(UPICC)中找到线索。PICC 中的第 2.1.19 条至第 2.1.22 条涉及一方或双方在订立合同时使用标准条款的特殊情况。①

例如,第 2.1.20 条规定了关于异常条款的问题:

"(1)任何格式条款中所包含的具有另一方不能合理预期的性质的条款均无效,除非该另一方已明确接受。

(2)在确定一个术语是否具有这种性质时,应考虑其内容、语言和表现形式。"

第 2.1.21 条规定了格式条款与非格式条款之间发生冲突时的解决办法:

"如果格式条款与非格式条款发生

In the previous chapter, I explored the questions about the validity of arbitration and the applicable law to the arbitration agreement. However, if we want to make sure the standard form contracts with arbitration clauses are valid, we should also know the requirements of the valid standard terms in contracts.

At international level, there are few international conventions or treaties about this issue. Even in the United Nations Convention on Contracts for the International Sale of Goods, we cannot find relevant provisions about validity of standard terms in contracts or standard form contracts. Nevertheless, we can find clues in the UPICC (UNIDROIT Principles of International Commercial Contracts). Article 2.1.19 to Article 2.1.22 in PICC deal with the special situation where one or both parties use standard terms in concluding a contract.①

For instance, Article 2.1.20 regulates the issue about surprising terms,

"(1) No term contained in standard terms which is of such a character that the other party could not reasonably have expected it, is effective unless it has been expressly accepted by that party.

(2) In determining whether a term is of such a character regard shall be had to its content, language and presentation."

Article 2.1.21 regulates the solution when the conflicts happen between standard terms and non-standard terms,

"In case of conflict between a standard term and a

---

① Available at:http://www.unidroit.org/english/principles/contracts/principles2010/integralversionprinciples2010-e.pdf (Last visited on May 12, 2016).

term which is not a standard term the latter prevails."

PICC have some provisions about standard terms, but they are just international principles for commercial contracts, not a law. It does have substantive effects on specific cases. The courts will decide the cases on the basis of the substantive laws in their countries. As for the issue of standard terms, different countries have their own opinions. Below are some examples to illustrate the issue about law applicable to standard terms.

1. China

In China, the standard form contract is widely used.[①] Although it has a long history of use in China, the legal system of the issue surrounding standard form contract is still not highly developed. Therefore, there is still some room for the advancement of legislation of the issue about the standard form contract.

First, the relevant provisions of the law on the standard form contract system are fragmented. It is difficult to have an effective legal system to protect the interests of weak parties in a standard form contract. China is a statute law country and most legal issues are regulated in law. The cases and disputes would be determined by court according to the statute law. In current Chinese law, only a few fragmented legal provisions are spotted in various laws.

The second problem is the lack of special legislation for the standard form contract. Most provisions are regulated in China Contract Law or the provisions about China Contract Law is scattered throughout other Chinese laws, such as law

冲突,以后者为准。"

PICC有一些关于格式条款的规定,但它们只是关于商业合同的国际原则,不是法律。它确实对具体的案件有实质性的影响。法院将根据其国家的实体法来裁决这些案件。关于格式条款的问题,不同的国家都有自己的意见。下面是一些例子来说明关于适用于格式条款的法律的问题。

一、中国

在中国,格式合同被广泛使用。[①]虽然格式合同在我国有着悠久的使用历史,但围绕格式合同问题的法律体系还没有被高度完善。因此,关于格式合同问题的立法仍有一定的推进空间。

第一,法律对格式合同制度的相关规定较零散。很难有一个有效的法律制度来保护格式合同中弱者的利益。中国是一个成文法国家,大多数法律问题都有法律规范。这些案件和纠纷将由法院根据成文法来裁定。在中国现行的法律中,在各种法律中只发现了少数零散的法律条款。

第二个问题是缺乏对格式合同的特殊立法。有关于格式合同的规定大多存在于中国《合同法》中,以及一些关于《合同法》的规定分散在其他法律法规中,例如中国《消费者权益保护法》《保险法》

---

① Smith, A. H. (1972). Standard Form Contracts in the International Commercial Transactions of the People's Republic of China. *International and Comparative Law Quarterly*, 21(1), 133-150, at 135.

《海商法》等。《合同法》第三十九、第四十、四十一条规定了格式合同的有效性和格式合同的解释问题。

第三，我国对格式合同没有特殊的法律程序。

本节中将讨论中国法律中对格式合同条款的规定。

（一）中国《消费者权益保护法》

中国《消费者权益保护法》第二十六条规定了保护消费者的格式合同的问题。在日常生活中，作为消费者，我们会处理许多格式合同，在这种情况下，我们就处于较弱的位置。中国法律禁止对消费者使用不合理或不公平的条款。此外，对格式条款的解释也将有利于处于弱势地位的消费者。

中国《消费者权益保护法》第二十六条规定：

"经营者不得以格式条款、通知、声明、店堂告示等方式，作出排除或者限制消费者权利、减轻或者免除经营者责任、加重消费者责任等对消费者不公平、不合理的规定，不得利用格式条款并借助技术手段强制交易。

格式条款、通知、声明、店堂告示等含有前款所列内容的，其内容无效。"

on Consumer Protection of Rights and Interests of Consumers, Insurance Law, Maritime Law, etc. Article 39, 40, 41 of the China Contract Law regulates the validity of the standard contract and the issue about the interpretation of the standard form contract.

Thirdly, there are no special law procedures for the standard form contract in China.

In this section, I will discuss the fragmented legal provisions for standard terms in Chinese law.

1.1 China's Law on Protection of Rights and Interests of Consumers

Article 26 of the China Consumer Protection of Rights and Interests of Consumers regulates the issue about the standard form contract for protecting consumers. In daily life we, as consumers, handle many standard form contracts and in that case, we are left in a weaker position. The unreasonable or unfair terms for consumers are forbidden in Chinese law. Also, the interpretation of the standard form clause would be in favor of the consumers in weaker positions.

Article 26 of the above-mentioned law regulates that:

"Business operators shall not impose unfair and unreasonable terms on consumers such as elimination or restriction of consumer rights, mitigation or disclaimer of business operator's liability, aggravation of consumer liability, etc. by way of standard clauses, notices, ments, entrance hall bulletins, etc., and shall not make use of standard clauses and compel transactions by way of technical means.

Standard clauses, notices, announcements, entrance hall bulletins, and soon with contents as listed in the preceding paragraph, the contents of such standard contracts, circulars, announcements and shop notices, etc., shall be invalid."

1.2 China Insurance Law

China Insurance Law[①] also regulates the issue about standard form contract. In Insurance Law, Article 18 stresses that the true intention of the parties conclude the standard insurance contract. Therefore, if the party does not realize that they sign a standard form contract, the insurance contract cannot be binding by the parties.

Article 18 of the China Insurance Law regulate that:

"If an insurance contract provides for the exemption of liabilities for the insurer, the insurer shall clearly state in before signing the insurance contract. If no clear statement is made about it, the clause shall not be binding"

China Insurance Law regulates that interpretations of standard terms in China Insurance would be favorable to the insured and beneficiaries. This provision presents that China Law protects the weaker party in the transaction.

Article 31 of the China Insurance Law regulates that:

"If the clauses of an insurance contract are in dispute among the insurer and the insurant, the insured or beneficiaries, the people's court or arbitration organizations shall make interpretations favorable to the insured and beneficiaries."

1.3 China Maritime Law

In China Maritime Law,[②] we can find provisions about the standard form contract. China Maritime Law has provisions regulating the circumstances where the standard form clauses in a contract of carriage would be null and void.

According to Article 126 of China Maritime Law,

"Any of the following clauses contained in a contract of carriage of passengers by sea shall be null and void:

---

① China Insurance Law, available at http://www.china. org.cn/english/DAT/214788.htm(Last visited on May12, 2016).

② China Maritime Law, available at: http://www.lawinfochina. com/display.aspx?lib=law&id=191 (Last visited on May 12, 2016).

（二）中国《保险法》

中国《保险法》[①]也对格式合同的问题进行了规定。该法第十七条第二款强调当事人订立保险合同的真实意思。因此，如果当事人没有意识到他们签订了一个格式合同，则该保险合同不受当事人的约束力。

中国《保险法》第十八条规定：

保险合同规定免除保险人的责任的，保险人应当在签订保险合同前明确说明。没有明确说明的，该条款不具有约束力。"

中国《保险法》规定，对中国保险的标准条款的解释将有利于被保险人和受益人。本规定表明，中国法律保护了交易中实力较弱的一方。

中国《保险法》第31条规定：

保险人与被保险人、被保险人、受益人之间的保险合同条款有争议的，人民法院、仲裁机构应当作出有利于被保险人和受益人的解释。

（三）中国《海商法》

中国《海商法》[②]中，我们可以找到关于格式合同的规定。中国《海商法》规定了运输合同中格式条款的无效情况。

根据中国《海商法》第一百二十六条：

"海上旅客运输合同中含有下列内容之一的条款无效：

（一）免除承运人对旅客应当承担的法定责任；

（二）降低本章规定的承运人责任限额；

（三）对本章规定的举证责任作出相反的约定；

（四）限制旅客提出赔偿请求的权利。

前款规定的合同条款的无效，不影响合同其他条款的效力。"

（四）中华人民共和国民法典

中国《合同法》不同于上述法律。中国合同法是处理合同纠纷的基本法。对于格式合同，中国《合同法》对这种复杂性有一些规定。《中华人民共和国民法典》（以下简称《民法典》）中亦有与格式合同相关的规则。

《民法典》第496条确定了格式合同的定义。格式合同是合同起草人提供格式条款，按照公平原则规定当事人的权利义务，合理提请对方注意该条款。

《民法典》第496条规定：

"采用格式条款订立合同的，提供格式条款的一方应当遵循公平原则确定当事人之间的权利和义务，并采取合理的方式提请对方注意免除或者限制其责任的条款，按照对方的要求，对该条款予以说明。格式条款是当事人为了重复使用而预先拟定，并在订立合同时未与对方协商的条款。"

《民法典》第497条规定，格式条款具有本法第五十二条和第五十三条规定情形的，或者提供格式条款一方免除其责任、加重对方责任、排除对方主要权利的，该条款无效。

(1) Any clause that exonerates the statutory responsibility of the carrier in respect of the passenger;

(2) Any clause that reduces the limitation of liability of the carrier as contained in this Chapter;

(3) Any clause that contains provisions contrary to those of this Chapter concerning burden of proof;

(4) Any clause that restricts the right of claim of the passenger.

The nullity and voidness of the clauses set out in the preceding paragraph shall not prejudice the validity of the other clauses of the contract."

1.4 Civil Code of the People's Republic of China

As for standard form contract, there are some provisions in Civil Code of the People's Republic of China concerning this complication.

Article 496 in Civil Code determines the definition of the standard form contract. Also the drafters of standard form contracts supply the standard terms and shall abide by the principle of fairness in prescribing the rights and obligations of the parties and shall, in a reasonable manner, call the other party's attention to the provision.

Article 496 in Civil Code regulates that:

"Duty to Call Attention Where a contract is concluded by way of standard terms, the party supplying the standard terms shall abide by the principle of fairness in prescribing the rights and obligations of the parties and shall, in a reasonable manner, call the other party's attention to the provision(s) whereby such party's liabilities are excluded or limited, and shall explain such provision(s) upon request by the other party.

Standard terms are contract provisions which were prepared in advance by a party for repeated use, and which are not negotiated with the other party in the course of concluding the contract."

Civil Code determines that a standard term is invalid if it falls into any of the circumstances. Article 144, Article146, Article153, Article154, Article505, Article506 in Civil Code regulates that term is invalid if the standard terms deprive the other of its material rights.

Article 144:

A civil juristic act performed by a person who has no capacity for performing civil juristic acts is void.

Article 146:

A civil juristic act performed by a person and another person based on a false expression of intent is void.

Article 153:

A civil juristic act in violation of the mandatory provisions of laws or administrative regulations is void, unless such mandatory provisions do not lead toinvalidity of such a civil juristic act. A civil juristic act that offends the public order or good morals is void.

Article 154:

A civil juristic act is void if it is conducted through malicious collusion between a person who

《民法典》第 498 条规定了中国法律对格式条款的解释。在中国，格式合同条款应按照常识进行解释。有两种以上解释的，需要按照格式合同被提供方有利的情形进行解释。格式条款与非格式条款的解释或约定不同的，应当以非格式合同的解释为准。

《民法典》第 498 条规定如下：

"对格式条款的理解发生争议的，应当按照通常理解予以解释。对格式条款有两种以上解释的，应当作出不利于提供格式条款一方的解释。格式条款和非格式条款不一致的，应当采用非格式条款。"

以上已经介绍了关于格式合同条款的主要规定。然而，格式条款同时也是合同中的一个普通条款。《民法典》第 153 条、154、505、506 条列出了合同的无效情形。例如，通过欺诈或胁迫等手段订立合同，可能会导致合同条款的无效。或者当事人恶意串通，损害国家、集体或者第三人的利益的，合同条款或者标准形式条款可能无效。

相关规定如下：

《民法典》第一百四十四条：

"无民事行为能力人实施的民事法律行为无效。"

《民法典》第一百四十六条：

"行为人与相对人以虚假的意思表示实施的民事法律行为无效。以虚假的意思表示隐藏的民事法律行为的效力，依照有关法律规定处理。"

《民法典》第一百五十三条：

"违反法律、行政法规的强制性规定的民事法律行为无效。但是，该强制性规定不导致该民事法律行为无效的除外。违背公序良俗的民事法律行为无效。"

《民法典》第一百五十四条：

"行为人与相对人恶意串通，损害他人合法权益的民事法律行为无效。"

《民法典》第五百零五条：

"当事人超越经营范围订立的合同的效力，应当依照本法第一编第六章第三节和本编的有关规定确定，不得仅以超越经营范围确认合同无效。"

《民法典》第五百零六条：

合同中的下列免责条款无效：

（一）不包括一方对对另一方造成的人身伤害的责任；

（二）不包括一方因故意或重大过失给另一方造成的财产损失的责任。"

众所周知，中国有两个特别行政区，一个是香港，另一个是澳门。由于历史原因，这两个地区的法律、法律制度是不同的。下面介绍适用于香港和澳门标准条款的法律。

（五）香港及澳门的条例

香港是一个英美法系地区，对格式条款的法定救济极少。《不合理合约条例》①（下简称 UCO）列举了一些不公平条款的例子。UCO 中承认的不公平条款可能无法强制执行。UCO 的第 6 节是 UCO 中的一个重要部分。它列举了一些关于不公平条款的例子，包括供应商在不通知消费者的情况下单方面改变合同条款、提前取消合同服务等。然而，UCO 并没有提供对不合理条款的

performs the act and a counterparty thereof and thus harms the lawful rights and interests of another person.

Article 505:

Where the parties conclude a contract beyond their scope of business, the validity of the contract shall be determined according to the provisions in Section 3 of Chapter VI of Book One of this Code and this Book, and the contract shall not be determined as invalid solely on the ground that it is beyond their scope of business.

Article 506:

An exculpatory clause in a contract exempting the liability on the following acts are void:

(1) causing physical injury to the other party; or

(2) causing losses to the other party's property intentionally or due to gross negligence.

As is well-known, China has two special administrative regions: one is Hong Kong, and the other is Macao. Due to historical reasons, the laws and the legal systems are different in these two areas. Next, I will introduce the laws applicable to standard terms in Hong Kong and Macao.

1.5 Regulations in Hong Kong and Macao

Hong Kong is a common law jurisdiction. There is little statutory recourse to standard terms. Unconscionable Contracts Ordinance① (UCO) lists some examples of unfair terms. The terms recognized unfair in the UCO may be unenforceable. Section 6

---

① Hong Kong Unconscionable Contracts Ordinance, available at: https://www.elegislation.gov.hk/hk/cap 458 (Last visited on September 8, 2022).

of the UCO[①] is an important section in the UCO. It sets out some examples about unfair terms, including a supplier to unilaterally vary the terms of a contract without notifying the consumer, early cancellation of a contracted service, etc. However, the UCO does not provide a clear definition of unconscionable terms. There are only some non-exhaustive factors listed in Section 6 of the UCO.

In addition to the UCO, the Control of Exemption Clauses Ordinance, Misrepresentation Ordinance, Supply of Services (Inplied Terms) Ordinance also have provisions about standard terms. The Control of Exemption Clauses Ordinance attempts to limit the business to exempt themselves from liability. The Misrepresentation Ordinance limits the parties to exclude or restrict liability for misrepresentation by standard terms. The Supply of Services (Inplied Terms) Ordinance stipulates that a supplier's liability arising from standard terms cannot be exempted or limited by

明确定义。在 UCO[①]的第 6 节中，只列出了一些非详尽的因素。

除 UCO 外，香港《管制免责条款条例》《失实陈述条例》《服务提供（隐含条款）条例》还有有关标准条款的规定。香港《管制免责条款条例》试图限制企业为自己免除责任。《失实陈述条例》限制当事人以标准条款排除或限制失实陈述的责任。《服务提供（隐含条款）条例》指出，供应商因标准条款而产生的法律责任，不能因参照合同条款而被豁免或限制。然而，上面提到的这些条款只是以标准条款规定了豁免条款的具体实例，还有许多在 UCO 中没有提到的其他情况。因此，香港法院必须求助于普通法寻求判例，因为该条例在香港的标准条款上缺乏效力。香港有需要改革该条例。

---

①   Section 6 of the Unconscionable Contracts Ordinance:"

(1) In determining whether a contract or part of a contract was unconscionable in the circumstances relating to the contract at the time it was made, the court may have regard to (among other things)—

(a) the relative strengths of the bargaining positions of the consumer and the other party;

(b) whether, as a result of conduct engaged in by the other party, the consumer was required to comply with conditions that were not reasonably necessary for the protection of the legitimate interests of the other party;

(c) whether the consumer was able to understand any documents relating to the supply or possible supply of the goods or services;

(d) whether any undue influence or pressure was exerted on, or any unfair tactics were used against, the consumer or a person acting on behalf of the consumer by the other party or a person acting on behalf of the other party in relation to the supply or possible supply of the goods or services; and

(e) the amount for which, and the circumstances under which, the consumer could have acquired identical or equivalent goods or services from a person other than the other party.

(2) In determining whether a contract or part of a contract was unconscionable in the circumstances relating to the contract at the time it was made—

(a) the court shall not have regard to any unconscionability arising from circumstances that were not reasonably foreseeable at the time the contract was made; and

(b) the court may have regard to conduct engaged in, or circumstances existing, before the commencement of this Ordinance.

(3) In considering the exercise of its powers under section 5 to grant relief in respect of a contract or part of a contract found to be unconscionable, the court may have regard to the conduct of the parties to the proceedings in relation to the performance of the contract since it was made."

至于澳门，其法律基本上是基于葡萄牙的法律。澳门的法律体系是大陆法系，成文法是主要的法律渊源。《通用合同条款法》①（第 17/92/M 号法律）规定了"通用合同条款"的具体实例。通用合同条款的概念与汉语中的"格式条款"的概念相似。通用合同条款是指一方事先准备好的条款，另一方只能接受通用合同条款中的条款和条件。目前《通用合同条款法》②尚未翻译成英文，只有中文和葡萄牙语版本。③《通用合同条款法》倾向于保护通用合同条款中实力较弱的一方。该法也规定了当事人的一些义务，如第五条、第六条、第九条至第十三条列出了一些禁止的情况。第 5 章规定了有关通用合同条款的程序问题。在笔者看来，与香港 UCO 相比，《通用合同条款法》的内容更适用于通用合同条款，其内容完整，满足法律实践中的需要。

二、德国

格式合同的问题在德国合同法中

reference to a contract term. However, these provisions I have mentioned above just provide for specific instances of exemption clauses in standard terms. Many other circumstances are not mentioned in the UCO. Therefore, the courts in Hong Kong have to turn to common law for precedents for the lack of efficacy of the ordinance to standard terms in Hong Kong. There are some needs to reform the ordinance in Hong Kong.

As for Macao, the laws in Macao is broadly based on the Portuguese law. The legal system of Macao is civil law. Statute laws are the main source for cases.① Law 17/92/M (Law on General Contract Clauses) provide for specific instances of "general contract clauses". The concept of general contract clauses is similar to that of standard terms in Chinese. General contract clauses are the clauses prepared by one party in advance. The other party can only accept the terms and conditions in general contract clauses.② Law 17/92/M has not been translated into English.③ It only has Chinese and Portuguese versions. Law 17/92/M tends to protect the weaker party in general contract clauses. It regulates some obligations of parties. For instance, Article 5, Article 6, and Article 9 to Article 13 list some prohibited circumstances. Chapter 5 in Law 17/92/M regulates the procedural issue pertaining to the general contract clauses. In my opinion, compared with Hong Kong UCO, Law 17/92/M is a law more suitable to general contract clauses. The content of Law 17/92/M is complete and meets the needs in practice.

2. Germany

The issue of standard terms of contract or standard form contracts plays a significant role in German

---

① Fan, J., & Pereira, A. D. (2011). *Commercial and Economic Law in Macao*. Kluwer Law International, at 29.

② Article1of Law17/92/M.

③ The Chinese and Portuguese version is available at: http://bo.io.gov.mo/bo/i/92/39/lei17_cn.asp (Last visited on May 12, 2016).

contract law. In Germany, AGBs[①] were traditionally the act on standard terms of business. However, these statutory rules were integrated into the German Civil Code in 2002.[②] Germany is a civil law country, meaning that written laws are the source of laws. Legislature regulates the laws in all major areas.[③]

As for the issue of standard form contract, the German Civil Code has some provisions about it. One of the features of the German Civil Code is the code not only regulates the substantive issue about the standard form contract, but also the procedural issue pertaining to the standard form contract.

The users of standard business terms are faced with problems from two aspects:

Firstly, the counterparty of the contract may be unfamiliar with the content of the standard business terms. In some contracts, the font size of standard business terms may be very small and the terms not noticeable, or some standard business terms may contain many technical terms, and they may be difficult to understand for the average person.

Secondly, the counterparty of the contract with standard business terms may be clearly aware of the unfair position, but they still accept these standard business terms. Sometimes the counter party has no other choice and if they do not accept these standard business terms, they cannot conclude the contract.

To protect the users of standard business terms, the German Civil Code regulates the issue at two levels. The first level is that the standard business terms meet the requirements as a standard business term. Or the standard business terms cannot be a part of the contract.

---

① AGB is short for "allgemeine Geschäftsbedingungen", which means "terms of business".

② Lowisch, M. (2003). New Law of Obligations in Germany. *Ritsumeikan Law Review*, 20, 141-156, at 142.

③ Merryman, J. H., & Pérez-Perdomo, R. (2007). *The Civil Law Tradition: An Introduction to the Legal Systems of Europe and Latin America*. Stanford University Press, at 20.

是重要的内容。德国的 AGB 法案[①]是传统意义上管理格式合同有关问题的法律法规。然而，AGB 法案于 2002 年被纳入德国民法典。[②]德国是一个大陆法系国家，这意味着成文法是德国法律的渊源，成文法规定了各种制度，司法机关将会依据成文法进行裁判。[③]

关于合同标准的问题，德国民法典有一些规定。德国民法典的特点之一是它不仅规范了有关格式合同的实质性问题，还规范了有关格式合同的程序问题。

格式合同的使用者面临着两个方面的问题：

首先，合同的另一方可能不熟悉商业格式条款的内容。在一些合同中，格式条款可能书写得非常小而且不太明显，或者一些格式条款可能包含许多专业术语，对普通人来说可能难以理解。

其次，具有格式条款的合同对方当事人可能清楚地意识到自己在该合同中不公平的地位，但他们仍然接受这些商业格式条款。有时对方当事人没有其他选择，如果他们不接受这些格式条款，他们就不能签订合同。

为了保护这些使用格式条款的用户，德国民法典将该问题分为两个层次。第一级是使格式条款满足作为格式条款的要求，或者要求格式条款不能成为合同的一部分。第二级是格式条款的内容不能与法律相冲突，否则格式条款无效。

《德国民法典》第 305 节至第 310 节涵盖了有关标准条款的实质性问题。下面将讨论从第 305 节到第 310 节的细节。

（一）德国民法典第 305 条

《德国民法典》第 305 条规定：①

"1. 格式条款是指为了使合同一方（合同使用者）在签订合同时提交给另一方两份以上的合同而预先制定的所有合同条款。这些条款无论是采用合同中独立部分的形式，还是成为合同文件本身的一部分，无论数量多少，使用什么字体以及合同采用什么形式，都无关紧要。如果双方已经详细谈判，那么合同条款不能是格式条款。

2. 仅在下列情形，并且合同另外一方当事人同意适用一般交易条款的，一般交易条款才构成合同的组成部分：

（1）使用人在订约时明确向另外一方当事人指明一般交易条款，或者因订约性质而仅在克服过巨困难的情况下始可以明确指明时，以在订约地清楚陈列的方式指明一般交易条款；并且

（2）使用人在订约时，以可合理期待的方式使另外一方当事人取得知悉一般交易条款内容的可能性，同时应适当考虑能够为使用人所辨识的另外一方当事人的身体障碍。

3. 合同双方在遵守上述第 2 款规定的要求的同时，可以事先同意将特定的格式条款适用于特定类型的法律交易。"

The second level is that contents of the standard business terms cannot conflict with the law, otherwise the they cannot be valid. Section 305 to Section 310 in the German Civil Code cover the substantive issue about the standard terms. I will discuss the details of Section 305 to Section 310 below.

2.1 Section 305 in German Civil Code

Section 305 in the German Civil Code regulates:①

"(1) Standard business terms are all contract terms pre-formulated for more than two contracts which one party to the contract (the user) presents to the other party upon the entering into of the contract. It is irrelevant whether the provisions take the form of a physically separate part of a contract or are made part of the contractual document itself, what their volume is, what typeface or font is used for them and what form the contract takes. Contract terms do not become standard business terms to the extent that they have been negotiated in detail between the parties.

(2) Standard business terms only become a part of a contract if the user, when entering into the contract,

1. refers the other party to the contract to them explicitly or, where explicit reference, due to the way in which the contract is entered into, is possible only with disproportionate difficulty, by posting a clearly visible notice at the place where the contract is entered into, and

2. gives the other party to the contract, in an acceptable manner, which also takes into reasonable account any physical handicap of the other party to the contract that is discernible to the user, the opportunity to take notice of their contents,
and if the other party to the contract agrees to their applying.

<hr>

① German Civil Code, available at: https://www.gesetze-im-internet.de/englisch_bgb/englisch_bgb.html (Last visited on May 12, 2016).

(3) The parties to the contract may, while complying with the requirements set out in subsection (2) above, agree in advance that specific standard business terms are to govern a specific type of legal transaction."

Under the German Civil Code Article 305(1), we can find that the standard business terms in German civil law mainly includes the following aspects: (1) The standard business terms can be effectively incorporated into the contract. The issue should be based on Article 305 to Article 305c of the German Civil Code. (2) The definition is the "pre-formulated" business terms for similar and frequent transactions. (3) The standard business terms should be proposed by one of the parties. If the terms have been negotiated by both sides, they will not be considered as standard form terms. (4) The standard business terms should be proposed before the conclusion of the contract. The notification of the standard business terms after the conclusion of the contract is not recognized as a standard business term, unless the parties reach a new agreement about the issue.

Under the German Civil Code Article 305(2), we can find that: (1) The drafters of standard business terms should make a clear indication of the terms, before the conclusion of the contract. Otherwise it could result in an invalid contract. (2) The drafter of the standard business terms has an obligation to make a clear indication of business standard terms, but should also make the "average consumer" (Durschschnittskunden) aware of the meaning of standard business terms.

In addition to Article 305a, Article 305b in the German Civil Code regulates[①] if the parties reached individually agreed terms, they take priority over standard business terms.

Under Article 305c of the German Civil Code,[②] we can find that: (1) Surprising and ambiguous terms cannot become part of the contract, because "surprising

---

① Section 305b in the German Civil Code regulates: "Individually agreed terms take priority over standard business terms."

② Section 305c in the German Civil Code regulates: "(1) Provisions in standard business terms which in the circumstances, in particular with regard to the outward appearance of the contract, are so unusual that the other party to the contract with the user need not expect to encounter them, do not form part of the contract. (2) Any doubts in the interpretation of standard business terms are resolved against the user."

根据《德国民法典》第 305 条第 1 款，我们可以发现德国民法的格式条款主要包括以下几个方面：(1) 格式条款可以有效地纳入合同。该问题应以德国民法典第 305 条至第 305c 条为依据。(2) 格式条款是指针对类似和频繁交易"预先制定好"的商业条款。(3) 格式条款应由合同当事人中的一方提出。如果这些条款已由双方协商过，它们将不被视为格式条款。(4) 在合同签订前应提出格式条款。在合同签订后，对格式条款的通知不会被确认为格式条款，除非双方就该问题达成新的协议。

根据《德国民法典》第 305 条第 2 款，我们可以发现：(1) 格式条款的起草者应在合同签订前明确指出合同中含有格式条款。否则可能会导致该合同无效。(2) 格式条款的起草者有义务明确指出格式条款，但也应使"普通消费者"（消费者）了解该格式条款的含义。

除了《德国民法典》[①]第 305a，第 305b 条还规定，如果双方达成了单独商定的条款，它们将优先于格式条款。

根据《德国民法典》[②]第 305c 条，我们可以发现：(1) 异常条款和模棱两可的条款不能成为合同的一部分。因为"异常条款和模棱两可的条款"可能会导致对另外一方当事人的不公平。(2) 异常条款的起草者应承担在解释异常条款时产生疑问的风险。如果合同的起草者在解释合同中的格式条款时有模糊不清或犹豫的情形，格式条款的解释将采取利于合同另一方的方式进行解释。

and ambiguous terms" may lead to unfairness for the other party. (2) The drafter of standard business terms should burden the risks of the doubts in the interpretation of standard business terms. If there is ambiguity or hesitation in the clarification, "any doubts in the interpretation of standard business terms are resolved against the user."

（二）德国民法典第306条

2.2 Section 306 in German Civil Code

《德国民法典》第306条规定：

"1.如果全部或部分的格式条款没有成为合同的一部分或无效，则合同的剩余部分仍然有效。"

2.如果格式条款未成为合同的一部分或无效，则合同的内容将由法定条款确定。

3.如果考虑到上述第2款规定的变更对一方来说是不合理的困难，则合同无效。"

从第306条中我们可以发现，如果格式条款的部分或全部没有成为合同的一部分或无效，则合同条款的其余部分仍然有效。主合同不会因格式条款无效而无效。第306条构成"放宽条款"，是指在特殊情况下，无效条款不能导致主合同无效。在笔者看来，第306条第3款为法官的自由裁量权留下了空间。

Section 306 in the German Civil Code regulates:

"(1) If standard business terms in whole or in part have not become part of the contract or are ineffective, the remainder of the contract remains in effect.

(2) To the extent that the terms have not become part of the contract or are ineffective, the contents of the contract are determined by the statutory provisions.

(3) The contract is ineffective if upholding it, even taking into account the alteration provided in subsection (2) above, would be an unreasonable hardship for one party."

From Section 306 we can find that if standard business terms in part or whole have not become part of the contract or are ineffective, the remainder of the contract terms remains in effect. The main contract would not be invalid due to the invalid standard terms. Section306 constitutes "relaxation terms," meaning that under special circumstances, the invalid terms cannot cause the main contract to be invalid. In my opinion, Section 306(3) leaves room for the judge's discretion.

（三）德国民法典第307条

2.3 Section 307 in German Civil Code

《德国民法典》第307条规定：

1. "合同中的格式条款，如果违反诚信要求，对另外一方当事人存在不合理

Section 307 in the German Civil Code regulates:

"(1) Provisions in standard business terms are ineffective if, contrary to the requirement of good faith, they unreasonably disadvantage the other party to the contract with the user. An unreasonable disadvantage may also arise from the provision not being clear and comprehensible.

(2) An unreasonable disadvantage is, in case of doubt, to be assumed to exist if a provision

1. is not compatible with essential principles of the statutory provision from which it deviates, or

2. limits essential rights or duties inherent in the nature of the contract to such an extent that attainment of the purpose of the contract is jeopardized.

(3) Subsections (1) and (2) above, and sections 308 and 309 apply only to provisions in standard business terms on the basis of which arrangements derogating from legal provisions, or arrangements supplementing those legal provisions, are agreed. Other provisions may be ineffective under subsection (1) sentence 2 above, in conjunction with subsection (1) sentence 1 above."

According to Section 307(1), if standard business terms violate the principle of good faith or hurt the interests of the counterparty (unangemessene Benachteiligung), the standard business terms will be invalid. Section 307(2) regulates the situations where an unreasonable disadvantage is assumed to exist.

2.4 Section 308 in German Civil Code

Section 308 in the German Civil Code provides:

"In standard business terms the following are in particular ineffective

1. (Period of time for acceptance and performance) a provision by which the user reserves to himself the right to unreasonably long or insufficiently specific periods of time for acceptance or rejection of an offer or for rendering performance; this does not include the reservation of the right not to perform until after the end of the period of time for withdrawal under section 355 subsections (1) and (2);

…

8. (Unavailability of performance) the agreement,

的不利, 则无效。由于规定不清楚和不可理解, 也可能产生不合理的不利条件。

2. 如条款存在以下情况, 则不合理的不利条件, 如有疑问, 应假定存在:

(1) 该条款不符合法定条款的基本原则, 或

(2) 该条款限制了合同性质中固有的基本权利或义务, 以至于危及了合同目的的实现。

3. 上述第 1 和 2 款以及第 308 和 309 条仅适用于格式条款的规定, 在此基础上同意减损法律条款的安排或补充这些法律条款的安排。根据上述第 1 款第 2 句, 以及上述第 1 款第 1 句, 其他条款可能无效。"

根据第 307 条第 1 款, 如果格式条款违反了诚信原则或损害了交易另一方的利益 (不合理的不利), 格式条款将会无效。第 307 条第 2 款规定了认为存在不合理的不利条件的情况。

(四) 德国民法典第 308 条

《德国民法典》第 308 条规定:

"就格式条款而言, 以下情况无效:

1. (接受和履行的期限) 一方当事人保留不合理地延长或设定不够具体的时间以接受或拒绝要约或履行要约的权利; 这不包括保留在第 355 条第 1 和 2 款规定的合同退出期限结束后才履行的权利;

……

8. (无法履行合同) 根据第 3 款允

许的协议，当事人在以下情况下仍保留在无法履行合同的情况下免除履行合同的权利：

a) 使用人无义务不迟延地向合同相对人告知不可处分性；并且

b) 使用人无义务不迟延地归还合同相对人的对待给付。

《德国民法典》第 308 条规定了可能被进行评估的禁止条款。第 308 节列出了 8 种特别无效的格式条款。[①]例如，条款要求不合理的长时间或不够具体的

admissible under no. 3, of the reservation by the user of a right to free himself from the duty to perform the contract in the absence of availability of performance, if the user does not agree to

(a) inform the other party to the contract without undue delay, of the unavailability, and

(b) reimburse the other party to the contract for consideration, without undue delay."

Section 308 of the German Civil Code identifies prohibited clauses with the possibility of evaluation. Section 308 lists 8 kinds of standard business terms that are in particular ineffective.[①] For example, "a provision by which the user reserves to himself the right to unreasonably long or insufficiently specific periods

---

① Section 308 in the German Civil Code regulates: "

In standard business terms the following are in particular ineffective

1. (Period of time for acceptance and performance) a provision by which the user reserves to himself the right to unreasonably long or insufficiently specific periods of time for acceptance or rejection of an offer or for rendering performance; this does not include the reservation of the right not to perform until after the end of the period of time for withdrawal under section 355 subsections (1) and (2);

2. (Additional period of time) a provision by which the user, contrary to legal provisions, reserves to himself the right to an unreasonably long or insufficiently specific additional period of time for the performance he is to render;

3. (Reservation of the right to revoke) the agreement of a right of the user to free himself from his obligation to perform without any objectively justified reason indicated in the contract; this does not apply to continuing obligations;

4. (Reservation of the right to modify) the agreement of a right of the user to modify the performance promised or deviate from it, unless the agreement of the modification or deviation can reasonably be expected of the other party to the contract when the interests of the user are taken into account;

5. (Fictitious declarations) a provision by which a declaration by the other party to the contract with the user, made when undertaking or omitting a specific act, is deemed to have been made or not made by the user unless

a) the other party to the contract is granted a reasonable period of time to make an express declaration, and

b) the user agrees to especially draw the attention of the other party to the contract to the intended significance of his behavior at the beginning of the period of time;

6. (Fictitious receipt) a provision providing that a declaration by the user that is of special importance is deemed to have been received by the other party to the contract;

7. (Reversal of contracts) a provision by which the user, to provide for the event that a party to the contract revokes the contract or gives notice of termination of the contract, may demand

a) unreasonably high remuneration for enjoyment or use of a thing or a right or for performance rendered, or

b) unreasonably high reimbursement of expenses;

8. (Unavailability of performance) the agreement, admissible under no. 3, of the reservation by the user of a right to free himself from the duty to perform the contract in the absence of availability of performance, if the user does not agree to

a) inform the other party to the contract without undue delay, of the unavailability, and

b) reimburse the other party to the contract for consideration, without undue delay."

of time for acceptance or rejection of an offer or for rendering performance"[①] , or "a provision by which the user, contrary to legal provisions, reserves to himself the right to an unreasonably long or insufficiently specific additional period of time for the performance he is to render"[②] , etc.

2.5 Section 309 in German Civil Code

Section 309 in the German Civil Code provides: "
"Even to the extent that a deviation from the statutory provisions is permissible, the following are ineffective in standard business terms:

1. (Price increases at short notice) a provision providing for an increase in payment for goods or services that are to be delivered or rendered within four months of the entering into of the contract; this does not apply to goods or services delivered or rendered in connection with continuing obligations;
......

13. (Form of notices and declarations) a provision by which notices or declarations that are to be made to the user or a third party are tied to a more stringent form than written form or tied to special receipt requirements."

Article 309 deals with the prohibited clauses without the possibility of evaluation. If standard business terms violate Article 309, they would be invalid. For instance, "a provision providing for an increase in payment for goods or services that are to be delivered or rendered within four months of the entering into of the contract; this does not apply to goods or services delivered or rendered in connection with continuing obligations"[③] , or "a provision by which the other party to the contract with the user is deprived of the right to set off a claim that is uncontested or has been finally and non-appealably established".[④] Section 309 holds the mandatory rules, and the standard

时间来接受或拒绝要约或履行要约[①]，或条款与法律规定相反，要求一段不合理的长时间或不够具体的额外时间来履行合同的义务。[②]

（五）德国民法典第309条

《德国民法典》第309条规定：

"即使允许偏离法定条文，下列格式条款也无效：

1.（短时间内的价格上涨）规定在合同签订后四个月内交付或提供的货物或服务增加付款的条款；这不适用于为持续义务交付或提供的货物或服务；

......

13.（通知和声明的形式）条款中，向用户或第三方作出的通知或声明采取了比书面形式更严格的形式或与特殊收据要求有关的形式。"

《德国民法典》的第309条阐述的是禁止类条款。如果格式条款违反了第309条，则该格式条款将无效。例如，"规定在合同签订后四个月内交付或提供的货物或服务增加付款的条款；这不适用于为持续义务交付或提供的货物或服务"[③]或"合同的另一方被剥夺撤销合同的权利，或当事人之间无争议或最终法院确立该争议不可上诉没有索赔的权利"。[④]由此可见，第309条是强制性

---

① Section 308(1) of the German Civil Code.
② Section 308(2) of the German Civil Code.
③ Section 309(1) of the German Civil Code.
④ Section 309(3) of the German Civil Code.

规则，违反该法条的格式条款在德国民法典中被认为无效。

（六）德国民法典第 310 条

《德国民法典》第 310 条规定：

"1. 第 305 条第 2 和第 3 条以及第 308 和 309 条不适用于与企业家、公法下的法人或公法下的特别基金订立的合同中使用的格式条款。然而，第 307 条第 1 和第 2 款仍然适用于第一句的情形，这导致了第 308 和 309 条中规定的合同条款无效；必须合理考虑适用于商业交易的惯例和习惯。根据第一句，（第 307 条第 1 款和第 2 款不适用于签订合同时适用的版本中规定的个别条款内容的合同。）

......

4. 本条款不适用于继承法、家庭法和公司法等领域的合同，也不适用于集体协议和私营部门工程协议或公共部门机构协议。这些条款在适用于劳动合同时，必须合理考虑到适用于劳动法的特殊性；第 305 条第 2 和第 3 款不得适用。集体协议和私营部门工程协议或公共部门机构协议等同于第 307 条第 3 款所指的法律规定。"

《德国民法典》第 310 条监督了合同中格式条款的范围。根据《德国民法典》第 310 条，有关公司、继承、家庭的案件不属于格式条款的范围。但是，劳

business terms violating Section 309 cannot be valid under the German Civil Code.

2.6 Section 310 in German Civil Code

Section 310 in the German Civil Code provides:

"(1) Section 305 (2) and (3) and sections 308 and 309 do not apply to standard business terms which are used in contracts with an entrepreneur, a legal person under public law or a special fund under public law. Section 307 (1) and (2) nevertheless apply to these cases in sentence 1 to the extent that this leads to the ineffectiveness of the contract provisions set out in sections 308 and 309; reasonable account must be taken of the practices and customs that apply in business dealings. In cases coming under sentence 1, section 307 (1) and (2) do not apply to contracts in which the entire Award Rules for Building Works, Part B [Vergabe-und Vertragsordnung für Bauleistungen Teil B-VOB/B] in the version applicable at the time of conclusion of the contract are included without deviation as to their content, relating to an examination of the content of individual provisions.

...

(4) This division does not apply to contracts in the field of the law of succession, family law and company law or to collective agreements and private-sector works agreements or public-sector establishment agreements. When it is applied to employment contracts, reasonable account must be taken of the special features that apply in labor law; section 305 (2) and (3) must not be applied. Collective agreements and private-sector works agreements or public-sector establishment agreements are equivalent to legal provisions within the meaning of section 307 (3)."

Section 310 of the German Civil Code oversees the scope of standard business terms of the contract. In accordance with Section 310, the cases about companies, inheritance, and families do not fall within the scope of standard business terms. However, the labor contract cases are not completely excluded from the scope of application.

The German Civil Code is a complete law to standard terms and has detailed provisions to regulate them. The German Civil Code is also a model for many statute law countries. In addition, the German Injunctions Act (Unterlassungsklagengesetz, UKlaG) is the procedure law for the issue of standard terms.[1] For instance, UKlaG allows the parties to use the class action to deal with the disputes of standard terms. And UKlaG stipulates that the courts should follow the procedures to record the process of standard term cases etc.[2] UKlaG is a feature of German law, because there are not many countries in the world that regulate the issue about the standard form contract in procedure law.

All in all, the legislation about the issue of the standard form contract in Germany more advanced than most nations. It is superior because not only does it cover regulations about substantive law, but it also handles the procedure law. The German Civil Code should be used as a model for other countries when dealing with the law on standard form contracts.

3. United States

In the United States, a standard form contract is usually called an adhesion contract[3] and has been widely applied to business practices. In the United States, the most popular doctrine for examining the enforcement of adhesive dispute settlement clauses

动合同案件并没有完全排除在适用范围之外。

德国民法典是一部完整格式条款法律，并有详细的规定来规范格式条款。德国民法典也是许多成文法国家的典范。此外，德国的《德国禁令法案》（UKlaG）是针对格式条款问题的程序法。[1]例如，UKlaG允许当事人使用集体诉讼来处理格式条款的纠纷。并且，UKlaG规定，法院应该遵循程序来记录格式条款案件的程序等。[2]UKlaG是德国法律的一个特色，因为世界上没有多少国家在程序法中规范关于格式合同的问题。

总之，德国关于格式合同的立法比大多数国家更先进。它之所以优越，是因为它不仅涵盖了有关实体法的规定，还处理了程序法。德国民法典可以作为其他成文法国家制定格式合同相关法律时的示范。

三、美国

在美国，格式合同通常被称为附和合同，[3]并已被广泛应用于商业实践中。在

---

① The details about UKlaG are available at: http://www.collectiveredress.org/collective-redress/reports/germany/consumerlaw (Last visited on May 12, 2016).

② Su, H.P.. (2004). A Study on Standard Contract Clauses, Beijing: China Renmin University Press, 114-121, at 115.

③ Zhang, M. (2008). Contractual Choice of Law in Contracts of Adhesion and Party Autonomy. *Akron L. Rev.*, 41, 123-142, at 125.

美国,审查附和纠纷解决条款或附和合同执行情况的最普遍的原则是不公平原则。[①]

最初,不公平原则是合同案件[②]中一种衡平法上的救济,主要用于拒绝合同的具体履行。[③]20 世纪 40 年代,不公平原则已成为适用于所有货物销售合同的一般规则。

美国《统一商法典》(U.C.C.)第 2-302 条也采用了不公平原则。《统一商法典》并不是针对格式合同的特殊法律,但大多数不公平的条款都可能与格式合同有关。在此法典中,第 1-201 条(3)、第 1-203、2-302、9-201、9-203 条也有类似的规定。但最著名的是第 2-302 条。

第 2-302 条规定:

"(1)如果法院依法认定合同或任何合同条款在订立合同时是不合理的,法院可以拒绝执行合同,或者它可以执行合同的其余部分,不包括不合理的条款,以避免任何不合理的结果。

(2)当法院声称或认为合同或其任何条款可能不合情理时,双方应有合理机会提供有关其商业环境、目的和效果的证据,以协助法院作出决定。"

《统一商法典》第 2-302 条规定,如

or contracts of adhesion in general is the doctrine of unconscionability.[①]

Originally the doctrine of unconscionability was an equitable remedy in contract cases[②] and available mostly to refuse specific performance.[③] In the 1940s, the doctrine of unconscionability has become a general rule applicable to all contracts for the sale of goods.

The doctrine of unconscionability was also adopted in Section 2-302 of the Uniform Commercial Code (U.C.C.). The Uniform Commercial Code is not a special law for standard form contracts, but most unconscionable terms may be related to the standard form contract. In this code, Sections 1-201(3), 1-203, 2-302, 9-201, 9-203 have the similar regulations. But the most famous section is 2-302.

Section 2-302 regulates:

"(1) If the court as a matter of law finds the contract or any clause of the contract to have been unconscionable at the time it was made the court may refuse to enforce the contract, or it may enforce the remainder of the contract without the unconscionable clause as to avoid any unconscionable result.

(2) When it is claimed or appears to the court that the contract or any clause thereof may be unconscionable the parties shall be afforded a reasonable opportunity to present evidence as to its commercial setting, purpose and effect to aid the court in making the determination."

From Section 2-302 it is evident that if the contract

---

① Id.

② Blum, B. A. (2007). Contracts: Examples & Explanations. Aspen Publishers Online, at 164.

③ Zhang, M. (2008). Contractual Choice of Law in Contracts of Adhesion and Party Autonomy. *Akron L. Rev.*, 41, 123-142, at 125.

is found unconscionable, the court may refuse to enforce it, or the court may enforce the remainder of the contract without the unconscionable clause as to avoid any unfair results. On the other hand, the parties shall be afforded a reasonable opportunity to present evidence as to its commercial setting, purpose and effect to aid the court in making the determination. Later, Section 2-302 of the U.C.C. was extended to apply to all contracts through Section 208 of the Restatement (Second) of Contracts.[①] These sections empower the courts to refuse a contract if the contract is unconscionable; under the sections, the party can remove or modify the unconscionable provisions.

果合同被发现不合理，或者合同的部分条款被发现不合理，法院可以拒绝执行以避免任何不公平的结果。另一方面，双方应获得合理的机会以提出有关合同或部分条款的商业环境、目的和实施效果的证据，以帮助法院作出决定。之后，《统一商法典》第 2-302 条的适用范围通过《第二次合同法重述》第 208 条扩展到所有类型的合同。[①]这些条款授权法院在合同不合理时认定合同无效，或者当事人可以删除或修改不合理的条款。

3.1 Fundamental Fairness

The leading case *Williams v. Walker Thomas Furniture Co.*[②] is an example. In this case, Walker Thomas Furniture Company provided a contract in printed form for Williams and there was a "cross collateralization" clause in the contract. The disputes between the parties over excess interest arised out of previous dealings. Mrs. Williams sued the furniture company for the excess interest amount. The United States Court of Appeals for the District of Columbia determined that the clause was unconscionabile.

In this case, Judge Wright had an opinion about the "two-pronged test" on the doctrine of unconscionability. The first was whether there was an absence of a choice

（一）公平原则

著名的威廉姆斯诉沃克·托马斯家具公司案就是一个例子。[②]这个案例中，沃克·托马斯家具公司为威廉姆斯提供了印刷形式的格式合同，合同中有一个"交叉担保"条款。当事人此前的交易因该条款而产生超额利息的纠纷。威廉姆斯起诉家具公司要求超额利息。美国哥伦比亚特区上诉法院裁定，该格式合同中的条款是不公平的。

在这个案件中，赖特法官根据不公平原则中的"双管齐下检验法"对案件进行检验。法官第一个检验问题是当

---

① Section 208 of Restatement (Second) of Contracts provides, "If a contract or term thereof is unconscionable at the time the contract is made a court may refuse to enforce the contract, or may enforce the remainder of the contract without the unconscionable term, or may so limit the application of any unconscionable term as to avoid any unconscionable result."

② Williams v. Walker Thomas Furniture Co., 350 F.2d 445 (D.C. Cir. 1965), the District of Columbia Court of Appeals, available at: http://law.justia.com/cases/federal/appellate-courts/F2/350/445/74531/ (Last visited on May12, 2016).

事人在该合同中是否没有选择。第二个检验的内容是，合同条款是否对本案中的另一方不合理地有利。

自从有了威廉姆斯诉沃克·托马斯家具公司案这个判例，大多数法院都确立了"双管齐下检验法"这一原则。此外，"双管齐下检验法"的方法被发展成为"程序测试"和"实质性测试"。"程序测试"的重点是合同的形成过程。"实质测试"的重点是格式合同的内容。如果合同条款否定了"双管齐下检验法"，则可以拒绝使用合同中的格式条款。

在德韦恩·哈伯特诉戴尔公司一案中，①戴尔公司提供了"销售条款和条件"，其中包括一个仲裁条款。基于该格式合同中的仲裁条款，戴尔拒绝提起诉讼。巡回法院驳回了戴尔公司的动议，而上诉法院则支持戴尔公司的申请。上诉法院认为，双方当事人之间的合同并非不合理的。因此，格式合同中的仲裁条款在程序上仅是不够不合理。②此外，如果仲裁没有向仲裁当事方收取额外费用，则仲裁条款实质上并不是不合理的。③

另一个著名的案例是嘉年华邮轮公司诉舒特案。④该案研究讨论了格式合同中选择条款的有效性问题。在这个

of the parties. The second was whether the contract terms were unreasonably favorable to the other party in the case.

Since this famous case of *Williams v. Walker Thomas Furniture Co.*, most courts have recognized the "two-pronged test". What is more, the method of "two-pronged test" was developed into the "procedural test" and "substantive test". The "procedural test" is focused on the formation process of contract. The "Substantive test" is focused on the contents of the standard form contract. If the contract clause negates the "two-pronged test", the standard terms in the contract can be refused.

In the case *Dewayne Hubbert v. Dell Corp.*[①], the Dell Corporation provided the "Terms and Conditions of Sale," which included an arbitration clause. Based on the arbitration clause in this standard form contract, Dell refused to litigate. The Circuit Court denied the motion of Dell, while the Appellate Court supported the application of Dell. The Appellate Court held the opinion that the contract between the parties was not unconscionable. Therefore, the arbitration clause in the standard form contract was insufficient to be procedurally unconscionable.[②] Furthermore, the arbitration clause was not substantially unconscionable if there were no excess costs charged to parities to arbitration.[③]

Another recognized case, *Carnival Cruise Lines, Inc. v. Shute*[④], addressed the issue of the validity of choice of forum clauses in the standard form contract. In the case, Shute bought a seven-day cruise aboard

---

① Dewayne Hubbert v. Dell Corp., [2006] 844 N.E.2d 965, Illinois Court of Appeals, available at: http://www.internetlibrary.com/cases/lib_case487.cfm (Last visited on May 12, 2016).

② Goodman, B., &Honey, I. (1999). Shrink-Wrapped the Consumer: The Shrink-Wrap Agreement as an Adhesion Contract. *Cardozo L. Rev.*, 21, 319-360, at 327.

③ Id.

④ Carnival Cruise Lines, Inc. v. Shute, [1991] 499 U.S. 585, U.S., United States Supreme Court, available at: https://supreme.justia.com/cases/federal/us/499/585/case.html (Last visited on May12, 2016).

Carnival's ship. There was a forum selection clause on the back of the ticket[①]. The forum selection clause stated that "all disputes arising out of or related to the contract would be litigated in Florida".

During the cruise, Mrs. Shute was injured when she slipped on the wet deck. Shute sued Carnival Cruise Lines in the federal district court in the State of Washington for compensation. The court rejected the claims from Mrs. Shute according to the forum selection clause. The Appeal Court reversed the decision from the federal district court in the State of Washington. The Appeal Court held the opinion that the forum selection clause was invalid, because the forum selection clause was not freely bargained for between the parties. The Supreme Court reversed the decision of the federal district court. Patrick Borchers once commented on the case, "The significant impact of the Carnival Cruise Lines, Inc. v. Shute case is that it opened the door widely to hold the 'non-freely-bargained for' contracts *prima facie* valid and signaled that the adhesive nature of a contract is no longer a defense for enforcement of a forum selection agreement."[②] Nevertheless, Carnival establishes a precedent based on the fundamental fairness, where the choice of law clauses in the standard form contract can be applied. Since the case *Carnival Cruise Lines, Inc. v. Shute*, the "fundamental fairness" has been an important element for the dispute of the standard form contract.[③]

案例中, 舒特购买了一个为期七天的嘉年华游轮行程。[①]在票的背面有一个协议管辖条款。这个协议管辖条款规定, "所有因合同而引起的或与合同有关的争议都将在佛罗里达州提起诉讼"。

游轮巡航期间, 舒特夫人在潮湿的甲板上滑倒受伤了。她在华盛顿州的联邦地区法院起诉了嘉年华邮轮公司, 要求获得赔偿。法院驳回了舒特夫人的索赔要求。上诉法院推翻了华盛顿州联邦地区法院的判决。上诉法院认为, 该协议管辖条款无效。因为格式合同中的协议管辖条款不是在当事人之间经过自由讨论而达成的。最高法院推翻了联邦地区法院的判决。帕特里克·博尔切斯曾评论过此案: "嘉年华邮轮公司诉舒特案是有重大影响的。这个案件使得'非自由讨论'的合同初步有效, 并表明格式合同并非抗辩的理由。[②]然而, 嘉年华确立了一个基于基本公平原则的格式合同范例, 当事人可以适用格式合同中的法律条款进行选择。自从嘉年华邮轮公司诉舒特案开始, "基本公平"就成为了格式合同纠纷的一个重要因素。[③]

[①] On the ticket, Paragraph 8 provided that "All disputes and matters whatsoever arising under, in connection with or incident to this Contract shall be litigated, if at all, in and before a Court located in the State of Florida, U.S.A. to the exclusion of the Courts of any other state or country."

[②] Borchers, P. J. (1992). Forum Selection Agreements in the Federal Courts after Carnival Cruise: A Proposal for Congressional Reform. *Wash. L. Rev.*, 67, 55-70, at 67.

[③] Zhang, M. (2008). Contractual Choice of Law in Contracts of Adhesion and Party Autonomy. *Akron L. Rev.*, 41, 123-142, at 127.

（二）合理的沟通

除了"基本公平"原则外，"合理沟通"原则也是格式合同的重要安排。例如，宏伟案例，[①]争议是轮船乘客是否受到船票细则中"示范"条件的约束。西尔维斯特里诉意大利航海协会案[②]也是一个例子。在本案中，法官认为，关于这个格式合同中的条款是否真实有效的测试是"尽一切合理努力警告乘客，这些条款和条件是影响其合法权利的重要合同事项。"

黛布拉·沃德诉十字湾渡轮公司一案也对"合理沟通"存在争议。原告起诉了十字湾渡轮公司，因为他们认为机票背面的格式合同是 7 号 Arial 字体，字体太小，无法阅读。此外，他们在登机前两到三分钟拿到了两张票，但他们没有足够的时间阅读船票背面的文字。地方法院认为，格式合同的起草人应确保格式条款能够"清晰"、合理地引起注意，并且对另一方进行合理通知具有重要意义。这一类案件，如德尼科拉诉冠达航运有限公司[③]、西尔维斯特里诉意大利航海协会案等[④]，都被美国的法院认为应当考虑"合理的沟通能力"的重要意义。

一般来说，在美国，法律处理格式合同争议的方法和处理其他类型合同是

3.2 Reasonable Communicativeness

Besides the "fundamental fairness", the "reasonable communicativeness" is also an important arrangement for the standard form contract. For instance, the Majestic case,[①] where the disputes were whether the steamship passengers are bound by "boilerplate" conditions in the fine print of the ticket. *Silvestri v. Italia Societa Per Azione di Navigazione*[②] would also be an example. In this case, Judge held the opinion that the test in terms of whether the company has the terms as *"done all it reasonably could to warn the passenger that the terms and conditions were important matters of contract affecting his legal rights."* The case *Debra Ward v. Cross Sound Ferry* also had disputes about the "reasonable communicativeness".

The plaintiff sued the Cross Sound Ferry Company because they held that the standard form contract on the reverse side of the ticket appeared in seven-point Arial type font which was too small to read. Also, they obtained both their tickets two to three minutes before boarding, which did not allow ample time for them to read it. The district court held the opinion that the drafter of the standard form contract should ensure the standard terms could be "clearly", reasonably noticed and the reasonable notices for the other party were of significant importance. There are also some similar cases, such as *DeNicola v. Cunard Line Ltd*[③], *Silvestri v. Italia Societa Per Azione di Navigazione*[④], to name a few. The courts in the United States held the opinion that "reasonable communicativeness" was of great significance.

Generally speaking, in the United States, the law deals with standard form contracts the same way as it

---

① Silvestri v. Italia Societa Per Azione di Navigazione, [1897] 166 U.S. 375, United States Court of Appeals Second Circuit, available at: http://law.justia.com/cases/federal/appellate-courts/F2/388/11/160413/ (Last visited on May 16 2016).

② Carnival Cruise Lines, Inc. v. Shute, [1991] 499 U.S. 585, U.S., United States Supreme Court, available at: https://supreme.justia.com/cases/federal/us/499/585/case.html (Last visited on May12, 2016).

③ DeNicola v. Cunard Line Ltd, [1981] 642 F.2d 5, United States Court of Appeals First Circuit, available at: http://openjurist.org/642/f2d/5/claire-denicola-v-cunard-line-limited (Last visited on May 16, 2016).

④ Supra note 256.

deals with any other contract. When disputes happen, different jurisdictions may have special rules for dealing with the issue. For instance, Louisiana has its own Civil Code about the issue of the standard form contract.[1] Different U.S. states may have different laws about the same issue.

Therefore, I take the U.C.C. as an example, because it is the uniform code for the United States. The courts make decisions based on previous cases or special rules. Also, if there are ambiguous or unclear provisions in a standard form contract, most rules will be interpreted in favor of the party that did not prepare the contract. In addition, the drafters should pay attention to the "reasonable communicativeness". The drafters of standard form contracts should make sure the opposing parties have noticed the standard terms in the contracts.

4. Other Areas

As for the issue of the validity of standard form contract, various legal systems have their own particular ways to resolve this problem and there are many different approaches to this issue.[2] Some of the civil law countries have broad code provisions, while others may have enacted code provisions specifically directed to the issue. For instance, the Italian Civil Code also has regulations about this issue. Article 1341, 1342, and 1370 of the Italian Civil Code of 1942 have special provisions for the issue. Article 1341 of the Italian Civil Code of 1942 regulates:

"General conditions, prepared by one of the parties, are binding on the other party [are incorporated into the contract] if known by the latter at the time when the contract was concluded or if he might have

一样的。当争议发生时,不同的司法管辖区可能会有特殊的规则来处理这个问题。例如,路易斯安那州就格式合同的问题有自己的民法典。[1]美国不同的州可能对同一问题有不同的法律。

因此,本书取美国《统一商法典》作为一个例子,因为《统一商法典》是美国的统一商法典。法院根据以前的案件或特殊规则作出裁决。此外,如果在格式合同案件中有不明确的规定,大多数规则的解释将有利于未准备合同的一方。此外,起草者应注意"合理的沟通能力"。格式合同的起草者应确保对方当事人已经注意到合同中的格式条款。

四、其他地域

至于格式合同的有效性问题,各种法律体系都有自己独特的方法来解决这个问题,也有许多不同的方法。[2]一些大陆法系国家有广泛的法典规定,而其他一些国家专门针对这个问题制定了相关法典进行规制。例如,《意大利民法典》中也有关于这个问题的规定。1942 年的《意大利民法典》第 1341 条、第 1342 条和第 1370 条对这个问题有特别的规定。1942 年《意大利民法典》第 1341 条规定:

"由一方准备的格式条件,如在另一方订立合同时知道合同,或者他可能通过一般勤勉知道,则对另一方具有约

---

① Hersbergen, R. L. (1982). Contracts of Adhesion under the Louisiana Civil Code. *La. L. Rev.*, 43, 1-29, at 7.

② Id.

束力（已纳入合同）。

但是，除非特别书面批准，下列条件未产生效力：

1. 条件限制了准备了一般条件的一方的责任，或给予其退出合同或中止执行合同的权力。

2. 对另一方行使提出抗辩的权利或限制的时间限制，或对与第三人的合同自由的限制，或默许延长或延长合同的条件。

3. 规定仲裁或仲裁条项或裁判管辖的变更等。"

1942 年《意大利民法典》第 1342 条规定：

"在采用为统一规定某些合同关系而编制的格式所订立的合同中，在这种格式中加入的条款，即使与原来的规定条款不相容，即使原来的规定条款并没有被删除，也要优于原来的规定条款。

另外，还适用前一条第二款的规定。"

1942 年《意大利民法典》的这些规定强调了格式合同的定义。它规定，援引格式合同的一方有义务提供通知、宣传的证据。格式合同的规则也应根据双方当事人共同的经验进行解释。这意味着对于有争议的条款的解释应当符合普通人的常识，并且对于格式合同的解释也应遵循诚实守信的原则。

以色列也在格式合同立法方面拥有赞誉。以色列于 1964 年制定了《格式合同法》，该法以其内容完整性和先

known thereof by using ordinary diligence.

The following conditions, however, have no effect [are not incorporated] unless specifically approved in writing:

1. Conditions limiting the liability of the party who has prepared the general conditions, or giving the said party a power to withdraw from the contract or to suspend the execution thereof.

2. Conditions burdening the other party with time limits for the exercise of a right or limitations to such party's power to raise defenses, or with restrictions on freedom of contract with third persons, or with tacit extension or renewal of the contract.

3. Clauses providing for arbitration or derogations from the normal venue or jurisdiction of the courts."

Article 1342 of the Italian Civil Code of 1942 regulates:

"In contracts made by subscribing to forms prepared for the purpose of regulating in a uniform manner certain contractual relationships, the clauses added to such forms prevail over the original formulary clauses, even if incompatible, and even though the latter have not been stricken out.

In addition, the provision of the second paragraph of the preceding Article is applicable."

These provisions of the Italian Civil Code of 1942 highlight the definition of the standard form contract. It stipulates that the party invoking the standard form contract should be obligated to provide evidence of notice and publicity. The rules of the standard form contract should also be interpreted in accordance to the common experience. That means that an ordinary man has the diligence and knowledge to agree to the interpretation. The interpretation of the standard form contract should also depend on the principle of reliance and interpretation in good faith promises.[1]

Israel is also an acclaimed country for the legislation of the standard form contract. Israel established the Standard Contract Law in 1964. The

---

[1] Gorla, G. (1962). Standard Conditions and Form Contracts in Italian Law. *The American Journal of Comparative Law*, 1-20, at 15.

Israel Standard Contract Law is famous because of the complete content and advanced legislative technique. The most creative impact of the Israel Standard Contract Law is that the law combines judicial and administrative controls to adjust the imbalances between the parties.[1] Even though the Israel Standard Contract Law fails to solve the practical problems and conceptual puzzles, the mode and rules still have a significant impact in today's legislation of standard contract law.

The U.K. has the Unfair Contract Terms Act of 1977 to regulate the standard form contract. The British Unfair Contract Terms Act impacts Hong Kong legislation. Therefore, Hong Kong has the Control of Exemption Clauses Ordinance for the issue of the standard form contract.

5. Comments

The statute law jurisdiction mainly relies on legislation to regulate the standard form contract issue in countries like China and Germany. Most statute countries use the dispersive lawmaking model, the provisions about the standard form contract scattered in different laws. For instance, in China, provisions about the standard form contract can be found in Chinese Contract Law, Chinese Insurance Law, Chinese Maritime Law, Chinese Law on Protection of Rights and Interests of Consumers, etc. However, some statute countries have specialized law to regulate the issue of the standard form contract. The Israel Standard Contract Law is a famous example of specialized law to resolve the issue of the standard form contract.

The common law jurisdiction often uses the precedents and to judge the issue of the standard form contract. For instance, the United States have a number of precedents regarding the issue of the standard form contract, but it also have provisions in the Uniform Commercial Code to regulate the issue.[2]

---

① Berg, K. F. (1979). The Israeli Standard Contracts Law 1964: Judicial Controls of Standard Form Contracts. *International and Comparative Law Quarterly*, 28(4), 560-574, at 566.

② In this code, Sections 1-201(3), 1-203, 2-302, 9-201, 9-203 have the regulations about the issue of the standard form contract.

进的立法技术而闻名。《以色列格式合同法》最具创造性的影响是,该法律结合了司法和行政管理,以调整各方之间的不平衡。[1]尽管《以色列格式合同法》未能解决实际问题和概念上的难题,但其模式和规则仍对今天的格式合同法立法产生重大影响。

英国有1977年的《不公平合同条款法案》来规范格式合同。《英国不公平合同条款法案》影响了香港的立法。因此,香港在格式合同方面设有《管制免责条款条例》。

五、评论

成文法国家管辖权主要依靠立法来规范格式合同问题。大多数成文法国家采用分散的立法模式,关于格式合同的规定分散在不同的法律中。例如,在中国,有关格式合同的规定可见于中国《民法典》《保险法》《海商法》《消费者权益保护法》等。然而,一些成文法国家有专门的法律来规范格式合同的问题。以色列的《格式合同法》就是解决格式合同问题的著名例子。

普通法管辖权经常使用判例和一些立法来判断格式合同的问题。例如,美国在格式合同的问题上有许多判例,它在《统一商法典》中也有规定来规范该问题。[2]

一般来说，维护当事人之间的基本公平、平衡格式合同中的不公平地位，是大多数国家立法的目标。在大多数情况下，如果格式合同对另一方不公平或使另一方负有义务，则合同条款可能无效。而在其他时候，整个合同不得因条款不公平而被视为无效。只有格式合同中的不公平条款才能无效或应由当事人修改。

综上所述，无论是属于成文法国家还是属于普通法国家，都应根据实际情况选择适当的法律作为适用依据。应仔细提及有关的判例和法律，因为每个国家都可能为同一问题制定了不同的法律和议定书。此外，适用于格式条款的法律可以确定本合同或格式合同中的仲裁条款的有效性。因此，选择适用的格式条款法律是仲裁的重要步骤。

Generally speaking, maintaining the fundamental fairness between the parties and balancing the unfair position in the standard form contract are the goals of legislation for most countries. In most cases, if the standard form contract holds unfairness or obligations for the other party, the contract terms may be void. While in other times, the whole contract may not be considered invalid due to the void unfair terms. Only the unfair terms in the standard form contract may be invalid or should be modified by the parties.

To sum up, whether it is in statute law jurisdiction or in common law jurisdiction, appropriate laws should be chosen for standard terms based on the actual situation. Relevant precedents and laws should be referred to carefully, as every country may have developed different laws and protocols for the same issue. Furthermore, the applicable law to standard terms can determine the validity of the contract or the arbitration clauses in the standard form contract. Thus, the choice of the applicable law for standard terms is an important step to arbitration.

六、合同的解释

6. Interpretation of Contract

每个国家对合同条款都有自己不同的意见。即使在同一个国家，法院也可能对同一问题有不同的答案。

Every country has its own different opinions to interpret the contract terms. Even in the same country, the courts may have different answers to the same issue.

例如，美国的法院有一个支持和执行仲裁条款的联邦政策。[1]然而，美国的一些法院适用《统一商法典》第2-207条来保护消费者不受不公平条款的影响，这可能会阻碍美国有利于仲裁的政策。[2]

For example, courts in the United States have a federal policy for favoring and enforcing the arbitration clauses.[1] However, some courts in the United States apply Section 2-207 of the Uniform Commercial Code to protect consumers from unfair terms, which may frustrate the arbitration -favoring policy in the United States.[2]

---

[1]　Mahdi, S. A. (2001). Gateway to Arbitration: Issues of Contract Formation under the UCC and the Enforceability of Arbitration Clauses Included in Standard Form Contracts Shipped with Goods. *Nw. UL Rev.*, 96, at 403.

[2]　Id.

In China, based on different cases, the result would be different. For instance, a case of Zhuhai Intermediate People's Court[①] concluded that the arbitration clauses in the standard form contracts were used in a unified font like other terms in the contract. Therefore, there was no obvious tip or specific guidance for consumers to realize the existence of the dispute settlement provisions. Finally, the court determined that the arbitration clause in the standard form contract was invalid.

According to another case from Xiamen Intermediate People's Court,[②] the court held the opinion that the arbitration clause in the standard form contract did not bring extra burden to the plaintiff. Therefore, the arbitration clauses in the standard form contract was valid.

In standard form contracts with arbitration clauses, the arbitration clauses are also deemed as a contract between the parties. Therefore, in general, the arbitration clauses are subject to the same type of rules of interpretation as the other contracts.[③] In conclusion, every court may have its own attitude toward the arbitration, so how to interpret the meaning of the arbitration clauses is very important.

The function of contract interpretation is to determinate the real intentions of both parties.[④] The process of contract interpretation is to give meaning to the words used by the parties in their contracts.[⑤] Several principles of contract interpretation are widely used in international commercial arbitration to be applied for

在中国，根据不同的情况，结果将会是不同的。例如，珠海中级人民法院[①]在案件审理中认为，格式合同中的仲裁条款与合同中的其他条款使用了统一的字体，因此，没有明显的提示或具体的指导让消费者认识到争议解决条款的存在。最后，法院认定格式合同中的仲裁条款是无效的。

另一个案件中，厦门中级人民法院认为，[②]格式合同中的仲裁条款不会给原告带来额外的负担，因此，格式合同中的仲裁条款是有效的。

在包含有仲裁条款的格式合同中，仲裁条款也被视为当事人之间的合同。因此，一般来说，仲裁条款应遵循与所有其他合同相同类型的解释规则。[③]总之，每个法院对仲裁都有自己的态度，所以如何解释仲裁条款的含义是非常重要的。

合同解释的作用是确定双方的真实意图。[④]合同解释的过程是赋予当事人在合同中使用的词语意义。[⑤]合同解释的几个原则被广泛应用于国际商事仲

① Case No. Min 243 (2016). Available at: http://gw.yjbys.com/zhongcaixieyishu/64130.html (Last visited on May 16, 2016).

② Case No. Xia Min-zhong-zi 200 (2015). Available at: http://gw.yjbys.com/zhongcaixieyishu/64130.html (Last visited on May 16, 2016).

③ Steingruber, A. M. (2009). Notion, Nature and Extent of Consent in International Arbitration (Doctoral dissertation), at 133. Available at: https://qmro.qmul.ac.uk/xmlui/bitstream/handle/123456789/415/STEINGRUBERNotionNature2009.pdf?sequence=1(Last visited on May 16, 2016).

④ Grenig, J. E. (1986). Principles of Contract Interpretation: Interpreting Collective Bargaining Agreements. *Cap. UL Rev.*, 16, at 31.

⑤ Id.

裁中，用于解释当事人的同意。因此，这些原则可能有助于确定在格式合同中出现模糊的仲裁条款时的情况。

（一）适用诚信原则进行解释

如上所述，诚信原则是合同解释中最被广泛接受的原则之一，它强调一方当事人的真实意图应始终优于其已宣布的意图。更具体来说，诚信原则的主要内容如下：

第一，对合同条款的解释应本着善意，并迎合当事人行为的真实意图。[①] 对合同条款应当进行合理的解释，并与普通人的认知能力相一致。[②]

第二，在案件中应考虑当事人的态度，[③] 因为它可以表明当事人如何看待有争议的合同条款。[④] 例如，如果一方发现格式合同中包含有仲裁条款，并反对立即同意该条款，那么即使这一方已经签署了格式合同，我们也不能确认各方都同意该合同中的条款。

第三，在解释合同条款时，必须考虑合同的组成部分。例如，如果仲裁条款和合同中的其他条款单独讨论，可能

interpreting parties' consent. Thus, these principles may help determine the cases when ambiguous arbitration terms appear in standard form contracts.

6.1 Interpretation in Good Faith

As discussed above, the good faith principle is one of the most widely accepted principles in contract interpretation. It stresses that a party's true intention should always prevail over its declared intention. To be more specific, the main contents of the good faith principle are as below.

First, the contract terms should be interpreted in good faith and cater to the true intention of the parties' conduct.[①] The contract terms should be interpreted reasonably and the interpretation should be consistent with ordinary people's cognition.[②]

Second, the attitude of the parties should be taken into consideration in the case,[③] as it can indicate how parties perceive the contract terms in dispute.[④] For instance, if one party finds the arbitration clauses in a standard form contract and objects to agree with the clauses immediately, then even if it has already signed the standard form contract, we cannot affirm that both parties agree to the terms in that contract.

Third, it is necessary to take into account the constituent parts of the contracts as a whole to interpret the contract terms. For instance, if arbitration clauses and other terms in contracts are discussed separately,

---

① Gaillard, E., & Savage, J.(Eds.). (1999). *Foucahrd Gaillard Goldman on International Commercial Arbitration.* Kluwer Law International, at 477.

② Steingruber, A. M. (2009). Notion, Nature and Extent of Consent in International Arbitration (Doctoral dissertation), at 133. Available at: https://qmro.qmul.ac.uk/xmlui/bitstream/handle/123456789/415/STEINGRUBERNotionNature2009.pdf?sequence=1(Last visited on May 16, 2016).

③ This rule is sometimes referred to as "practical and quasi-authentic interpretation" or "contemporary practical interpretation" and is usually applied in arbitral case law.

④ Steingruber, A. M., Supra note 316, at 133.

it may lead to difficulty in judging the true intention of the parties. Although sometimes the arbitration clauses seem well-designed, if put in the whole contract, they might go against the parties' real intentions. In some extreme examples, the parties may even fail to realize the existence of the arbitration clauses in the standard form contracts.

6.2 Effective Interpretation

Effective interpretation is also a famous principle that is widely adopted by many courts and arbitral tribunals. The effective interpretation principle emphasizes that if the contract terms are ambiguous, it would be better to give meaning to the terms rather than consider the terms useless or nonsensical.[①]

Nowadays, many courts uphold the pathological clauses based on the principle of effective interpretation, as they believe that when the parties insert the arbitration clause in their contracts, it indicates that the parties are willing to solve their disputes by arbitration. If the court determines that the pathological arbitration clause is invalid, it is not good for solving the disputes between the parties.

6.3 Interpretation *Contra Proferentem*

There are many laws and precedents about the *contra proferentem* principle in different countries. The *contra proferentem* is a Latin term meaning "interpretation against the draftsman".[②] This principle stresses that if there are any ambiguous contract terms, the courts may give favor to the parties who are not the drafter of the contract. This principle is usually applied in the standard form contracts. The supporters of this principle hold the opinion that in standard form contracts the drafters of contracts may take a monopoly

会导致当事人的真实意图难以判断。虽然有时仲裁条款似乎设计得很好，但如果放在整个合同中，它们可能会违背双方的真实意图。在一些极端的例子中，当事人甚至可能没有意识到格式合同中仲裁条款的存在。

（二）有效性解释

有效性解释也是一个著名的、被许多法院和仲裁法庭广泛采用的原则。有效性原则强调，如果合同条款模棱两可，最好赋予这些条款有效性，而不是认为这些条款无用或无意义。[①]

目前，许多法院坚持基于有效性原则解释具有瑕疵的仲裁条款，因为他们认为，当事人在合同中插入仲裁条款，表明当事人愿意通过仲裁来解决纠纷。如果法院轻易认定这类仲裁条款无效，则不利于解决当事人之间的纠纷。

（三）不利于提供方解释

不同国家有许多关于"不利于提供方"原则的法律和判例。*contra proferentem* 是一个拉丁法律术语，意思是"不利于提供方"。[②]这一原则强调，如果合同条款有任何含糊的地方，法院可以进行有利于非合同起草者的当事人一方的解释。这一原则通常适用于格式合同。这一原则的支持者认为，在格式合同中，合同的起草者可以采取垄断

---

① See ICC Award No. 1434 (1975), at 982.

② Horton, D. (2009). Flipping the Script: Contra Proferentem and Standard Form Contracts. *U. Colo. L. Rev.*, 80, at 431.

地位,因此法院可以支持实力较弱的一方,以平衡议价能力。

position, so the courts can give favor to the weaker parties to balance the bargaining power.

(四)评论

6.4 Comments

首先,世界上几乎每个国家都支持诚信原则,因此对格式合同中的仲裁条款应进行中立和客观的解释。法院的裁决应对各方公正,反映当事人将争议提交仲裁的真实意图。

First of all, almost every country in the world supports the principle of good faith. Therefore, the arbitration clauses in standard form contracts should be interpreted in a neutral and objective way. The courts' decision should be impartial to both parties and reflect the true intention of the parties to send their disputes to arbitration.

其次,仲裁协议书面形式的要求不被重视已成为一种普遍趋势。越来越多的国家法律正试图接受有利于仲裁的政策。因此,有效性解释的原则将在国际商事仲裁中得到广泛的应用。但是,人们应该区分对仲裁协议的有效性解释和广泛的解释。广泛的解释可能会扩大仲裁条款的含义,造成混淆和争议。虽然有效的解释是一种"有利于仲裁"的规则,但它旨在消除阻碍当事人同意仲裁的障碍。

Second, it has become a common trend that formal requirements of arbitration agreements are being taken less seriously. More national laws are trying to accept the arbitration-favoring policy. Thus, the principle of effective interpretation would be widely used in international commercial arbitration. However, people should distinguish the effective interpretation from the extensive interpretation of arbitration agreements. The extensive interpretation may expand the meaning of arbitration clauses and cause confusion and disputes. While the effective interpretation is a rule "in favor of arbitration", it aims at eliminating the barriers against parties' consent to the arbitration.

最后,"不利于提供方"原则只是被少数国家所接受,并不是所有国家都在格式合同中保护弱势一方。大多数法院可以根据实际情况作出自然判决,以维持各方之间的公平性。即便如此,一些国家法律的特别规定应该得到承认,法院可以作出"不利于提供方"裁决。

Lastly, the *contra proferentem* principle is just accepted by few countries and not all countries protect weak parties in the standard form contract. Most courts may make natural judgment based on the actual situation to maintain the fairness between both parties. Even so, special provisions in some national laws should be recognized and the courts may make the decision *contra proferentem*.

Chapter V GENCON 1994 as Case Study

第五章 以 GENCON 1994 作为案例研究

1. Brief Introduction to GENCON 1994

一、GENCON 1994 的概念

GENCON 1994 is a standard form contract provided by BIMCO, which is short for Baltic and International Maritime Council. BIMCO is a world famous leader for standard contracts in the maritime industry.[①] BIMCO has more than 100 years' history in the production and revision of standard maritime contracts and clauses. The documentary work of BIMCO has been one of the cornerstones of the current maritime industry.[②]

BIMCO provides a tangible contribution to trade facilitation, harmonization and the raising of contractual standards within the maritime industry. BIMCO also produces new standard form contracts and clauses and revises existing ones, with the aim to fairly represent the interests of both parties.

GENCON 1994 is one of the standard form contract provided by BIMCO and is BIMCO's Uniform General Charter. GENCON was revised in 1922, 1976 and 1994. Compared with the old versions, GENCON 1994 revised some outdated provisions and made some necessary deletions and additions. The additional provisions made the new model GENCON 1994 more complete. GENCON 1994 also made statements clearer, and exceedingly accurate.

In addition, the new version of GENCON 1994 added some optional provisions for parties. It is easier to

GENCON 1994 是由 BIMCO 提供的一种格式合同，BIMCO 是波罗的海国际航运工会的缩写。[①]BIMCO 是世界著名的海运行业格式合同的领导者，在制定和修订标准海事合同和条款方面有 100 多年的历史。BIMCO 的文书工作一直是当前海运行业的基石之一。[②]

BIMCO 为海运业内的贸易便利化、协调及合同标准的提高作出了切实的贡献。BIMCO 还制定新的格式合同和条款，并修改现有条款，旨在公平代表双方的利益。

GENCON 1994 是 BIMCO 提供的格式合同之一，是 BIMCO 的《统一杂货租船合同》。GENCON 分别于 1922 年、1976 年和 1994 年修订。与旧版本相比，GENCON 1994 修订了一些过时的条款，并进行了一些必要的删除和添加。额外的规定使新的 GENCON 1994 的内容更加完整，陈述更加清楚、准确。

此外，新版本的 GENCON 1994 还为缔约方增加了一些可选规定，根据实际情况更容易使用，更灵活。

---

① Aspragkathou D. (2007). Review of the GENCON Charter Clauses for the Commmencement of Laytime: Analysis of the "Time Lost in Waiting for a Berth to Count as Laytime or Time on Demurrage" *Clause. J. Mar. L. & Com.*, 38, 603-667.

② Id.

GENCON 1994 以规范的法律术语书写，其风格清楚地向双方传达了协议的风险和回报。使用本格式合同，可以减少商业当事人在合同和条款的解释方面发生争议的可能性。①

GENCON 1994 是海运行业当事人的热门选择。因此，本书将 GENCON 1994 作为案例研究，来讨论带有仲裁条款的格式合同。

GENCON 1994 的副本将放在下几页中。

二、关于 GENCON 1994 第十九条的评论

GENCON 1994 由两部分组成。第一部分是一个有很多空格的表格，当事人双方可以根据自己的需要来填空。第二部分是 GENCON 1994 的详细条款，本条款规定了双方之间的权利和义务。第十九条是 GENCON 1994 中的"法律和仲裁条款"。

GENCON 1994 第十九条有其优点，是具有仲裁条款的格式合同的一个例子。第一，第十九条对当事各方有可选的选择。双方可以根据自己的具体需要来选择条款。②根据 GENCON 1994 第十九条，当事人可以采用英国法律，选择 A 节进行仲裁，也可以根据《美国法典》和《美国海商法》选择 B 节进行仲裁。英国法律和美国法律在国际合同

use and more flexible for contracting parties in accordance with the actual situation. GENCON 1994 is written in legally sound language in a style that clearly conveys to both parties the risks and rewards of the agreement. By using this standard form contract, the likelihood of disputes arising over the interpretation of contracts and clauses by commercial parties can be reduced.①

GENCON 1994 is a popular choice for the parties in the maritime industry. Therefore, I would like to introduce GENCON 1994 as a case study to discuss the issue of the standard form contract with arbitration clauses.

The copies of GENCON 1994 are presented in the next pages.

2. Comments on GENCON 1994 Article 19

GENCON 1994 consists of two parts. The first part is a form with many blanks. The parties can fill in the blanks according to their own needs. The second part is the detailed articles of GENCON 1994. These articles regulate the rights and obligations between the parties. Article 19 is the "law and arbitration clauses" in GENCON 1994.

Article 19 has its merits and is an example of the standard form contract with arbitration clauses. First of all, Article 19 has optional choices for the parties. The parties can choose the terms based on their specific needs.② On the basis of Article 19 in GENCON 1994, the parties can choose Section A to have arbitration by applying English Law, or the party can choose Section B to have arbitration by applying the United States Code and the Maritime Law of the United States. English law and the law of the United States are

---

① The introduction of GENCON 1994, available at: https://www.bimco.org/Documentary.aspx (Last visited on May 16, 2016).

② Article 19 of GENCON 1994.

commonly used in international contracts; they are well -known in the legal community. Providing these two choices for parties is more convenient.

Second, the second part details the small claims procedure. Article 19 regulates that:

"For disputes where the total amount claimed by either party does not exceed the amount stated in Box 25** the arbitration shall be conducted in accordance with the Small Claims Procedure of the London Maritime Arbitrators Association."

The Small Claims Arbitration Procedure means the arbitration procedure is performed with expedition and simplicity, regarding a dispute over a claim not very expensive.[1] The procedure is also more user-friendly because parties can apply for the small claims procedure based on the actual situation, making it beneficial to both parties because it saves time and money.

Third, Article 19 regulates the procedural issue of arbitration, such as the selection of arbitrators in a case.[2] It can avoid the ambiguous rules that cause the disputes.

Fourth, it protects the validity of the main contract and promotes the transaction. Article 19 regulates:

"**Where no figure is supplied in Box 25 in Part

中很常用, 在法律界很有名。为当事人提供这两种选择, 更方便。

第二, 第二部分详细介绍了小额索偿金的程序。第十九条规定:

"对于任何一方索赔总金额不超过第 25 栏 ** 所述金额的争议, 仲裁应按照伦敦海事仲裁员协会的小额索赔程序进行。"

小额索赔仲裁程序意味着仲裁程序的执行快速而简单, 所涉争议的索赔不是很昂贵。[1]小额索赔仲裁程序也更方便使用, 因为当事人可以根据实际情况申请小额索赔仲裁程序, 节省了时间和金钱, 对双方都有利。

第三, 第十九条规定了仲裁的程序问题, 如案件中仲裁员的选择。[2]这可以避免导致争议的模糊规则。

第四, 保护主合同的有效性, 促进交易。第十九条规定:

"如第 1 部分第 25 栏中没有提供

---

[1] Rosenberg, M., & Schubin, M. (1961). Trial by Lawyer: Compulsory Arbitration of Small Claims in Pennsylvania. *Harvard Law Review*, 448-472, at 449.

[2] For example, Article 19 in GENCON 1994 regulates: "Unless the parties agree upon a sole arbitrator, one arbitrator shall be appointed by each party and the arbitrators so appointed shall appoint a third arbitrator, the decision of the three-man tribunal thus constituted or any two of them, shall be final. On the receipt by one party of the nomination in writing of the other party's arbitrator, that party shall appoint their arbitrator within fourteen days, failing which the decision of the single arbitrator appointed shall be final."

数字, 则本规定无效, 但除却本条以外的其他规定应完全有效并继续有效。"

在这条规则中, 无效条款不得导致整个合同无效。本条款旨在保护交易, 并且不解除主合同。

第五, 该格式合同有一个严格的设计。例如, 第十九条 (d) 提供了在当事人没有选择法律的情况下的解决办法。①此外, GENCON 1994 中对条款的陈述也很清晰, 并以严谨的法律术语进行书写, 清楚地向双方传达了该协议的风险和回报。使用这个格式合同可以帮助减少缔约方在合同的解释方面发生争议的可能性。

Ⅰ, this provision only shall be void but the other provisions of this Clause shall have full force and remain in effect."

In this rule, the void term may not cause the whole contract to be void. This provision is intended to protect the transaction and not dissolve the main contract.

Fifth, the standard form contract has a rigorous design. For example, Article19(d) provides the solutions in the situation of parties' absence in choice of law.① Also, the presentation of the articles in GENCON 1994 is clear and written in legally sound language that clearly conveys to both parties the risks and rewards of the agreement. Using this standard form contract can help reduce the likelihood of disputes arising over the interpretation of contracts by contracting parties.

---

① Article19(d) regulates that "If Box 25 in Part Ⅰ is not filled in, sub-clause (a) of this Clause shall apply."

1. Shipbroker	**RECOMMENDED** **THE BALTIC AND INTERNATIONAL MARITIME COUNCIL** **UNIFORM GENERAL CHARTER (AS REVISED 1922, 1976 and 1994)** (To be used for trades for which no specially approved form is in force) **CODE NAME: "GENCON"** Part I
	2. Place and date
3. Owners/Place of business (Cl. 1)	4. Charterers/Place of business (Cl. 1)
5. Vessel's name (Cl. 1)	6. GT/NT (Cl. 1)
7. DWT all told on summer load line in metric tons (abt.) (Cl. 1)	8. Present position (Cl. 1)
9. Expected ready to load (abt.) (Cl. 1)	
10. Loading port or place (Cl. 1)	11. Discharging port or place (Cl. 1)
12. Cargo (also state quantity and margin in Owners' option, if agreed; if full and complete cargo not agreed state "part cargo") (Cl. 1)	
13. Freight rate (also state whether freight prepaid or payable on delivery) (Cl. 4)	14. Freight payment (state currency and method of payment; also beneficiary and bank account) (Cl. 4)
15. State if vessel's cargo handling gear shall not be used (Cl. 5)	16. Laytime (if separate laytime for load. and disch. is agreed, fill in a) and b). If total laytime for load. and disch., fill in c) only) (Cl. 6)
17. Shippers/Place of business (Cl. 6)	a) Laytime for loading
18. Agents (loading) (Cl. 6)	b) Laytime for discharging
19. Agents (discharging) (Cl. 6)	c) Total laytime for loading and discharging
20. Demurrage rate and manner payable (loading and discharging) (Cl. 7)	21. Cancelling date (Cl. 9)
	22. General Average to be adjusted at (Cl. 12)
23. Freight Tax (state if for the Owners' account) (Cl. 13 (c))	24. Brokerage commission and to whom payable (Cl. 15)
25. Law and Arbitration (state 19 (a), 19 (b) or 19 (c) of Cl. 19; if 19 (c) agreed also state Place of Arbitration) (if not filled in 19 (a) shall apply) (Cl. 19)	
(a) State maximum amount for small claims/shortened arbitration (Cl. 19)	26. Additional clauses covering special provisions, if agreed

It is mutually agreed that this Contract shall be performed subject to the conditions contained in this Charter Party which shall include Part I as well as Part II. In the event of a conflict of conditions, the provisions of Part I shall prevail over those of Part II to the extent of such conflict.

Signature (Owners)	Signature (Charterers)

PART II
"Gencon" Charter (As Revised 1922, 1976 and 1994)

1. It is agreed between the party mentioned in Box 3 as the Owners of the Vessel 1
named in Box 5, of the GT/NT indicated in Box 6 and carrying about the number 2
of metric tons of deadweight capacity all told on summer loadline stated in Box 3
7, now in position as stated in Box 8 and expected ready to load under this 4
Charter Party about the date indicated in Box 9, and the party mentioned as the 5
Charterers in Box 4 that: 6
The said Vessel shall, as soon as her prior commitments have been completed, 7
proceed to the loading port(s) or place(s) stated in Box 10 or so near thereto as 8
she may safely get and lie always afloat, and there load a full and complete 9
cargo (if shipment of deck cargo agreed same to be at the Charterers' risk and 10
responsibility) as stated in Box 12, which the Charterers bind themselves to 11
ship, and being so loaded the Vessel shall proceed to the discharging port(s) or 12
place(s) stated in Box 11 as ordered on signing Bills of Lading, or so near 13
thereto as she may safely get and lie always afloat, and there deliver the cargo. 14

2. **Owners' Responsibility Clause** 15
The Owners are to be responsible for loss of or damage to the goods or for 16
delay in delivery of the goods only in case the loss, damage or delay has been 17
caused by personal want of due diligence on the part of the Owners or their 18
Manager to make the Vessel in all respects seaworthy and to secure that she is 19
properly manned, equipped and supplied, or by the personal act or default of 20
the Owners or their Manager. 21
And the Owners are not responsible for loss, damage or delay arising from any 22
other cause whatsoever, even from the neglect or default of the Master or crew 23
or some other person employed by the Owners on board or ashore for whose 24
acts they would, but for this Clause, be responsible, or from unseaworthiness of 25
the Vessel on loading or commencement of the voyage or at any time 26
whatsoever. 27

3. **Deviation Clause** 28
The Vessel has liberty to call at any port or ports in any order, for any purpose, 29
to sail without pilots, to tow and/or assist Vessels in all situations, and also to 30
deviate for the purpose of saving life and/or property. 31

4. **Payment of Freight** 32
(a) The freight at the rate stated in Box 13 shall be paid in cash calculated on the 33
intaken quantity of cargo. 34
(b) *Prepaid.* If according to Box 13 freight is to be paid on shipment, it shall be 35
deemed earned and non-returnable, Vessel and/or cargo lost or not lost. 36
Neither the Owners nor their agents shall be required to sign or endorse bills of 37
lading showing freight prepaid unless the freight due to the Owners has 38
actually been paid. 39
(c) *On delivery.* If according to Box 13 freight, or part thereof, is payable at 40
destination it shall not be deemed earned until the cargo is thus delivered. 41
Notwithstanding the provisions under (a), if freight or part thereof is payable on 42
delivery of the cargo the Charterers shall have the option of paying the freight 43
on delivered weight/quantity provided such option is declared before breaking 44
bulk and the weight/quantity can be ascertained by official weighing machine, 45
joint draft survey or tally. 46
Cash for Vessel's ordinary disbursements at the port of loading to be advanced 47
by the Charterers, if required, at highest current rate of exchange, subject to 48
two (2) per cent to cover insurance and other expenses. 49

5. **Loading/Discharging** 50
(a) Costs/Risks 51
The cargo shall be brought into the holds, loaded, stowed and/or trimmed, 52
tallied, lashed and/or secured and taken from the holds and discharged by the 53
Charterers, free of any risk, liability and expense whatsoever to the Owners. 54
The Charterers shall provide and lay all dunnage material as required for the 55
proper stowage and protection of the cargo on board, the Owners allowing the 56
use of all dunnage available on board. The Charterers shall be responsible for 57
and pay the cost of removing their dunnage after discharge of the cargo under 58
this Charter Party and time to count until dunnage has been removed. 59
(b) Cargo Handling Gear 60
Unless the Vessel is gearless or unless it has been agreed between the parties 61
that the Vessel's gear shall not be used and stated as such in Box 15, the 62
Owners shall throughout the duration of loading/discharging give free use of 63
the Vessel's cargo handling gear and of sufficient motive power to operate all 64
such cargo handling gear. All such equipment to be in good working order. 65
Unless caused by negligence of the stevedores, time lost by breakdown of the 66
Vessel's cargo handling gear or motive power - pro rata the total number of 67
cranes/winches required at that time for the loading/discharging of cargo 68
under this Charter Party - shall not count as laytime or time on demurrage. 69
On request the Owners shall provide free of charge cranemen/winchmen from 70
the crew to operate the Vessel's cargo handling gear, unless local regulations 71
prohibit this, in which latter event shore labourers shall be for the account of the 72
Charterers. Cranemen/winchmen shall be under the Charterers' risk and 73
responsibility and as stevedores to be deemed as their servants but shall 74

always work under the supervision of the Master. 75
(c) Stevedore Damage 76
The Charterers shall be responsible for damage (beyond ordinary wear and 77
tear) to any part of the Vessel caused by Stevedores. Such damage shall be 78
notified as soon as reasonably possible by the Master to the Charterers or their 79
agents and to their Stevedores, failing which the Charterers shall not be held 80
responsible. The Master shall endeavour to obtain the Stevedores' written 81
acknowledgement of liability. 82
The Charterers are obliged to repair any stevedore damage prior to completion 83
of the voyage, but must repair stevedore damage affecting the Vessel's 84
seaworthiness or class before the Vessel sails from the port where such 85
damage was caused or found. All additional expenses incurred shall be for the 86
account of the Charterers and any time lost shall be for the account of and shall 87
be paid to the Owners by the Charterers at the demurrage rate. 88

6. **Laytime** 89
* *(a) Separate laytime for loading and discharging* 90
The cargo shall be loaded within the number of running days/hours as 91
indicated in Box 16, weather permitting, Sundays and holidays excepted, 92
unless used, in which event time used shall count. 93
The cargo shall be discharged within the number of running days/hours as 94
indicated in Box 16, weather permitting, Sundays and holidays excepted, 95
unless used, in which event time used shall count. 96
* *(b) Total laytime for loading and discharging* 97
The cargo shall be loaded and discharged within the number of total running 98
days/hours as indicated in Box 16, weather permitting, Sundays and holidays 99
excepted, unless used, in which event time used shall count. 100
(c) Commencement of laytime (loading and discharging) 101
Laytime for loading and discharging shall commence at 13.00 hours, if notice of 102
readiness is given up to and including 12.00 hours, and at 06.00 hours next 103
working day if notice given during office hours after 12.00 hours. Notice of 104
readiness at loading port to be given to the Shippers named in Box 17 or if not 105
named, to the Charterers or their agents named in Box 18. Notice of readiness 106
at the discharging port to be given to the Receivers or, if not known, to the 107
Charterers or their agents named in Box 19. 108
If the loading/discharging berth is not available on the Vessel's arrival at or off 109
the port of loading/discharging, the Vessel shall be entitled to give notice of 110
readiness within ordinary office hours on arrival there, whether in free pratique 111
or not, whether customs cleared or not. Laytime or time on demurrage shall 112
then count as if she were in berth and in all respects ready for loading/ 113
discharging provided that the Master warrants that she is in fact ready in all 114
respects. Time used in moving from the place of waiting to the loading/ 115
discharging berth shall not count as laytime. 116
If, after inspection, the Vessel is found not to be ready in all respects to load/ 117
discharge time lost after the discovery thereof until the Vessel is again ready to 118
load/discharge shall not count as laytime. 119
Time used before commencement of laytime shall count. 120
* *Indicate alternative (a) or (b) as agreed, in Box 16.* 121

7. **Demurrage** 122
Demurrage at the loading and discharging port is payable by the Charterers at 123
the rate stated in Box 20 in the manner stated in Box 20 per day or pro rata for 124
any part of a day. Demurrage shall fall due day by day and shall be payable 125
upon receipt of the Owners' invoice. 126
In the event the demurrage is not paid in accordance with the above, the 127
Owners shall give the Charterers 96 running hours written notice to rectify the 128
failure. If the demurrage is not paid at the expiration of this time limit and if the 129
vessel is in or at the loading port, the Owners are entitled at any time to 130
terminate the Charter Party and claim damages for any losses caused thereby. 131

8. **Lien Clause** 132
The Owners shall have a lien on the cargo and on all sub-freights payable in 133
respect of the cargo, for freight, deadfreight, demurrage, claims for damages 134
and for all other amounts due under this Charter Party including costs of 135
recovering same. 136

9. **Cancelling Clause** 137
(a) Should the Vessel not be ready to load (whether in berth or not) on the 138
cancelling date indicated in Box 21, the Charterers shall have the option of 139
cancelling this Charter Party. 140
(b) Should the Owners anticipate that, despite the exercise of due diligence, 141
the Vessel will not be ready to load by the cancelling date, they shall notify the 142
Charterers thereof without delay stating the expected date of the Vessel's 143
readiness to load and asking whether the Charterers will exercise their option 144
of cancelling the Charter Party, or agree to a new cancelling date. 145
Such option must be declared by the Charterers within 48 running hours after 146
the receipt of the Owners' notice. If the Charterers do not exercise their option 147
of cancelling, then this Charter Party shall be deemed to be amended such that 148

the seventh day after the new readiness date stated in the Owners' notification 149
to the Charterers shall be the new cancelling date. 150
The provisions of sub-clause (b) of this Clause shall operate only once, and in 151
case of the Vessel's further delay, the Charterers shall have the option of 152
cancelling the Charter Party as per sub-clause (a) of this Clause. 153

10. Bills of Lading 154
Bills of Lading shall be presented and signed by the Master as per the 155
"Congenbill" Bill of Lading form, Edition 1994, without prejudice to this Charter 156
Party, or by the Owners' agents provided written authority has been given by 157
Owners to the agents, a copy of which is to be furnished to the Charterers. The 158
Charterers shall indemnify the Owners against all consequences or liabilities 159
that may arise from the signing of bills of lading as presented to the extent that 160
the terms or contents of such bills of lading impose or result in the imposition of 161
more onerous liabilities upon the Owners than those assumed by the Owners 162
under this Charter Party. 163

11. Both-to-Blame Collision Clause 164
If the Vessel comes into collision with another vessel as a result of the 165
negligence of the other vessel and any act, neglect or default of the Master, 166
Mariner, Pilot or the servants of the Owners in the navigation or in the 167
management of the Vessel, the owners of the cargo carried hereunder will 168
indemnify the Owners against all loss or liability to the other or non-carrying 169
vessel or her owners in so far as such loss or liability represents loss of, or 170
damage to, or any claim whatsoever of the owners of said cargo, paid or 171
payable by the other or non-carrying vessel or her owners to the owners of said 172
cargo and set-off, recouped or recovered by the other or non-carrying vessel 173
or her owners as part of their claim against the carrying Vessel or the Owners. 174
The foregoing provisions shall also apply where the owners, operators or those 175
in charge of any vessel or vessels or objects other than, or in addition to, the 176
colliding vessels or objects are at fault in respect of a collision or contact. 177

12. General Average and New Jason Clause 178
General Average shall be adjusted in London unless otherwise agreed in Box 179
22 according to York-Antwerp Rules 1994 and any subsequent modification 180
thereof. Proprietors of cargo to pay the cargo's share in the general expenses 181
even if same have been necessitated through neglect or default of the Owners' 182
servants (see Clause 2). 183
If General Average is to be adjusted in accordance with the law and practice of 184
the United States of America, the following Clause shall apply: "In the event of 185
accident, danger, damage or disaster before or after the commencement of the 186
voyage, resulting from any cause whatsoever, whether due to negligence or 187
not, for which, or for the consequence of which, the Owners are not 188
responsible, by statute, contract or otherwise, the cargo shippers, consignees 189
or the owners of the cargo shall contribute with the Owners in General Average 190
to the payment of any sacrifices, losses or expenses of a General Average 191
nature that may be made or incurred and shall pay salvage and special charges 192
incurred in respect of the cargo. If a salving vessel is owned or operated by the 193
Owners, salvage shall be paid for as fully as if the said salving vessel or vessels 194
belonged to strangers. Such deposit as the Owners, or their agents, may deem 195
sufficient to cover the estimated contribution of the goods and any salvage and 196
special charges thereon shall, if required, be made by the cargo, shippers, 197
consignees or owners of the goods to the Owners before delivery.". 198

13. Taxes and Dues Clause 199
(a) _On Vessel_ -The Owners shall pay all dues, charges and taxes customarily 200
levied on the Vessel, howsoever the amount thereof may be assessed. 201
(b) _On cargo_ -The Charterers shall pay all dues, charges, duties and taxes 202
customarily levied on the cargo, howsoever the amount thereof may be 203
assessed. 204
(c) _On freight_ -Unless otherwise agreed in Box 23, taxes levied on the freight 205
shall be for the Charterers' account. 206

14. Agency 207
In every case the Owners shall appoint their own Agent both at the port of 208
loading and the port of discharge. 209

15. Brokerage 210
A brokerage commission at the rate stated in Box 24 on the freight, dead-freight 211
and demurrage earned is due to the party mentioned in Box 24. 212
In case of non-execution 1/3 of the brokerage on the estimated amount of 213
freight to be paid by the party responsible for such non-execution to the 214
Brokers as indemnity for the latter's expenses and work. In case of more 215
voyages the amount of indemnity to be agreed. 216

16. General Strike Clause 217
(a) If there is a strike or lock-out affecting or preventing the actual loading of the 218
cargo, or any part of it, when the Vessel is ready to proceed from her last port or 219

at any time during the voyage to the port or ports of loading or after her arrival 220
there, the Master or the Owners may ask the Charterers to declare, that they 221
agree to reckon the laydays as if there were no strike or lock-out. Unless the 222
Charterers have given such declaration in writing (by telegram, if necessary) 223
within 24 hours, the Owners shall have the option of cancelling this Charter 224
Party. If part cargo has already been loaded, the Owners must proceed with 225
same, (freight payable on loaded quantity only) having liberty to complete with 226
other cargo on the way for their own account. 227
(b) If there is a strike or lock-out affecting or preventing the actual discharging 228
of the cargo on or after the Vessel's arrival at or off port of discharge and same 229
has not been settled within 48 hours, the Charterers shall have the option of 230
keeping the Vessel waiting until such strike or lock-out is at an end against 231
paying half demurrage after expiration of the time provided for discharging 232
until the strike or lock-out terminates and thereafter full demurrage shall be 233
payable until the completion of discharging, or of ordering the Vessel to a safe 234
port where she can safely discharge without risk of being detained by strike or 235
lock-out. Such orders to be given within 48 hours after the Master or the 236
Owners have given notice to the Charterers of the strike or lock-out affecting 237
the discharge. On delivery of the cargo at such port, all conditions of this 238
Charter Party and of the Bill of Lading shall apply and the Vessel shall receive 239
the same freight as if she had discharged at the original port of destination, 240
except that if the distance to the substituted port exceeds 100 nautical miles, 241
the freight on the cargo delivered at the substituted port to be increased in 242
proportion. 243
(c) Except for the obligations described above, neither the Charterers nor the 244
Owners shall be responsible for the consequences of any strikes or lock-outs 245
preventing or affecting the actual loading or discharging of the cargo. 246

17. War Risks ("Voywar 1993") 247
(1) For the purpose of this Clause, the words: 248
(a) The "Owners" shall include the shipowners, bareboat charterers, 249
disponent owners, managers or other operators who are charged with the 250
management of the Vessel, and the Master; and 251
(b) "War Risks" shall include any war (whether actual or threatened), act of 252
war, civil war, hostilities, revolution, rebellion, civil commotion, warlike 253
operations, the laying of mines (whether actual or reported), acts of piracy, 254
acts of terrorists, acts of hostility or malicious damage, blockades 255
(whether imposed against all Vessels or imposed selectively against 256
Vessels of certain flags or ownership, or against certain cargoes or crews 257
or otherwise howsoever), by any person, body, terrorist or political group, 258
or the Government of any state whatsoever, which, in the reasonable 259
judgement of the Master and/or the Owners, may be dangerous or are 260
likely to be or to become dangerous to the Vessel, her cargo, crew or other 261
persons on board the Vessel. 262
(2) If at any time before the Vessel commences loading, it appears that, in the 263
reasonable judgement of the Master and/or the Owners, performance of 264
the Contract of Carriage, or any part of it, may expose, or is likely to expose, 265
the Vessel, her cargo, crew or other persons on board the Vessel to War 266
Risks, the Owners may give notice to the Charterers cancelling this 267
Contract of Carriage, or may refuse to perform such part of it as may 268
expose, or may be likely to expose, the Vessel, her cargo, crew or other 269
persons on board the Vessel to War Risks; provided always that if this 270
Contract of Carriage provides that loading or discharging is to take place 271
within a range of ports, and at the port or ports nominated by the Charterers 272
the Vessel, her cargo, crew, or other persons onboard the Vessel may be 273
exposed, or may be likely to be exposed, to War Risks, the Owners shall 274
first require the Charterers to nominate any other safe port which lies 275
within the range for loading or discharging, and may only cancel this 276
Contract of Carriage if the Charterers shall not have nominated such safe 277
port or ports within 48 hours of receipt of notice of such requirement. 278
(3) The Owners shall not be required to continue to load cargo for any voyage, 279
or to sign Bills of Lading for any port or place, or to proceed or continue on 280
any voyage, or on any part thereof, or to proceed through any canal or 281
waterway, or to proceed to or remain at any port or place whatsoever, 282
where it appears, either after the loading of the cargo commences, or at 283
any stage of the voyage thereafter before the discharge of the cargo is 284
completed, that, in the reasonable judgement of the Master and/or the 285
Owners, the Vessel, her cargo (or any part thereof), crew or other persons 286
on board the Vessel (or any one or more of them) may be, or are likely to be, 287
exposed to War Risks. If it should so appear, the Owners may by notice 288
request the Charterers to nominate a safe port for the discharge of the 289
cargo or any part thereof, and if within 48 hours of the receipt of such 290
notice, the Charterers shall not have nominated such a port, the Owners 291
may discharge the cargo at any safe port of their choice (including the port 292
of loading) in complete fulfilment of the Contract of Carriage. The Owners 293
shall be entitled to recover from the Charterers the extra expenses of such 294
discharge and, if the discharge takes place at any port other than the 295
loading port, to receive the full freight as though the cargo had been 296

carried to the discharging port and if the extra distance exceeds 100 miles, 297
to additional freight which shall be the same percentage of the freight 298
contracted for as the percentage which the extra distance represents to 299
the distance of the normal and customary route, the Owners having a lien 300
on the cargo for such expenses and freight. 301

(4) If at any stage of the voyage after the loading of the cargo commences, it 302
appears that, in the reasonable judgement of the Master and/or the 303
Owners, the Vessel, her cargo, crew or other persons on board the Vessel 304
may be, or are likely to be, exposed to War Risks on any part of the route 305
(including any canal or waterway) which is normally and customarily used 306
in a voyage of the nature contracted for, and there is another longer route 307
to the discharging port, the Owners shall give notice to the Charterers that 308
this route will be taken. In this event the Owners shall be entitled, if the total 309
extra distance exceeds 100 miles, to additional freight which shall be the 310
same percentage of the freight contracted for as the percentage which the 311
extra distance represents to the distance of the normal and customary 312
route. 313

(5) The Vessel shall have liberty:- 314
(a) to comply with all orders, directions, recommendations or advice as to 315
departure, arrival, routes, sailing in convoy, ports of call, stoppages, 316
destinations, discharge of cargo, delivery or in any way whatsoever which 317
are given by the Government of the Nation under whose flag the Vessel 318
sails, or other Government to whose laws the Owners are subject, or any 319
other Government which so requires, or any body or group acting with the 320
power to compel compliance with their orders or directions; 321
(b) to comply with the orders, directions or recommendations of any war 322
risks underwriters who have the authority to give the same under the terms 323
of the war risks insurance; 324
(c) to comply with the terms of any resolution of the Security Council of the 325
United Nations, any directives of the European Community, the effective 326
orders of any other Supranational body which has the right to issue and 327
give the same, and with national laws aimed at enforcing the same to which 328
the Owners are subject, and to obey the orders and directions of those who 329
are charged with their enforcement; 330
(d) to discharge at any other port any cargo or part thereof which may 331
render the Vessel liable to confiscation as a contraband carrier; 332
(e) to call at any other port to change the crew or any part thereof or other 333
persons on board the Vessel when there is reason to believe that they may 334
be subject to internment, imprisonment or other sanctions; 335
(f) where cargo has not been loaded or has been discharged by the 336
Owners under any provisions of this Clause, to load other cargo for the 337
Owners' own benefit and carry it to any other port or ports whatsoever, 338
whether backwards or forwards or in a contrary direction to the ordinary or 339
customary route. 340

(6) If in compliance with any of the provisions of sub-clauses (2) to (5) of this 341
Clause anything is done or not done, such shall not be deemed to be a 342
deviation, but shall be considered as due fulfilment of the Contract of 343
Carriage. 344

18. General Ice Clause 345
Port of loading 346
(a) In the event of the loading port being inaccessible by reason of ice when the 347
Vessel is ready to proceed from her last port or at any time during the voyage or 348
on the Vessel's arrival or in case frost sets in after the Vessel's arrival, the 349
Master for fear of being frozen in is at liberty to leave without cargo, and this 350
Charter Party shall be null and void. 351
(b) If during loading the Master, for fear of the Vessel being frozen in, deems it 352
advisable to leave, he has liberty to do so with what cargo he has on board and 353
to proceed to any other port or ports with option of completing cargo for the 354
Owners' benefit for any port or ports including port of discharge. Any part 355
cargo thus loaded under this Charter Party to be forwarded to destination at the 356
Vessel's expense but against payment of freight, provided that no extra 357
expenses be thereby caused to the Charterers, freight being paid on quantity 358
delivered (in proportion if lumpsum), all other conditions as per this Charter 359
Party. 360
(c) In case of more than one loading port, and if one or more of the ports are 361
closed by ice, the Master or the Owners to be at liberty either to load the part 362
cargo at the open port and fill up elsewhere for their own account as under 363
section (b) or to declare the Charter Party null and void unless the Charterers 364
agree to load full cargo at the open port. 365

Port of discharge 366
(a) Should ice prevent the Vessel from reaching port of discharge the 367
Charterers shall have the option of keeping the Vessel waiting until the re- 368
opening of navigation and paying demurrage or of ordering the Vessel to a safe 369
and immediately accessible port where she can safely discharge without risk of 370
detention by ice. Such orders to be given within 48 hours after the Master or the 371
Owners have given notice to the Charterers of the impossibility of reaching port 372

of destination. 373
(b) If during discharging the Master for fear of the Vessel being frozen in deems 374
it advisable to leave, he has liberty to do so with what cargo he has on board and 375
to proceed to the nearest accessible port where she can safely discharge. 376
(c) On delivery of the cargo at such port, all conditions of the Bill of Lading shall 377
apply and the Vessel shall receive the same freight as if she had discharged at 378
the original port of destination, except that if the distance of the substituted port 379
exceeds 100 nautical miles, the freight on the cargo delivered at the substituted 380
port to be increased in proportion. 381

19. Law and Arbitration 382
* (a) This Charter Party shall be governed by and construed in accordance with 383
English law and any dispute arising out of this Charter Party shall be referred to 384
arbitration in London in accordance with the Arbitration Acts 1950 and 1979 or 385
any statutory modification or re-enactment thereof for the time being in force. 386
Unless the parties agree upon a sole arbitrator, one arbitrator shall be 387
appointed by each party and the arbitrators so appointed shall appoint a third 388
arbitrator, the decision of the three-man tribunal thus constituted or any two of 389
them, shall be final. On the receipt by one party of the nomination in writing of 390
the other party's arbitrator, that party shall appoint their arbitrator within 391
fourteen days, failing which the decision of the single arbitrator appointed shall 392
be final. 393
For disputes where the total amount claimed by either party does not exceed 394
the amount stated in Box 25** the arbitration shall be conducted in accordance 395
with the Small Claims Procedure of the London Maritime Arbitrators 396
Association. 397
* (b) This Charter Party shall be governed by and construed in accordance with 398
Title 9 of the United States Code and the Maritime Law of the United States and 399
should any dispute arise out of this Charter Party, the matter in dispute shall be 400
referred to three persons at New York, one to be appointed by each of the 401
parties hereto, and the third by the two so chosen; their decision or that of any 402
two of them shall be final, and for purpose of enforcing any award, this 403
agreement may be made a rule of the Court. The proceedings shall be 404
conducted in accordance with the rules of the Society of Maritime Arbitrators, 405
Inc.. 406
For disputes where the total amount claimed by either party does not exceed 407
the amount stated in Box 25** the arbitration shall be conducted in accordance 408
with the Shortened Arbitration Procedure of the Society of Maritime Arbitrators, 409
Inc.. 410
* (c) Any dispute arising out of this Charter Party shall be referred to arbitration at 411
the place indicated in Box 25, subject to the procedures applicable there. The 412
laws of the place indicated in Box 25 shall govern this Charter Party. 413
(d) If Box 25 in Part 1 is not filled in, sub-clause (a) of this Clause shall apply. 414
* *(a), (b) and (c) are alternatives; indicate alternative agreed in Box 25.* 415
** *Where no figure is supplied in Box 25 in Part 1, this provision only shall be void but* 416
the other provisions of this Clause shall have full force and remain in effect. 417

3. A Case about GENCON 1994 Article 19

3.1 Facts

It seems that GENCON 1994 is quite convenient for the parties to use. Due to the features of arbitration clauses and standard form contracts, some disputes still happen. Below, I will introduce a case containing an issue with GENCON 1994.

In the case *Shagang South-Asia (Hong Kong) Trading Co. Ltd v. Daewoo Logistics,*[①] a contract was concluded between the parties. In the Fixture Note,[②] the parties agreed on the clauses of "Arbitration in Hong Kong with English Law to apply." or "Arbitration to be held in Hong Kong. English Law to be applied." and other terms agreed on GENCON 1994. The dispute was that the arbitration clauses in GENCON 1994 and the arbitration clauses in the Fixture Note were different.

The Fixture Note between the parties regulate that:[③]

"23. ARBITRATION: ARBITRATION TO BE HELD IN HONGKONG. ENGLISH LAW TO BE APPLIED.

24. OTHER TERMS/CONDITIONS AND CHARTER PARTY DETAILS BASED ON GENCON 1994 CHARTER PARTY."

However, Article 19 in GENCON 1994 regulates that

---

① Shagang South-Asia (Hong Kong) Trading Co. Ltd v. Daewoo Logistics, [2015] EWHC 194 (Comm), High Court of England and Wales, available at: http://globalarbitrationnews.com/ shagang-south-asia-hong-kong-trading-co-ltd-v-daewoo-logistics-2015-ewhc-194-comm-20150414/ (Last visited on May12, 2016).

② Afixture note is a confirmation document for renting boats.

③ Available at: http://www.ccpit.org (Last visited on May12, 2016).

三、关于 GENCON 1994 第十九条案例

（一）案件事实

通常情况下，GENCON 1994 便利于当事人双方的使用。但是由于仲裁条款和格式合同的特殊性，仍会发生一些争议。下面将介绍一个包含 GENCON 1994 问题的案例。

在沙钢南亚（香港）贸易有限公司诉大宇物流公司案中①，双方共同签订了一份合同。在租船确认书中，②双方同意"在香港仲裁并且使用英国法律"或"将在香港进行的仲裁将适用英国法律"以及其他 GENCON 1994 条款。然而，争议在于租船确认书中的仲裁条款和 GENCON 1994 中的仲裁条款不同。

当事人双方之间的租船确认书规定：③

"23. 仲裁：将在香港举行的仲裁。仲裁程序将适用英国的法律。

24. 其他条款 / 条件及租约细节基于 GENCON 1994 的规定。"

然而，GENCON 1994 的第十九条规定：

"(a) 该租约应当使用英国法律进行裁决。由该租约引起的任何争议应当提交仲裁，并且按照伦敦仲裁法案 1950 年和 1979 年版本或任何法定修改或重新制定且暂时生效的版本进行仲裁。

除非双方同意一名单独仲裁员，否则双方应指定一名仲裁员，由此指定的仲裁员应指定第三名仲裁员；这样组成的三人法庭或其中任何两个人的决定应为最终决定。在一方收到另一方仲裁员的书面提名后，该一方应在十四天内指定其仲裁员，否则，指定的单一仲裁员的决定应为最终决定。

······

d) 如果未填写第 1 部分中的第 25 栏，则适用本条第 (a) 款。

*(a)、(b) 和 (c) 是替代方案；表示在第 25 栏中商定的替代方案。

** 如果在第 1 部分的第 25 栏中没有提供任何数字，则本条款无效，但本条款的其他规定应完全有效并继续有效。"

在本案中，[①]由于到岸的货物不足而存在争议。2014 年 2 月，大宇物流公司通知了沙钢南亚公司进行仲裁，并索赔 100 万美元的损失。与此同时，大宇公司任命蒂莫西·雷蒙特先生为其仲裁员，并要求沙钢南亚公司在指定的期限内指定其仲裁员。否则，大宇将任命蒂莫西·雷蒙特先生为唯一的仲裁员。

"(a) This Charter Party shall be governed by and construed in accordance with English law and any dispute arising out of this Charter Party shall be referred to arbitration in London in accordance with the Arbitration Acts 1950 and 1979 or any statutory modification or re-enactment thereof for the time being in force.

Unless the parties agree upon a sole arbitrator, one arbitrator shall be appointed by each party and the arbitrators so appointed shall appoint a third arbitrator, the decision of the three-man tribunal thus constituted or any two of them, shall be final. On the receipt by one party of the nomination in writing of the other party's arbitrator, that party shall appoint their arbitrator within fourteen days, failing which the decision of the single arbitrator appointed shall be final.

…

d) If Box 25 in Part Ⅰ is not filled in, sub-clause (a) of this Clause shall apply.

* (a), (b) and (c) are alternatives; indicate alternative agreed in Box 25.

** Where no figure is supplied in Box 25 in Part Ⅰ, this provision only shall be void but the other provisions of this Clause shall have full force and remain in effect."

In the case,[①] there was controversy due to short landed goods. Daewoo informed Shagang South-Asia of the arbitration and claimed $ 1 million for its loss in February 2014. At the same time Daewoo appointed Mr. Timothy Rayment as its arbitrator, and requested that Shagang South-Asia appoint its arbitrator within the specified period. Otherwise Daewoo would appoint Mr. Timothy Rayment as the sole arbitrator.

---

① The details of the case are available at: http://globalar-bitrationnews.com/shagang-south-asia-hong-kong-trading-co-ltd-v-daewoo-logistics-2015-ewhc-194-comm-20150414/ (Last visited on May 12, 2016).

For various reasons, Shagang South-Asia did not make any response to the notice of arbitration to Daewoo. Daewoo then appointed Mr. Timothy Rayment as the sole, designated arbitrator. On March 18, 2014 Mr. Timothy Rayment accepted to be the sole arbitrator in the case and sent notice to Shagang South-Asia. Later, Shagang South-Asia appointed lawyer Reed Smith Richards Butler. After receiving the commission, the Hong Kong lawyer Reed Smith Richards Butler immediately challenged jurisdiction of the tribunal on the grounds that the seat of arbitration should be in Hong Kong. He believed that the Hong Kong Arbitration Ordinance should apply to the case. According to the Hong Kong Arbitration Ordinance,[1] if the arbitration clause does not specify the number of arbitrators, the number of arbitrators shall be decided by the Hong Kong International Arbitration Center.

After the written statements of the parties were presented, the arbitral tribunal considered "ARBITRATION TO BE HELD IN HONGKONG" just meant the place of arbitration (venue / place of the arbitration) was to be Hong Kong, and that the arbitration clause in the Fixture Note did not refer to the seat of the arbitration. Besides, "ENGLISH LAW TO BE APPLIED" means the arbitration procedure law would apply the English Arbitration Act 1996. In addition, according to Article 19 of GENCON 1994[2], the tribunal decided that the appointment of the sole arbitrator was effective and the arbitrator had jurisdiction for this arbitration case.

Shagang South-Asia appealed to the British Appeal Court, and attempted to apply for revocation of

由于各种原因，沙钢南亚没有对大宇的仲裁通知作出任何回应。大宇随后将蒂莫西·雷蒙特作为唯一的指定仲裁员。2014 年 3 月 18 日，蒂莫西·雷蒙特先生接受任命成为本案的唯一仲裁员，并向沙钢南亚发出通知。后来，沙钢南亚任命了律师里德·史密斯·理查兹·巴特勒。该律师收到委托后，立即质疑仲裁法庭的管辖权，理由是仲裁地点应在香港。他认为该案件应适用于《香港仲裁条例》。根据《香港仲裁条例》，[1]如仲裁条款没有指明仲裁员的人数，则仲裁员的人数应由香港国际仲裁中心决定。

双方发表书面陈述后，仲裁庭认为"在香港进行仲裁"仅指仲裁地点（地点/仲裁地点）为香港，租船确认书中的仲裁条款并未提及仲裁所在地。此外，"适用英国法律"是指仲裁程序法将适用 1996 年的《英国仲裁法》。此外，根据 GENCON 1994 第十九条[2]，法庭认定任命唯一一名仲裁员有效，该仲裁员对该仲裁案件具有管辖权。

沙钢南亚公司向英国上诉法院提出上诉，并试图申请撤销仲裁裁决。沙

---

① It regulates in Part 4, Composition of Arbitral Tribunal, Hong Kong Arbitration Ordinance. Available at: http://www.legco.gov.hk/yr10-11/english/ord/ord017-10-e.pdf (Last visited on May12, 2016).

② Article 19(a) of GENCON 1994 statesthat "…Unless the parties agree upon a sole arbitrator, one arbitrator shall be appointed by each party and the arbitrators so appointed shall appoint a third arbitrator; the decision of the three-man tribunal thus constituted or any two of them shall be final. On the receipt by one party of the nomination in writing of the other party's arbitrator, that party shall appoint their arbitrator within fourteen days, failing which the decision of the single arbitrator appointed shall be final…"

钢南亚声称,仲裁庭没有适当地成立,仲裁庭没有管辖权。

英国上诉法院支持沙钢南亚的索赔要求。沙钢南亚认为,对租船确认书中第二十三条说明最合理的解释是,仲裁应在香港举行。因此,程序法应适用《香港仲裁条例》,但实质问题应适用英国法律。

法院还认为,合同中的争议解决条款可以包括两个方面,一是仲裁的地点,另一个是适用哪个法律来解决实质性争议。因此,双方选择在香港进行仲裁,但由英国法律管辖实质问题这一现象非常普遍。法院认为,如果当事各方希望仲裁所在地与仲裁地点不同,则应在合同中明确规定并具体规定仲裁所在地。

最后,法院认为,租船确认书中的第二十三条不符合 GENCON 1994 第十九条的规定。因此,该案中 GENCON 1994 的第十九条不能并入租船确认书中的第二十四条并适用本案。英国法院进一步发现,即使 1996 年的《英国仲裁法》适用于本案,蒂莫西·雷蒙特先生仍然不能成为唯一的仲裁员。

（二）案例分析

本案是海运行业的一个重要案例,也为法律界提供了启示,特别是在具有

the arbitral award. Shagang South-Asia claimed that the arbitral tribunal was not properly constituted and the arbitral tribunal had no jurisdiction.

The British Appeal Court supported the claims of Shagang South-Asia. Shagang South-Asia held the opinions that the most reasonable interpretation of Article 23 of the Fixture Note is that the arbitration should be held in Hong Kong. Therefore, the procedural law should be the Hong Kong Arbitration Ordinance, but for the substantive issue, the English law should apply.

The court also holds that the dispute resolution clauses in the contracts may contain two aspects; one is the location of the arbitration, and the other is which law to apply in order to resolve the substantive dispute. Therefore, the parties chose to hold arbitration in Hong Kong, but it was very common that the substantive issue was governed by the English law. The court held that if the parties wished the seat of the arbitration to be different from the place of the arbitration, it should be clearly stated in the contract and specify the seat of arbitration.

Finally, the Court held that Article 23 of the Fixture Note was not consistent with Article 19 of GENCON 1994. Therefore, Article 19 of GENCON 1994 could not be incorporated into Article 24 of the Fixture Note to apply to the case. The British Court further found that, even if the English Arbitration Act 1996 could be applied in this case, Mr. Timothy Rayment still could not be the sole arbitrator.

3.2 Case Analysis

This case is an important case in the maritime industry, and it also provides inspiration for the legal community, especially in the area of standard form contracts with arbitration clauses.

(a) Call for Clear Arbitration Clauses

The terms in standard form contracts should be clear because ambiguous terms may lead to disputes. As I have stated in previous paragraphs, not only the Shagang case but many cases in practice show that if parties do not specifically state the applicable law for their arbitration agreement, then this may cause the disputes.

For instance, in the *Shagang South-Asia (Hong Kong) Trading Co. Ltd v. Daewoo Logistics*[①] case, disputes arose because of the lack of a clear indication of the applicable law of arbitration. Consequently, the parties have disputes regarding whether to apply Hong Kong law or English law.

To be on the safe side, it would be better to have clear choices at every stage of arbitration. To determine the validity of an arbitration agreement, we should choose the law governing the arbitration agreement in advance. To protect the process of arbitration, we should have a clear choice of *lex arbitri*. In order to avoid arbitral awards being challenged because of the procedure issue. Lastly, it is also important to decide which law is applicable to the substantive issues. This law may ultimate decide the substantive disputes between the parties.

(b) Arbitration Clauses Incorporated by Reference

Nowadays, arbitration clauses incorporated by reference are usually used in international commercial arbitration. In practice, parties may not have arbitration clauses in their contracts but refer to a separate document that has the arbitration clause. This situation may happen in standard form contracts, general business conditions, or a charter party bill of landing, just like the case of *Shagang South-Asia (Hong Kong) Trading Co. Ltd v. Daewoo Logistics*[②] that I discussed above. Disputes arise due to the separate documents regarding the arbitration clauses.

---

①   Supra note 327.
②   Supra note 327.

仲裁条款的格式合同领域。

1. 要求有明确的仲裁条款

格式合同中的仲裁条款应该明确，因为含糊不清的条款可能会导致争议。正如前几段中所述，不仅是沙钢案，而且在实践中的许多案例都表明，如果双方没有具体说明其仲裁协议的适用法律，那么这可能会导致争议。

例如，在沙钢南亚（香港）贸易有限公司诉大宇物流公司[①]案中，争议发生是因为缺乏明确的适用仲裁法。因此，双方就是否适用香港法律或是否适用英国法律存在争议。

为了安全起见，最好在仲裁的每个阶段都有明确的选择。要确定仲裁协议的有效性，我们应事先选择管辖仲裁协议的法律。为了保护仲裁程序，我们应该有一个明确的仲裁法选择。为了避免仲裁裁决因程序问题而受到质疑。最后，决定哪项法律适用于实质性问题也很重要。该法可以最终裁决当事人之间的实质性纠纷。

2. 用于援引的仲裁条款

目前，在国际商事仲裁中，仲裁条款可能存在于附随的指引文件中。在实践中，当事人在合同中可能没有仲裁条款，但是可能存在具有仲裁条款的单独文件可供参考。这种情况可能发生在格式合同、一般商业合同或船舶租约中，就像上述讨论的沙钢南亚（香港）贸易有限公司诉大宇物流公司案件[②]一样，由于有关仲裁条款的单独文件而产生争议。

《纽约公约》中所规定的形式要件要求并没有得到统一的解释。因此，有必要讨论"通过引用其他文件而纳入的仲裁条款"是否可以被视为不同法域之下的当事人之间有效的仲裁协议。

例如，蒂尔麦蒂克公司诉艾伯皮特汀公司案件①中，法院倾向于"相对不完美"理论。法院裁定，国际交易协议对包含仲裁条款的格式合同的国际引用必须被视为有效和具有约束力。理由如下：第一，符合《纽约公约》第二条中有关于仲裁协议成立的条件。第二，法院认为，作为一个合格的企业主按照常理应该知道主合同中的标准规则。

同样的结论也可以在法国的一个案例中找到：博玛石油公司诉突尼斯石油公司。②该案中有一个格式合同包括"其他条件"。"其他条件"是指国际商会的仲裁协议。法院认定通过参考文件（例如一般条件表格）而纳入的仲裁协议是有效的。此外，法院认为原告在签订合同时就知道了该文件的内容。

The formal requirements set out by the New York Convention have not been construed uniformly. Thus, there is a need to discuss whether "an arbitration clause incorporated by reference" can be regarded as a valid arbitration agreement between the parties in diverse jurisdictions.

For instance, the case *Del Medico & C. SAS v. Iberprotein Sl*① is inclined to adopt the "*relatio imperfecta*" theory. The court ruled that the global reference made by an international transaction agreement to a standard form contract containing an arbitration clause must be regarded as valid and binding. The reasons are as follows: First, Article II of the New York Convention admits the arbitration agreement, which is based on general reference. Second, the court believes that a qualified business is supposed to know the standard rules in the main contract.

The same conclusion can be found in a French case— *Société Bomar Oil N.V. v. Entreprise tunisienne d'activités pétrolières*.② There is a standard form contract that includes the "other conditions." The "other conditions" refers to an ICC arbitration agreement. The court made the decision that the arbitration agreement incorporated by reference to a document, such as a general conditions form, is valid. Also, the court thinks the plaintiff was aware of the content of the document at the time when the parties entered into the contract.

---

① Del Medico & C. SAS v. Iberprotein Sl, [2011] Case No. 13231, Italy, Corte di Cassazione. Available at: http://newyorkconvention1958.org/index.php?lvl=notice_display&id=1404 (Last visited on May12, 2016).

② Société Bomar Oil N.V. v. Entreprise tunisienne d'activités pétrolières

However, Italian courts adopt a different approach on this matter. In the case *Louis Dreyfus Commodities v. Cereal Mangimi Srl*[①], the Italian Court held the opinion that only when both parties explicitly know about the existence of the reference to arbitration contained in a document other than the main contract, the arbitration clauses may be valid, whereas a mere generic reference to the separate document or form containing the arbitration clauses is not enough.

Even though there are a lot of divergent precedents that can be found on this matter, in my opinion, most countries hold the opinion that the validity of an arbitration agreement depends on whether the parties are aware of the incorporation of the arbitration clause and whether the parties have full effective consent to arbitrate.[②] Also, there is a trend to have an open opinion on the interpretation of Article II of the New York Convention on the issue of arbitration clauses incorporated by reference. Some courts will recognize the arbitration clauses that are incorporated by reference as valid.

To date, there is no univocal position expressed by jurisprudence or any international or domestic rules clarifying the requirements for proper incorporation. Therefore, I strongly recommend that parties explicitly mention the arbitration clause contained in a secondary document. This can help to avoid some unnecessary risks about arbitration clauses that are incorporated by reference.

3.3 Some Important Factors that Need to be Considered

The drafter should take many factors into consideration that may affect the process of arbitration. For instance, the usage of trade, industry practice, the number of arbitrators, the language of arbitration, and confidentiality terms must be considered.

---

① Louis Dreyfus Commodities v. Cereal Mangimi Srl [2009], Cases No. 11529, Italy, Corte di Cassazione. Available at: http://www.forwarderlaw.com/library/view.php?article_id=877 (Last visited on May12, 2016).

② Kronke, H., Supra note 96, at 87-88.

然而，意大利法院在这个问题上采取了不同的办法。在路易斯·德雷福斯大宗商品公司诉谷物饲料有限公司案中①，意大利法院认为只有当双方明确知道主合同以外的文件中提到了仲裁时，仲裁条款才可能是有效的，而仅仅通用引用单独的文档或包含仲裁条款是不够的。

在笔者看来，尽管有很多不同的判例，可以发现在这个问题上，大多数国家认为仲裁协议的有效性取决于当事人是否意识到格式合同中具有仲裁条款，以及当事人是否充分同意仲裁。②与此同时，有一种倾向是持有开放的观点，认为根据《纽约公约》第二条的解释，一些法院承认根据指引文件而被纳入的仲裁条款是有效的。

到目前为止，判例或任何国际或国内规则都没有明确表达立场来澄清引用其他文件中的仲裁条款合并入合同的有效性问题。因此强烈建议当事各方为避免一些不必要的风险，应当在约定中明确提出在其他文件中所载的仲裁条款。

（三）需要考虑的一些重要因素

起草者应考虑到许多可能影响仲裁程序的因素。例如，必须考虑国际贸易中的行业惯例、仲裁员的数量、仲裁的语言以及保密条款。

上面讨论过的沙钢南亚（香港）贸易有限公司诉大宇物流有限公司案中，我们可以发现，仲裁所在地法律在这个案件中发挥了重要的作用。

In the case of *Shagang South-Asia (Hong Kong) Trading Co. Ltd v. Daewoo Logistics*, which I discussed above, we can find that the law of the seat of arbitration played an important role in the case.

首先，该条款应明确规定仲裁的所在地。在大多数情况下，仲裁的所在地将决定支配仲裁的程序规则。[1]仲裁的所在地可能会影响使用哪种法律来管理仲裁。[2]例如，如果仲裁所在地是巴黎，那么程序规则将受大陆法系的管辖，可能不同于英国等普通法管辖的情况。

Primarily, the clause should specify the seat of arbitration. In most cases, the seat of arbitration will determine the procedural rules that govern the arbitration.[1] The seat of arbitration may influence which law to use to govern the arbitration.[2] For example, if the seat of arbitration is Paris, then the procedural rule would be governed by the civil law jurisdiction and may be different from the position in a common law jurisdiction such as England.

其次，我们应该能够解读仲裁所在地和"仲裁地点"之间的区别。在沙钢南亚（香港）贸易有限公司诉大宇物流有限公司案件中双方就"仲裁地点"和"仲裁所在地"存在争议。仲裁地点是指仲裁字面上的地点。然而，仲裁的所在地是一个法律概念。仲裁所在地与某一地点有关。该地点的法律可以决定管理仲裁的程序或规则。它还可以决定哪些国家法院可以干预仲裁过程以及这种干预的程度。因此，在国际商事仲裁中，当事人通常选择一个"中立"国家作为其仲裁所在地。双方认为，中立的选择将有利于公正的仲裁程序。

Secondly, we should be able to decipher the difference between the seat of arbitration and "the place of arbitration." In the case of *Shagang South-Asia (Hong Kong) Trading Co. Ltd v. Daewoo Logistics*, which I discussed above, the parties had a dispute about "the place of arbitration" and "the seat of arbitration." The place of arbitration refers to the literal location of the arbitration. However, the seat of arbitration is a legal concept. The seat of arbitration is tied to a certain location. The law of this location may determine the procedure or rules that govern the arbitration. It may also determine which national court can intervene in the process of the arbitration and the extent of this intervention. Therefore, in international commercial arbitration, parties usually choose a "neutral" country as their seat of arbitration.[3] The parties believe that the neutral choice will be beneficial to just arbitration processes.

---

[1]   I have disused the details in Chapter III.

[2]   Lew, J. D., Mistelis, L. A., & Kröll, S., Supra note 7, at 231.

[3]   Redfern, A., Supra note 6, at 104.

Lastly, by selecting a place or seat for arbitration, we should pay attention to a country's mandatory national laws that are applicable to the arbitration. There would be a wide divergence between the extent of court intervention during the process of arbitration. Failure to do so may make the involved parties face the risk of being challenged during the process of arbitration.

In addition to the seat of arbitration, the International Bar Association (IBA) provides a good example with suggestions for drafting an arbitration agreement. For more information, we can see the IBA Guidelines on drafting international arbitration clauses.[①] There are some elements mentioned in the IBA Guidelines, such as document production, the allocation of costs and fees, qualifications of arbitrators, time limits, and finality. These are some important elements that will affect arbitration. I think IBA Guidelines may be a good model for the parties to draft a better arbitration agreement.

最后，通过选择仲裁地点或仲裁所在地，我们应该注意一个国家适用于仲裁的强制性国家法律。在仲裁过程中，法院干预的程度会有很大区别。如果不这样做，可能会使相关当事人在仲裁过程中面临被质疑的风险。

除了仲裁所在地之外，国际律师协会（IBA）还为起草仲裁协议提供了很好的例子和建议。为获取更多信息，我们可以查阅国际律师协会关于起草国际仲裁条款的指南。IBA 指南中提到了一些要素，如文件的制作、成本和费用的分配、仲裁员的资格、时限和最终结果。这些都是影响仲裁的一些重要因素。我认为 IBA 指南可能是双方起草更好的仲裁协议的一个好范例。

---

① IBA Guidelines on Drafting International Arbitration Clauses, available at: http://www.ibanet.org/Publications/publications_IBA_guides_and_free_materials.aspx (Last visited on May 12, 2016)

第六章 结论

Chapter VI Conclusions

仲裁的定义及其在格式合同中的设计是一个有趣的话题。①仲裁是诉讼的一个有用的选择。为确保仲裁条款在格式合同中有效,应注意以下条件:

第一,有必要在格式合同中加入明确的仲裁条款指示,以便所有各方都意识到他们未来的纠纷将由仲裁来决定。推荐格式合同中的仲裁条款采用粗体字体或改变颜色,以提醒当事人仲裁条款的重要性。如果不强调,处在弱势一方的当事人可能会辩称他们不知道这些条款并且是被迫进行仲裁。此外,法院可以裁定仲裁条款因违反了当事人的自治原则而无效。

第二,仲裁条款的设计要精确。任何措辞的歧义都会引起争议。法院可能会根据国家法律或法院采用的解释原则来解释有缺陷的仲裁条款,导致不确定的情况和不必要的结果。

第三,起草者应谨慎选择仲裁适用的法律,因为法律可以决定实质性纠纷的结果、仲裁条款的有效性、仲裁的程序问题等。现在对这个问题有很多理论和观点。然而,由于国家法院面临着不同的案件和情况,理论不能盲目采用。

The definition of arbitration and its design in standard form contracts is an intriguing topic. Arbitration is a useful alternative to litigation.① In order to make sure that arbitration clauses are valid in a standard form contract, the following conditions should be noticed:

Firstly, it is necessary to include clear instructions of arbitration clauses in standard form contracts so that all parties are aware of the fact that their future disputes will be determined by the arbitration. Bold fonts or change of the font color of the arbitration clauses in the standard form contracts are recommended to remind parties of the importance of arbitration clauses. If not highlighted, weak parties may argue that they are unaware of the clauses and forced into the arbitration. What is more, the court may decide that the arbitration clause is invalid because it violates the autonomy of the parties.

Secondly, arbitration clauses should be designed with precision. Any ambiguity of wording will bring controversies and the courts may interpret the defective arbitration clauses on the basis of national laws or the interpretation principles that the courts adopt, leading to uncertain situations and unwanted outcomes.

Thirdly, drafters should be careful with the choice of applicable laws in the arbitration, as the laws can decide the results of substantive disputes, the validity of arbitration clauses, the procedural problem of the arbitration and so on. There are many theories and

---

① Coakley, C. (2000). Growing Role of Customized Consent in International Commercial Arbitration, *The. Ga. J. Int'l & Comp. L.*, 29, 127-149, at 129.

standpoints toward this issue nowadays. However, theories cannot be adopted blindly, as national courts face different cases and circumstances. For instance, some national courts do not uphold the delocalization theory because they believe that the theory may hurt the judicial sovereignty of their countries.

Fourthly, drafters should pay attention to some important elements while designing the arbitration clauses, such as the seat of arbitration, language of arbitration, institutional or *ad hoc* clauses, confidentiality terms, etc., which may affect the result of the arbitration. For instance, the choice of arbitration seat will be related to the applicable law of the arbitration and affect the place where the arbitration is held. The choice of language will determine the translation of documents.

Fifthly, it would be a wise way to design the arbitration clauses based on business practices. Different industries have different business practices and custom usages. As for the validity of arbitration clauses or standard terms, the courts may determine the case according to different business practices. For instance, the *lex mercatoria* is widely applied in many maritime cases.

To sum up, according to what I have discussed in previous chapters, nowadays many scholars propose new and modern viewpoints of arbitration and they stress the importance of absolute parties' autonomy and delocalization. New and modern theories and discussions may provide insights for academic researches, but they may not be suitable to be applied in arbitration practices.[1]

Just as Professor Simões points out, "Law in books is of no use if it cannot meet the needs of the everyday business world."[2]

例如，一些国家法院不支持离域理论，因为他们认为该理论可能会损害他们国家的司法主权。

第四，起草者在设计仲裁条款时应注意一些重要的因素，如仲裁所在地、仲裁语言、机构条款或临时条款、保密条款等，这可能会影响仲裁的结果。例如，仲裁所在地的选择将与仲裁的适用法律有关，并影响到仲裁的举行地点。语言的选择将决定文件的翻译。

第五，根据商业惯例设计仲裁条款是一种明智的方法。不同的行业有不同的商业惯例和定制用法。对于仲裁条款或标准条款的有效性，法院可以根据不同的商业惯例来裁决案件。例如，*lex mercatoria* 被广泛应用于许多海事案件。

综上所述，根据前几章中所讨论的内容，现在许多学者提出了新的、现代的仲裁观点，他们强调了绝对当事人自治和离域原则的重要性。全新的现代理论和讨论可能为学术研究提供见解，但它们可能不适合应用于仲裁实践。[1]

正如思摩斯教授所指出的那样："书中的法律如果不能满足日常商业世界的实践需求，那么它便是无用的。"[2]

---

① For instance, some countries do not accpet the delocalizaiton theory. It may cause the national courts to challenge the arbitral awards on such grounds.

② Simões, F. D., Supra note 27.

仲裁条款的设计应满足实际商业惯例的要求，因为格式合同将被多次重复使用。此外，许多国家认为起草者有责任起草一份清晰、组织良好的格式合同，否则格式合同以及该合同中的仲裁条款的有效性将受到国家法院的质疑。因此，格式合同中的仲裁条款应精确设计，以满足相关国家强制性规则的要求。更重要的是，选择适用的法律应该全面考虑，以确保它们遵循特定行业的实际商业实践。此外，阅读和研究类似的案例和相关的法律，将有利于设计格式合同中的实用仲裁条款。

Arbitration clauses should be designed to meet the requirements of real business practices, as the standard form contracts will be reused for many times. In addition, many countries hold drafters responsible for drafting a clear and well-organized standard form contract, or the validity of the standard form contract and arbitration clauses will be challenged by national courts. Therefore, arbitration clauses in standard form contracts should be designed precisely to meet the requirements of mandatory rules of relevant countries. What is more, applicable laws should be chosen with a comprehensive consideration to make sure they follow actual business practices in the specific industry. Besides, reading and studying similar cases and relevant laws would be beneficial for the design of practical arbitration clauses in standard form contracts.

法律法规
Laws and Regulations

American Arbitration Association - International Arbitration Rules, 2000
<Available at: http://www.jus.uio.no/lm/american.arbitration.association.rules.2000/>

Civil Procedure Law of the People's Republic of China, 2012
< Available at: http://www.inchinalaw.com/wp-content/uploads/2013/09/PRC-Civil-Procedure-Law-2012.pdf>

Contract Law of the People's Republic of China, 1999
< Available at:http://www.npc.gov.cn/englishnpc/Law/2007-12/11/content_1383564.htm>

England Arbitration Act,1996
<Available at: http://www.legislation.gov.uk/ukpga/1996/23/data.pdf>

German Civil Code, 2013
<Available at: http://www.gesetze-im-internet.de/englisch_bgb/englisch_bgb.html>

Hong Kong Arbitration Ordinance, 2010
<Available at: It regulates in Part 4, Composition of Arbitral Tribunal, Hong Kong Arbitration Ordinance. Available at: http://www.legco.gov.hk/yr10-11/english/ord/ord017-10-e.pdf (Last visited on May12, 2016).>

Hong Kong Unconscionable Contracts Ordinance, 2021
< Available at: Hong Kong Unconscionable Contracts Ordinance, available at: https://www.elegislation.gov.hk/hk/cap 458 (Last visited on September 8, 2022).

IBA Guidelines on Drafting International Arbitration Clauses, 2010
<Available at: http://www.ibanet.org/Publications/publications_IBA_guides_materials.aspx>

Insurance Law of the People's Republic of China, 2002
<Available at: http://www.npc.gov.cn/englishnpc/Law/2007-12/12/content_1383720.htm>

International Chamber of Commerce Arbitration Rules, 1998
<Available at: http://gjpi.org/wp-content/uploads/icc-rules-of-arbitration-en.pdf>

Italian Civil Code, 2014
<Available at: http://www.altalex.eu/content/italian-civil-code-translated-english>

Law of the People's Republic of China on Protection of Consumer Rights and Interests, 2013
<Available at: http://www.wipo.int/edocs/lexdocs/laws/en/cn/cn174en.pdf>

London Court of International Arbitration Arbitration Rules, 2014
<Available at: http://www.lcia.org/Dispute_Resolution_Services/lcia-arbitration-rules-2014.aspx>

Maritime Law of the People's Republic of China, 1992
<Available at: http://www.lawinfochina.com/display.aspx?lib=law&id=191>

UN Convention on the Recognition and Enforcement of Foreign Arbitral Awards, 1958
<Available at: http://www.newyorkconvention.org/English>

UNCITRAL Model Law on International Commercial Arbitration (1985), with amendments as adopted in 2006
<Available at: http://www.uncitral.org/sites/uncitral.un.org/files/media-documents/uncitral/en/19-09955_e_ebook.pdf>

Uniform Commercial Code, 2010
<Available at: https://www.law.cornell.edu/ucc>

United Nations Commission on International Trade Law Arbitration Rules, 2010
<Available at: https://www.uncitral.org/sites/uncitral.un.org/files/media-documents/uncitral/en/arb-rules-revised-2010-e.pdf>

United Nations Convention on Contracts for the International Sale of Goods, 2010
<Available at: https://www.uncitral.org/pdf/english/texts/sales/cisg/V1056997-CISG-e-book.pdf>

参考文献
Bibliography

Books

Atiyah, P. S. (1979). *The Rise and Fall of Freedom of Contract* (Vol. 61). Oxford: Clarendon Press.

Bhatia, V. K., Candlin, C., & Gotti, M. (Eds.). (2012). *Discourse and Practice in International Commercial Arbitration: Issues, Challenges and Prospects.* Ashgate Publishing, Ltd.

Binder, P., & Sekolec, J. (2005). *International Commercial Arbitration and Conciliation in UNCITRAL Model Law Jurisdictions.* Sweet & Maxwell.

Blum, B. A. (2007). *Contracts: Examples & Explanations.* Aspen Publishers Online.

Bockstiegel, K., Kröll, S., & Nacimiento, P. (2014). *Arbitration in Germany: The Model Law in Practice.* Kluwer Law International.

Born, G. (2010). *International Arbitration and Forum Selection Agreements: Drafting and Enforcing.* Kluwer Law International.

Brown, H. J., & Marriott, A. L. (1999). *ADR Principles and Practice.* London: Sweet & Maxwell.

Bühring-Uhle, C., Kirchhoff, L., & Scherer, G. (2006). *Arbitration and Mediation in International Business.* Kluwer Law International.

Craig, W. L., Park, W. W., & Paulsson, J. (1985). *International Chamber of Commerce Arbitration.* Oceana Publications.

DiMatteo, L. A., & Dhooge, L. J. (2006). *International Business Law: A Transactional Approach.* Thomson/Southwestern.

Dore, I. I. (1986). *Arbitration and Conciliation under the UNCITRAL Rules: A Textual Analysis.* Martinus Nijhoff Publishers.

Fan, J., & Pereira, A. D. (2011). *Commercial and Economic Law in Macao.* Kluwer Law International.

Gaillard, E., & Savage, J. (Eds.)(1999). *Foucahrd Gaillard Goldman on International Commercial Arbitration.* Kluwer Law International.

Kjos, H. E. (2013). *Applicable Law in Investor-State Arbitration.* Oxford University Press.

Kronke, H. (2010). *Recognition and Enforcement of Foreign Arbitral Awards: A Global Commentary on the New York Convention.* Kluwer Law International.

Kuang, M.W., & Hong, L.Y. (2013). *The Theories and the Development of the International Commercial Arbitration.* Hanlu Press.

Lew, J. D., Mistelis, L. A., & Kröll, S. (2003). *Comparative International Commercial Arbitration.* Kluwer Law International.

Merryman, J. H., & Pérez-Perdomo, R. (2007). *The Civil Law Tradition: An Introduction to the Legal Systems of Europe and Latin America.* Stanford University Press.

Onyema, E. (2010). *International Commercial Arbitration and the Arbitrator's Contract.* Routledge.

Poudret, J. F., & Besson, S. (2007). *Comparative Law of International Arbitration.* Sweet & Maxwell.

Redfern, A. (2004). *Law and Practice of International Commercial Arbitration.* Sweet & Maxwell.

Reisman, W. M. (1997). *International Commercial Arbitration: Cases, Materials and Notes on the Resolution of International Business Disputes.* Foundation Press.

Rouche, J., & Pointon, G. H. (2003). *French Arbitration Law and Practice.* Kluwer Law International.

Rubino-Sammartano, M. (2001). *International Arbitration Law.* Kluwer Law International.

Steingruber, A. M. (2012). *Consent in International Arbitration.* OUP Oxford.

Su, H.P. (2004). *A Study on Standard Contract Clauses.* China Renmin University Press.

Šulija, G. (2011). *Standard Contract Terms in Cross-Border Business Transactions: A Comparative Study from the Perspective of European Union Law.* P. Lang.

Schmitthoff, C. M. (1981). *Commercial Law in a Changing Economic Climate* (Vol. 20). London: Sweet & Maxwell.

Tao, J. (2008). *Arbitration Law and Practice in China.* Kluwer Law International.

Trebilcock, M. J. (1997). *The Limits of Freedom of Contract.* Harvard University Press.

Tweeddale, A., & Tweeddale, K. (2005). *Arbitration of Commercial Disputes: International and English Law and Practice.* Oxford University Press.

Van, D. B. (1996). *Yearbook Commercial Arbitration Vol. XXXI.* Kluwer Law International.

Yates, D., & Hawkins, A. J. (1986). *Standard Business Contracts: Exclusions and Related Devices.* Sweet & Maxwell.

Articles

Arsić, J. (1997). International Commercial Arbitration on the Internet—Has the Future Come Too Early? *Journal of International Arbitration*, 14(3), 209-221.

Aspragkathou, D. (2007). Review of the GENCON Charter Clauses for the Commencement of Lay time: Analysis of the "Time Lost in Waiting for a Berth to Count as Laytime or Time on Demurrage" *Clause. J. Mar. L. & Com.*, 38, 603-667.

Bakos, Y., Marotta-Wurgler, F., & Trossen, D. R. (2014). Does Anyone Read the Fine Print? Consumer Attention to Standard Form Contracts. *Journal of Legal Studies*, 43(1), 9-40.

Barcelo III, J. J. (2003). Who Decides the Arbitrators' Jurisdiction? Separability and Competence-Competence in Transnational Perspective. *Vand. J. Transnat'l L.*, 36, 1115-1202.

Berger, K. P. (2006). Re-examining the Arbitration Agreement: Applicable Law—Consensus or Confusion? *International Arbitration*, 301-334.

Berg, K. F. (1979). The Israeli Standard Contracts Law 1964: Judicial Controls of Standard Form Contracts. *International and Comparative Law Quarterly*, 28(4), 560-574.

Burger, W. E. (1984). State of Justice, The. *ABAJ*, 70, 62-67.

Bolgar, V. (1972). Contract of Adhesion—A Comparison of Theory and Practice. *The. Am. J. Comp. L.*, 20, 53-67.

Borchers, P. J. (1992). Forum Selection Agreements in the Federal Courts after Carnival Cruise: A Proposal for Congressional Reform. *Wash. L. Rev.*, 67, 55-70.

Brunet, E. (2002). Seeking Optional Dispute Resolution Clauses in High Stakes Employment Contracts. *Berkeley J. Emp. & Lab. L.*, 23, 107-130.

Bělohlávek, A. J. (2013). Importance of the Seat of Arbitration in International Arbitration:

Delocalization and Denationalization of Arbitration as an Outdated Myth. *ASA Bulletin*, 31(2), 262-292.

Byrnes, J., & Pollman, E. (2003). Arbitration, Consent and Contractual Theory: The Implications of EEOC v. Waffle House. *Harvard Negotiation Law Review*, 8, 289-312.

Carbonneau, T. E. (2003). Exercise of Contract Freedom in the Making of Arbitration Agreement, *The Vand. J. Transnat'l L.*, 36, 1189-1211.

Chi, M. (2008). Is Chinese Arbitration Act Truly Arbitration-Friendly? Determining the Validity of Arbitration Agreement under Chinese Law. *Asian International Arbitration Journal*, 4(1), 104-120.

Chukwumerije, O. (1994). Applicable Substantive Law in International Commercial Arbitration. *Anglo-American Law Review*, 23(3), 265-310.

Coakley, C. (2000). Growing Role of Customized Consent in International Commercial Arbitration, *The. Ga. J. Int'l & Comp. L.*, 29, 127-149.

Drahozal, C. R. (1999). Privatizing Civil Justice: Commercial Arbitration and the Civil Justice System. *Kan. JL & Pub. Pol'y*, 9, 578-599.

Egle, A. V. (2003). Back to Prima Paint Corp. v. Flood and Conklin Manufacturing Co.: To Challenge an Arbitration Agreement You Must Challenge the Arbitration Agreement. *Wash. L. Rev.*, 78, 199-230.

Fisher, R. D., & Haydock, R. S. (1995). International Commercial Disputes Drafting an Enforceable Arbitration Agreement. *Wm. Mitchell L. Rev.*, 21, 941-987.

Franck, S. (2005). Role of International Arbitrators, The. ILSA J. Int'l & Comp. L., 12, 499-530.

Gaillard, E. (1999). The Enforcement of Awards Set Aside in the Country of Origin. *ICSID Review*, 14, 16-45.

Goldring, J. (1976). Australian Law and International Commercial Arbitration. *Columbia Journal of Transnational Law*, 15(2), 265-310.

Goodman, B., & Honey, I. (1999). Shrink-Wrapped the Consumer: The Shrink-Wrap Agreement as an Adhesion Contract, *Cardozo L. Rev*, 21, 319-360.

Gorla, G. (1962). Standard Conditions and Form Contracts in Italian Law. *The American Journal of Comparative Law*, 11(1), 1-20.

Granier, T. (2015). Unilateral Termination of an Arbitration Agreement by a Party After the Arbitration Has Commenced. *Revista Brasileira de Arbitragem*, 12(45), 108-124.

Green, E. D. (1997). International Commercial Dispute Resolution: Courts, Arbitration, and Mediation—Introduction. *BU Int'l LJ, 15*, 175-198.

Gravel, S., & Peterson, P. (1991). French Law and Arbitration Clauses—Distinguishng Scope from Validity: Comment on ICC Case No. 6519 Final Award. *McGill LJ, 37*, 510-515.

Habib, S. (2013). Delocalized Arbitration Myth or Reality? Analyzing the Interplay of the Delocalization Theory in Different Legal Systems. <Available at: http://bspace.buid.ac.ae/bitstream/1234/361/1/100149.pdf> (Last visited on May 12, 2016).

Hersbergen, R. L. (1982). Contracts of Adhesion under the Louisiana Civil Code. *La. L. Rev., 43*, 1-29.

Hillman, R. A., & Rachlinski, J. J. (2002). Standard-Form Contracting in the Electronic Age. *NYUL Rev.*, 77, 429-495.

Hober, K., & Magnusson, A. (2008). The Special Status of Agreements to Arbitrate: The Separability Doctrine, Mandatory Stay of Litigation. *The Disp. Resol. Int'l*, 2, 65-75.

Horton, D. (2009). Flipping the Script: Contra Proferentem and Standard Form Contracts. *U. Colo. L. Rev., 80*, at 429-432.

Kessler, F. (1943). Contracts of Adhesion—Some Thoughts about Freedom of Contract. *Colum. L. Rev.*, 43, 629-677.

Korobkin, R. (2003). Bounded Rationality, Standard Form Contracts, and Unconscionability. *The University of Chicago Law Review*, 70(4), 1203-1225.

Lando, O. (1985). The Lex Mercatoria in International Commercial Arbitration. *ICLQ, 34*(4), 747-768.

Lenhoff, A. (1961). Contracts of Adhesion and the Freedom of Contract: A Comparative Study in the Light of American and Foreign Law. *Tul. L. Rev.*, 36, 481-497.

Lowisch, M. (2003). New Law of Obligations in Germany. *Ritsumeikan Law Review*, 20, 141-156.

Mahdi, S. A. (2001). Gateway to Arbitration: Issues of Contract Formation under the UCC and the Enforceability of Arbitration Clauses Included in Standard Form Contracts Shipped with Goods. *Nw. UL Rev.*, 96, 401-413.

Mann, F. A. (1984). England Rejects "Delocalised" Contracts and Arbitration. *International and Comparative Law Quarterly*, 33(1), 190-199.

Marotta-Wurgler, F. (2007). What's in a Standard Form Contract? An Empirical Analysis of Software License Agreements. *Journal of Empirical Legal Studies*, 4(4), 677-713.

Martinez, R. (1990). Recognition and Enforcement of International Arbitral Awards under the United Nations Convention of 1958: The "Refusal" Provisions. *The International Lawyer*, 487-518.

Olatawura, O. O. (2003). Delocalized Arbitration under the English Arbitration Act 1996: An Evolution or a Revolution. *Syracuse J. Int'l L. & Com.*, 30, 45-57.

Park, W. W. (1984). Arbitration of International Contract Disputes. *The Business Lawyer*, 1783-1799.

Piersol, C. V. (1984). Insurance Arbitration and the Standard Form Contract after Southland. *SDL Rev.*, 30, 617-637.

Rensmann, T. (1998). Anational Arbitral Awards—Legal Phenomenon or Academic Phantom. *Journal of International Arbitration*, 15(2), 37-65.

Rosenberg, M., & Schubin, M. (1961). Trial by Lawyer: Compulsory Arbitration of Small Claims in Pennsylvania. *Harvard Law Review*, 448-472.

Sales, H. B. (1953). Standard Form Contracts. *The Modern Law Review*, 16(3), 318-342.

Schmitz, A. (2002). Ending a Mud Bowl: Defining Arbitration's Finality Through Functional Analysis. *Georgia Law Review*, 37, 123-204.

Siegel, T. M. (1995). Is Arbitration Final & (and) Binding—Public Policy Says, Not Necessarily—Exxon Shipping Company v. Exxon Seamen's Union. *J. Disp. Resol.*, 351-380.

Simões, F. D. (2015). Harmonization of Arbitration Laws in the Asia-Pacific: Trendy or Necessary? <Available at: http://www.victoria.ac.nz/law/research/publications/about-nzacl/publications/special-issues/hors-serie-volume-xvi,-2013/Dias-Simoes.pdf> (Last visited on May 12, 2016).

Slawson, W. D. (1971). Standard Form Contracts and Democratic Control of Lawmaking Power. *Harvard Law Review*, 529-566.

Smith, A. H. (1972). Standard Form Contracts in the International Commercial Transactions of the People's Republic of China. *International and Comparative Law Quarterly*, 21(1), 133-150.

Steingruber, A. M. (2009). Notion, Nature and Extent of Consent in International Arbitration (Doctoral dissertation) < Available at: https://qmro.qmul.ac.uk/xmlui/bitstream/handle/123456789/415/STEINGRUBERNotionNature2009.pdf?sequence=1> (Last visited on May 16, 2016).

Strong, S. I. (2012). What Constitutes an Agreement in Writing in International Commercial

Arbitration? Conflicts Between the New York Convention and the Federal Arbitration Act. *Stanford Journal of International Law*, 47-75.

Tetsuya, N. (2000). The Place of Arbitration—Its Fictitious Nature and Lex Arbitri, *Mealey's International Arbitration Report*, 15(10), at 23-29.

Thomas, G. (2012). What Are the Limits of Competence-Competence for Arbitral Tribunals? <Available at www.heintzmanadr.com> (Last visited on May 12, 2016).

Warkentine, E. R. (2007). Beyond Unconscionability: The Case for Using Knowing Assent as the Basis for Analyzing Unbargained-for Terms in Standard Form Contracts. *Seattle UL Rev., 31*, 469-499.

Wilson, N. S. (1965). Freedom of Contract and Adhesion Contracts. *International and Comparative Law Quarterly,* 14(1), 172-193.

Yackee, J. W. (2003). A Matter of Good Form: The (Downsized) Hague Judgments Convention and Conditions of Formal Validity for the Enforcement of Forum Selection Agreements. *Duke Law Journal*, 53(3), 1179-1214.

Zhang, M. (2008). Contractual Choice of Law in Contracts of Adhesion and Party Autonomy. *Akron L. Rev., 41*, 123-142.

Zuberbühler, T. (2008). Non-signatories and the Consensus to Arbitrate. *ASA Bulletin, 26(1)*, 18-34.

Cases

ACC Limited v. Global Cements Ltd., [2012] SCC 71, the Supreme Court of India.
<Available at: http://www.cnica.org/images/cnica18.pdf> (Last visited on May 12, 2016).

Arsanovia Ltd & Ors v. Cruz City Mauritius Holdings, [2012] EWHC 3702 (Comm), High Court of England and Wales.
<Available at: http://hsfnotes.com/arbitration/2013/03/01/high-court-applies-sulamerica-test-in-arsanovia-and-gives-rise-to-unexpected-results/> (Last visited on May12, 2016).

B.P. Exploration Company (Libya) Limited v. Government of the Libyan Arab Republic. (1973) 53 I.L.R. 297, Lagergren, Sole Arbitrator.
<Available at: https://zh.scribd.com/document/190391346/BP-Exploration-v-Libyan-Arab-Republic-53-I-L-R-297-1973> (Last visited on May 12, 2016).

Beijing Jianlong Heavy Industry Group v. Golden Ocean Group Ltd & Ors, [2013] EWHC 1063, King's Bench High Court.
<Available at: http://www.cnarb.com/Item/5989.aspx> (Last visited on May 12, 2016).

Carnival Cruise Lines, Inc. v. Shute, [1991] 499 U.S. 585, U.S., United States Supreme Court.
<Available at: https://supreme.justia.com/cases/federal/us/499/585/case.html > (Last visited on May12, 2016).

Concordia Trading B.V. v. Nantong Gangde Oil Co., Ltd, [2009] MinSiTaZi No. 22, China Supreme People's Court.
<Available at: http://newyorkconvention1958.org/index.php?=notice_ &id=1501&opac_view=2> (Last visited on May 12, 2016).

Dewayne Hubbert v. Dell Corp., [2006] 844 N.E.2d 965, Illinois Court of Appeals.

<Available at: http://www.internetlibrary.com/cases/lib_case487.cfm> (Last visited on May 12, 2016).

Fiona Trust v. Privalov, [2015] EWHC 527, High Court of England and Wales.

<Available at: https://www.cliffordchance.com/briefings/2014/06/singapore_highhtml> (Last visited on May 12, 2016).

First Link Investments Corp Ltd v. GT Payment Pte Ltd and Others, [2014] SGHCR 12, Singapore High Court.
<Available at: http://hsfnotes.com/arbitration/2015/03/19/fiona-trust-v-privalov-in-the-high-court/> (Last visited on May 12, 2016).
Gao Haiyan and another v. Keeneye Holdings and another, CACV79/2011, Hong Kong Court of Appeal.
<Available at: http://www.onlinedmc.co.uk/index.php/> (Last visited on May12, 2016).
Harbor Assurance Co. Ltd. v. Kansa General International Insurance Co. Ltd., [1993] 1 Lloyd's Rep. 455, House of Lords.
<Available at: http://translex.uni-koeln.de/302700> (Last visited on May 12, 2016).

Heyman v. Darwins Ltd., [1942] AC 356, House of Lords.
<Available at: https://webstroke.co.uk/law/cases/heyman-v-darwins-1942> (Last visited on May 12, 2016).

Klöckner Pentaplast Gmbh & Co Kg v. Advance Technology (H.K.) Company Limited, [2010] HCA1526, Hong Kong Court of First Instance.
<Available at: http://uk.practicallaw.com/D-021-8481?source=relatedcontent> (Last visited on May12, 2016).

Paklito Investment Limited v. Klockner Ease Asia Limited, [1993] HKCU 0613, Hong Kong High Court.
<Available at: http://neil-kaplan.com/wp-content/uploads/2013/08/Paklito-Investment-Ltd-v-Klockner-East-Asia-Ltd-HCMP2219-of-1991.pdf> (Last visited on May12, 2016).

Paul Smith Ltd v. H and S International Holdings Incorporation, [1991] Llyods Rep 127, Queen's Bench Division Commercial Court.
<Available at: http://cn.lexology.com/library/detail.aspx?g=c7b3d230-b0dd-4d7e-b2e6-a5a5df1a9086> (Last visited on May 12, 2016).

Piallo GmbH v. Yafriro International Pte Ltd, [2013] SGHC 260, Singapore High Court.
<available at: http://www.singaporelaw.sg/sglaw/laws-of-singapore/case-law/free-law/high-court-judgments/15435-piallo-gmbh-v-yafriro-international-pte-ltd-2013-sghc-260> (Last visited on May 12, 2016).

Prima Paint Corp. v. Flood & Conklin Mfg. Co., [1967] Co. 388 U.S. 395, United States Supreme

Court.

　　<Available at: https://supreme.justia.com/cases/federal/us/388/395/case.html> (Last visited on May 12, 2016).

　　Progressive Casualty Insurance Co v. C.A. Reaseguradora Nacional De Venezuela, [1993]991F.2d.42, United States Court of Appeals Second Circuit.
　　<Available at: http://openjurist.org/991/f2d/42/progressive-casualty-insurance-co-v-ca-reaseguradora-nacional-de-venezuela > (Last visited on May 12, 2016).

　　Shagang South-Asia (Hong Kong) Trading Co. Ltd v. Daewoo Logistics, [2015] EWHC 194 (Comm), High Court of England and Wales.
　　<Available at: http://globalarbitrationnews.com/shagang-south-asia-hong-kong-trading-co-ltd-v-daewoo-logistics-2015-ewhc-194-comm-20150414> (Last visited on May12, 2016).

　　Sonatrach Petroleum Corporation (BVI) v. Ferrell International Limited, [2001] APP.L.R. 10/04, High Court of England and Wales.
　　<Available at: http://www.nadr.co.uk/articles/published/ArbLR/Sonatrach%2> (Last visited on May12, 2016).

　　Specht v. Netscape Communications Corporation, [2002] 306 F.3d 17, United States Court of Appeals for the Second Circuit.
　　<Available at: http://www.casebriefs.com/blog/law/contracts/contracts-keyed-to-murphy/the-bargain-relationship/specht-v-netscape-communications-corporation/> (Last visited on May 12, 2016).

　　Sulamerica CIA Nacional de Seguros SA and Others v. Enesa Engenharia SA and Others, [2012] EWHC 42 (Comm), High Court of England and Wales.
　　<Available at: https://www.cliffordchance.com/briefings/2014/06/singapore_high_court.html> (Last visited on May 12, 2016).

　　Union of India v. McDonnell Douglas Corporation, [1993] 2 Lloyd's Rep. 48, Queen's Bench Division Commercial Court.
　　<Available at: https://www.i-law.com/ilaw/doc/view.htm?id=149987> (Last visited on May12, 2016).

　　Whitworth Street Estates (Manchester) Ltd v. James Miller & Partners Ltd, [1970] A.C. 583, 603, House of Lords.
　　<Available at: http://swarb.co.uk/whitworth-street-estates-manchester-ltd-v-james-miller-partners-ltd-hl-1970/> (Last visited on May12, 2016).

　　Williams v. Walker Thomas Furniture Co., 350 F.2d 445 (D.C. Cir. 1965), the District of Columbia Court of Appeals.
　　<Available at: http://law.justia.com/cases/federal/appellate-courts/F2/350/445/74531> (Last visited on May12, 2016).